MYSTICISM

in the

WESLEYAN TRADITION

MYSTICISM

in the

WESLEYAN TRADITION

Robert G. Tuttle, Jr.

Foreword by Bishop William R. Cannon

69-1002

FRANCIS ASBURY PRESS
of Zondervan Publishing House
Grand Rapids, Michigan

MYSTICISM in the WESLEYAN TRADITION
Copyright © 1989 by Robert G. Tuttle, Jr.

Francis Asbury Press is an imprint of Zondervan Publishing House,
1415 Lake Drive, S.E., Grand Rapids, Michigan 49506.

Library of Congress Cataloging in Publication Data

Tuttle, Robert G.
   Mysticism in the Wesleyan tradition / Robert G. Tuttle, Jr.
     p.   cm.
   Bibliography: p.
   Includes index
   ISBN 0-310-75430-5
   1. Mysticism—England—History—18th century. 2. Mysticism.
  3. Wesley, John, 1703–1791—Contributions in mysticism.
  4. Methodist Church—Doctrines—History. I. Title.
BV5077.G7T88   1989
248.2'2'092—dc20   89-6896
                                                        CIP

Edited by Robert D. Wood

Printed in the United States of America

89 90 91 92 93 94 95 / AF / 10 9 8 7 6 5 4 3 2 1

To
My Colleagues and Students
at Garrett-Evangelical Theological Seminary

contents

On Social Justice: the Inevitable Fruit

acknowledgments

May 24, 1988, marked the 250th anniversary of John Wesley's Aldersgate experience. This book is an outgrowth of a lecture delivered at a celebration of that event held in Nashville, Tennessee, under the auspices of the United Methodist Renewal Services Fellowship. Special appreciation is expressed to the executive director of the UMRSF, Ross Whetstone, who first suggested the topic "Mysticism in the Wesleyan Tradition" for that lecture.

Special appreciation must also be extended to Helen Hauldren whose long hours with this manuscript have made enjoyable work that much more enjoyable.

To the editor and staff of Zondervan/Francis Asbury Press, who saw the potential of this project and offered the necessary encouragement to see it to completion, my sincere thanks as well.

fOREWORd

This book, *Mysticism in the Wesleyan Tradition,* is an almost perfect example of the use of the Hegelian method in philosophy in solving a vexing and difficult theological problem in the thought and practice of John Wesley. The Hegelian method sets two opposite and contradictory principles in juxtaposition to one another and then works out a synthesis, displaying the essential elements in each and showing that one without the other is an incomplete rendition, even distortion, of reality. There are in Hegel's philosophy always the thesis, the antithesis, and the synthesis. For example, Hegel takes what he calls Subjective Mind, that is, the thoughts and feelings of persons, which form the substance of anthropology and psychology, and sets it over against Objective Mind, which actualizes itself in concrete social institutions that are the subject matter of history, sociology, and politics, and of the two forms the synthesis of the subjective and objective, which brings Spirit into complete self-consciousness, displayed in art, philosophy, and religion. The thesis is Subjective Mind. The antithesis is Objective Mind. And the synthesis is Absolute Spirit.

This is precisely what Dr. Tuttle does in his explication of mysticism and the role it plays in the thought and teaching ministry of John Wesley. There is no indication that Dr. Tuttle is deliberately employing the Hegelian method, nor need there be, for his work is a highly original handling of the Wesleyan theological materials; and generally the province of the theologian, especially a biblical theologian such as Dr. Tuttle, is far removed from that of the philosopher. Nonetheless, the clarity and precision and the skillful balance of judgment in assessing what Wesley says in one instance in favor of mysticism and what he says against it in another and arriving at a logic that makes sense of both show Dr. Tuttle to be, at least in his role as an interpreter of Wesley's treatment of the mystics, as adept in the use of the Helgelian method in theology as Hegel himself was in philosophy.

Indeed, by this means Dr. Tuttle has given us a new understanding and at the same time appreciation of mysticism in the Wesleyan tradition. Heretofore, we have thought of mysticism as merely a passing phase in the development of John Wesley's thought. He fell under the spell of the mystics through the writings of William Law, but then later he became aware of the inadequacy of Law's teachings and repudiated him and mysticism altogether. Just as Augustine in his pre-Christian years was for a time a Manichaean, only to disavow Manichaeism and look on it as the work of the devil when he became a Christian, so we have interpreted Wesley's thinking as tinged with mysticism for a short time during his Oxford years and perhaps shortly thereafter only to have all vestiges of mysticism swept away by the Aldersgate experience and replaced by the objective grace of God given by faith in Jesus Christ. We have dealt with mysticism in Wesley chronologically rather than ontologically, that is, as something temporary and transient rather than essential to the abiding substance of his theology and a necessary ingredient of his practical divinity.

In this book Dr. Tuttle shows us that Wesley was much more than a passing and temporary mystic. Rather, mysticism belonged to his thought and was essential to his theology to the very end. Indeed, it was the bulwark to his doctrine of Christian Perfection. The mystic concept of union with God is the equivalent of Wesley's concept of perfect love. We cannot obtain perfect love unless God brings it to us by taking personal possession of us and dwelling in our hearts so that we become his temples on this earth.

The clue to Dr. Tuttle's interpretation lies in the fact that after Wesley repudiated mysticism, especially the mysticism of William Law, he continued to read the writings of the mystics, to recommend them to his followers, and to include many of them in his *Christian Library,* which he edited, published, and distributed widely throughout the English-speaking world. Many of these writings of the mystics he had personally to translate from the Romantic languages into English. They must have meant a lot to him spiritually for him to expend so much time and energy to make them available to his reading public.

To employ the Hegelian method to his book, we will call the thesis Wesley's repudiation of mysticism as seen in the arresting statement he made in a letter to his older brother in 1736: "I think the rock on which I nearest made shipwreck of the faith was the writings of the Mystics." The antithesis would be his continued use of the writings of the mystics and his constant citing of their lives as sterling examples of piety and unselfish Christian devotion. It is they who most nearly display his concept of Perfect Love, which he himself never claimed to possess. The synthesis, then, is the combination of the Reformation teaching of the grace of God given freely to miserable and undeserving sinners through their faith in Jesus Christ for his atoning death for them on the cross, which mysticism seems to Wesley to lack, and the Roman Catholic teaching of sanctification, which so many of the mystics so beautifully exemplify. Dr. Tuttle rightly identifies the Atonement as the missing link that alone can tie mysticism to an effective and complete order of salvation, binding a person to God and enabling that person to receive the power of the Holy Spirit to live a life well pleasing to God and worthy of heaven in the end.

The plan of the book is admirable. It moves logically from chapter to chapter as one floor upon another in an orderly and well-constructed building, displaying the plan of its architect, which in turn is a blueprint of the mind and heart of John Wesley. It begins with a clear and fulsome definition of mysticism and shows the impact it made on the young Mr. Wesley, his experiments with it and even acceptance of it. Then, it points out what Wesley found to be its inadequacies and his rejection of it only to rediscover in the end its gold among the dross so that he could reemploy it in modified form to the edification of his own soul and the nurturing of the souls of others. One could not improve on the design of the book if he tried, and its thesis is sound and sensible and will hold up under the most careful scrutiny.

I have been a conscientious student of Wesley's thought for almost fifty years. Yet it did not occur to me that mysticism had much, if any, influence on Wesley after Aldersgate until I read *Mysticism in the Wesleyan Tradition*. But through this book, Dr. Tuttle has opened my eyes to a whole new dimension in Wesleyan thought, and for this I am deeply grateful.

Though the author sticks rigidly to his theme throughout the book and does not deviate from it in the least, still the wealth of material he uses to substantiate his thesis provides the reader with a broad knowledge both of mysticism in the variety of its expression and of Wesleyan theology in general. The author has a good style, swift, direct, and pungent. The book provides interesting, even fascinating, reading. Tuttle's style is remarkably similar to Wesley's. The student has stayed so close to his master that the master's way of thinking and writing has become his very own.

I cannot recall when I have read a finer monograph on Wesley's thought than this one. It will enhance Dr. Tuttle's already proud reputation as a significant Wesleyan scholar. Indeed, it will secure for him a place among the very best interpreters of the mind of John Wesley in this generation.

William R. Cannon
A Bishop of The United Methodist Church and Honorary President of The World Methodist Council

preface

At various points early on in John Wesley's ministry he writes, "I think the rock on which I had the nearest made shipwreck of the faith was the writings of the Mystics,"[1] for "they stab [Christian faith] in the vitals: and its most serious professors are most likely to fall by them. May I praise Him who hath snatched me out of this fire,"[2] this "fairest of Satan's devices,"[3] this "specious snare of the devil,"[4] this "mystery of iniquity."[5] Yet throughout his life Wesley continues to use the mystic lives as the standard of measurement to which his doctrine of Christian perfection is compared.[6]

In 1764 Wesley writes to his old friend Lady Maxwell commending two well-known seventeenth-century mystics: "I want you to be all a Christian;—such a Christian as the Marquis de Renty or Gregory Lopez was."[7] About the same time, Wesley responds to James Hervey's charge that Wesley was *"half"* a papist. He retorts, "What if he had *proved* it, too? What if he had proved I was a *whole* Papist? (though he might as easily have proved me a Mahometan). Is not a Papist a child of God? Is Thomas à Kempis, Mr. de Renty, Gregory Lopez gone to hell? Believe it who can. Yet still of such (though Papists) the same is my brother and sister and mother."[8]

Nehemiah Curnock says that John Wesley was "no martyr to the

---

[1] John Wesley, *The Letters of the Rev. John Wesley, A.M.*, ed. John Telford. 8 vols. (London: Epworth, 1931), 1:207.

[2] John Wesley, *The Journal of the Rev. John Wesley, A.M.*, ed Nehemiah Curnock. 8 vols. (London: Epworth, 1909), 1:420.

[3] John Wesley, *Wesley's Standard Sermons*, ed. E. H. Sugden. 2 vols. (London: Epworth, 1921), 1:378n.

[4] *Journal*, 6:10.

[5] *Notes Upon the New Testament*, 2 Thess. 2:7. (London: Epworth, 1950 reprint)

[6] *Letters*, 6:67; 8:18.

[7] John Wesley, *The Works of the Rev. John Wesley, A.M.*, ed. Thomas Jackson, 14 vols. (London: Wesleyan–Methodist Conference Office, 1872), 4:327.

[8] *Letters*, 4:293.

bugbear of consistency."[9] While that may be true of many of us, the question still remains: How can Wesley condemn the mystics one day and then use their lives to illustrate perfection the next? As one might imagine, that problem has puzzled many a Wesleyan scholar of no small stature or mean reputation. Obviously, there was something about mysticism that Wesley hated and despised and something about the mystics that he loved and admired. This book is an attempt to sort out this apparent inconsistency while describing Wesley's wider appreciation of mysticism (especially in his later years) and then speak a word of caution and hope to the contemporary scene that has been sometimes thrilled, sometimes duped, and sometimes deeply enriched by the experiences known to mysticism.

Let's begin by way of synopsis. John Wesley's Puritan/high church heritage made it impossible for him to give himself completely to the mystical system as taught by the mystics that he read and abridged. Their mystical piety, to a large extent Roman Catholic, so deeply impressed him, however, that he came dangerously close at one point to the mystic way. Aldersgate marks the end of a nineteen-month struggle against the mystical system. Wesley, although retaining a common end with the mystics (manifested particularly in his doctrine of perfection), substituted an evangelical doctrine of justification by faith for the "dark night of the soul" (the mystic fourth stage). In so doing he drove a wedge between the tenets of mysticism that were dark, speculative, passive, and unsocial on the one hand (epitomized by Law and the German mystics) and a practical pietistic mysticism on the other (epitomized by the Roman Catholic mystics whom he abridged), that is, a "mysticism of service."

The ultimate influence after the crisis of 1738 is varied, and Wesley from 1738 to 1764 is particularly ambivalent. Consciously, he stood firm against the mystic extravagances (the Moravian "stillness," for example), but he still managed to read, recommend, and even publish abridgments of mystical works (de Renty, Guyon and those in *The Christian Library*). During the period 1764 to 1767 Wesley seems to undergo a theological readjustment as he reveals a wider appreciation for certain aspects of the Christian faith in general and mysticism in particular. Perhaps John Fletcher, a mystic in many ways, reintroduced Wesley to a higher appreciation of mysticism. This renewed appreciation (although still not without variation) then remained with Wesley until his death. He, therefore, although never fully committed to the

---

[9] *Journal*, 1:33.

mystic way, was deeply influenced by the mystics who consequently provided considerable impetus to the perpetuation of the Evangelical Revival.

At this point it is important to note that Wesley's struggle with mysticism has a relevance for today that was perhaps unmatched even by his own day. Mysticism in one form or another has been used or abused as fertile ground for a veritable legion of religious experiences. Much of this is built on deceit and superstition, a cancer on the otherwise healthy body of mysticism. Some of this is insight and access to the very mind of God. Obviously, a great deal is at stake. Wesley realized that the difference between mystic gold and mystic dross could mean for some the difference between heaven and hell. Too strong? Read on and come to your own conclusion.

1

mysticism defineδ[1]

Anyone who has studied mysticism seriously realizes the importance of defining the term accurately. This obstacle successfully passed can lead to a rewarding study, but if neglected it can lead to impossible confusion.

MYSTICISM: AN OVERVIEW

Due to almost endless diversification, mysticism, commonly so-called or as it has developed traditionally over the years, has few common denominators. Dean Inge hardly need tell us that no word has been used more loosely.[2] One author suggests that the term " 'mysticism' belongs to that totally useful family of words whose meanings are in their atmosphere and suggestions, rather than in their mathematical precision."[3] Ronald Knox states that mysticism is a "direction of the mind, not a bunch of conclusions."[4] In fact, if one is honest, no one definition can be said to be right and no one can be said to be wrong; one is usually *more* or *less* a mystic. Nonetheless, if we are to establish the

---

[1] This chapter should not place the reader under any illusion with respect to mysticism. A working definition is provided here only as a necessary means to establishment of common ground. Ultimately, the full meaning of mysticism is understood only as it grows upon one gradually through the continuing process of dealing with what mysticism stands for in principle.

[2] W. R. Inge, *Christian Mysticism* (London: Methuen, 1899), 3.

[3] G. G. Atkins, *Making of the Christian Mind* (Garden City, NY: Doubleday, 1929), 217.

[4] Ronald Knox, *Enthusiasm* (Oxford: Clarendon Press, 1950), 260.

necessary common ground upon which at least a part of this study is to be built, some sort of an attempt at a definition must be made.

Perhaps as good a definition as any could begin with the statement that mysticism is anything that gets one in touch with reality beyond the physical senses. Furthermore, mysticism embraces a "right brain" awareness of God and all mystics stress (more or less) the essential unity of God, nature, and humankind; therefore, union with God can be achieved (more or less) through the mystical contemplation of that unity.[5] More specifically, mysticism is in essence that "deep sense of union with God in the inmost depths of the soul," an immediate awareness of a unique relationship wih God.[6] "It is religion in its most acute, intense, and living stage."[7] A paraphrase of a section in Inge's *Christian Mysticism* summarizes these thoughts—the innate consciousness of the beyond is both the origin and raw material of religious experience, and mysticism arises when one tries to bring this higher consciousness into close relation with the other contents of the mind.[8] Herein lies the essence of mysticism.

If one can accept this "intimate union with God" as the essence of mysticism, the origin, character, and fulfillment of the *esse* should now be discussed. Briefly, the origin of the term *mystic* can be found in connection with the well-known Greek mysteries. A mystic was one initiated into some esoteric knowledge of divine things. Whether or not this has any relation to Christian mysticism is a topic which has been freely debated. It seems likely that Christian mysticism developed through the Christian Platonists at Alexandria. Both Origen and Clement of Alexandria distinguish between the active and the contemplative lives. From Alexandria mysticism almost certainly spread to the Asian church and Gregory of Nyssa who so strongly influenced St. Macarius, the earliest mystic abridged by John Wesley.[9] While many strongly deny any Neoplatonic origin for Christian mysticism, the

---

[5] Brazier Green, *John Wesley and William Law* (London: Epworth, 1945), 84. Inge also states that "the unity of all existence is the fundamental doctrine of mysticism." Inge, *Mysticism*, 28.

[6] John Lawson, *Notes on Wesley's Forty-Four Sermons* (London: Epworth, 1946), 255.

[7] R. Jones, *Studies in Mystical Religions* (London: Macmillan, 1936), xv.

[8] Inge, *Mysticism*, 5f.

[9] John Wesley abridged and published ten mystical treatises during the revival years. Since most of these treatises are products of those within the so-called Counter or Catholic Reformation, a brief history of that movement is included in this chapter, and a discussion of Wesley's method of abridgment and the conclusions drawn from a study of these works appears in chapter 5.

Neoplatonists by this time had obviously adopted certain aspects of the mystical scheme to connote a kind of discipline or rule of life congenial to their own speculative views of religion.[10] Inge devotes considerable space to the discussion of the theory concerning the Neoplatonic origin of Christian mysticism, emphasizing the Hellenistic term *logos*, which for the Neoplatonist represents the underlying nature of all things.[11] Both Plotinus and Augustine regarded the world as a living organism in which mystical stages secure higher and higher levels of divine participation.[12] Consequently, mysticism by the end of the fourth century (and probably earlier) had combined Christian, Greek, and even Persian thought into a categorical system of spiritual ascent.

Also important for this study is the character of mysticism. Several characteristics have been listed as common to all mystical experience.[13] First of all, mysticism defies expression, and its ineffable character makes it virtually impossible for mystics to describe their experiences adequately. Another characteristic of mysticism lies in its "noetic quality."[14] To understand mysticism one must experience mysticism. Its thoroughly esoteric nature plunges the soul into depths of truth unplumbed by the discursive intellect. The mystical experience is also transitory because the mystical heights cannot be sustained for long, but this is not to imply that no growth has taken place. Ideally, after each experience the mystic returns to a level of devotion even higher than before. In fact, these "mystical heights" are nonessential to mysticism and can be justified only if the mystic returns to the senses with a higher level of devotion.

It is the character of the mystic to emphasize progression; holiness is achieved only through the perpetual acquisition of knowledge. Yet another characteristic has been described as "passivity." It is not uncommon for the mystic to feel suspended by a superior power. Having attained the ecstatic (but not essential) state of consciousness, the mystic feels as if one's own will were one with the divine will; the

---

[10] Evelyn Underhill, *The Mystic Way* (London: Dent, 1913), 59. Underhill writes that "to see Christian mysticism descending from Neoplatonism is the result of a fundamental misunderstanding of mysticism." She insists that the Bible is the only possible source for Christian mysticism.

[11] Ibid., Lectures 3 and 4, pp. 22ff.

[12] Ibid., 27.

[13] William James, *Varieties of Religious Experience* (New York: Longmans, Green, 1919), 379f. James lists four characteristics which I have woven into this paragraph: ineffability, the noetic quality, transiency and passivity.

[14] D. Knowles, *The English Mystical Tradition* (London: Burnes and Oates, 1966), 2. He describes mystic theology as a kind of third knowledge over and above natural and revealed theology.

mystic becomes like a "statue" or even a "corpse in the hands of God."[15] Finally, the mystic character is flexible; mysticism in general leans more to antinomianism than legalism, more to Platonism than Aristotelianism.

We must now turn our attention to the mystic way of fulfillment. We have already seen that the mystic emphasizes growth, a process which is based on several presuppositions. First of all, the mystic believes that the soul can see and perceive; that one must partake of the divine nature to know God; that purification removes barriers (without holiness no one may see God); and finally, that one's guide to purification is perfect love (a pure "disinterested" or *agape* love desiring nothing in return).[16] From these presuppositions the mystics have developed their scheme, and over the years precedents have been established and digested into a system of mystical theology.

The basis of this system is "orison" or meditation which is then methodically applied to the disposition of the soul that it might be elevated toward God.[17] Several levels of mystical consciousness are involved, and while mystics in general are by no means unanimous in their description of these levels, an overall pattern does emerge. The pattern usually assumes three (but sometimes four or even five) stages.[18]

The first is the *purgative* stage (usually preceded by some sort of religious awakening) involving ascetical exercises and roughly analogous to the training of an athlete. This rigid discipline, aimed at purifying the body, buffets the flesh that it might not inhibit the spirit. This stage has led some to describe mysticism on the whole as morbid, but one must carry on to "judge a tree by its fruits, not by its roots."[19] The first stage, characterized by mortification, must lead to a second stage, the *illuminative* stage. Illumination, a somewhat misleading term involving mystical faith, requires one to concentrate all of one's faculties on God.[20] This frequently involves a delicate balance between agony and ecstasy as one must ultimately learn to trust God further than one can

---

[15] Both Sales and Loyola describe their experiences in this manner.

[16] Inge, *Mysticism,* 6ff.

[17] James, *Varieties,* 406.

[18] Underhill, *Mystic Way,* 52–55; and Inge, *Mysticism,* 10ff. Both describe these stages in detail.

[19] Inge, *Studies of English Mystics* (London: John Murray, 1906), 20.

[20] One should remember that mystical "faith" is not to be confused with the terminology of the Reformers. Reformed theology emphasizes more the assurance of faith (Heb. 11:1), but mystical faith emphasizes blind trust in the absence of assurance. It would be good to keep this difference in mind.

see. During this illuminative stage, God sends shafts of light into the soul which provide the mystic with "sensible comforts." At this point, however, most would insert an additional stage as the illuminative eyes of faith lead into the all important mystical "death," where (according to the mystic) God withdraws these shafts of light, forcing the mystic to come to God by "naked faith."[21] St. John of the Cross describes this death as the "dark night of the soul" where a supreme moral crisis is constituted as the human will completely surrenders to the will of God.[22]

The final stage in the mystical path is the *unitive* stage, which has been frequently misinterpreted. While much of the more unguarded language of mystical union has the odor of pathological deification, most mystics understand this "complete" union with God as an almost unreachable ideal. Even the greatest mystics were involved in an infinite process of growth in which they continued until death.

If this explanation establishes at least some common ground, it should now be remembered that mysticism also has countless diversifications. Some would speak only of a "pure New Testament mysticism," which usually involves little more than the essence of Christian experience. The mysticism discussed here is that mysticism that, according to consensus, has gradually developed from the earliest times. There are, however, many types and measures of mysticism, and when studying a particular aspect it does little good to speak of mysticism as it ought to be ideally or even as it has developed traditionally over the years. When studying the influence of mysticism on John Wesley, for example, one must describe the mysticism of those mystics known and read by him. Having described the more general context, therefore, we now turn our attention to mysticism as understood by Wesley, especially where it either diverges from or strongly amplifies that type of mysticism already discussed.

MYSTICISM AS UNDERSTOOD BY JOHN WESLEY

For the most part, the greatest span of Christian mysticism developed along the lines mentioned above.[23] Mysticism as understood

---

[21] The Pauline phrase "to live is Christ, to die is gain" is frequently used.

[22] Underhill, *Mystic Way*, 55.

[23] At least until the Middle Ages when the pseudo-Dionysian writings began to subordinate the ascetical for the speculative. This period is largely omitted here because Wesley, as we shall see, had little interest in medieval mysticism.

by John Wesley, however, had a distinctly Roman Catholic flavor. Furthermore, most of the Roman Catholics abridged by Wesley were post-Reformation mystics; Macarius, for example, being an exception. For this reason our attention turns quickly to some of the characteristics of Roman Catholic mysticism in general and then more specifically to the so-called Counter or (more correctly) Catholic Reformation mystics since these were the ones who most attracted Wesley's attention.

The Roman Catholics

Although Protestant mysticism has been sporadic, the Catholics have maintained a remarkable continuity of mysticism since the Reformation.[24] Since mysticism is "pure" religion, the church has never been able to exist without it, but it has similarly been unable to harness it for its own aims. By its very nature it is difficult to control. At the time of the Reformation, two mystical trends began to appear among the Roman Catholics.[25] One trend continued along the lines of medieval mysticism which, in an effort to counterbalance formalism in the church, had lost the perspective of its already unstable synthesis between Christian dogma and Neoplatonic thought. The Rhineland mystics like Eckhart, Tauler, and the author of the fourteenth-century treatise *Theologia Germanica* had become increasingly involved in a speculative, near-pantheistic philosophy aimed at the "progressive deification" of the soul. Behmen, and later William Law, were influenced by this school which epitomizes the kind of mysticism that Wesley would grow to despise the most. A second trend, however, centered in Spain and France and usually associated with the so-called Counter Reformation, is of particular interest to us here.

The post-Reformation mystics abridged by John Wesley can all be identified with the Catholic Reformation.[26] This second trend empha-sized the ascetical stage of mysticism, after the example of the pre-medieval mystics and the fifteenth-century quasi-mystic, Thomas à Kempis. Several scholars have attempted to label this second trend, but the most basic characteristic is "activity."[27] The great Spanish mystic

---

[24] James, *Varieties,* 406.

[25] The lines here are by no means clear since both trends must appear to a certain extent in all mystics.

[26] Again, this Catholic Reformation period is so important for our particular study that this necessarily brief introductory statement will be expanded later on in this chapter.

[27] M. Schmidt tags it, "Romanic mysticism"; H. Lindström, "practical" and John Fletcher, "evangelical." One need hardly add that these far from exhaust the possibilities.

Ignatius Loyola wanted to create active and heroic rather than contemplative Christians.[28] This, of course, is not to imply that these mystics were no longer concerned with contemplation; indeed they were, and if not, they would cease to be mystics.[29] Properly speaking, mysticism is a combination of the ascetical and contemplative lives: one leads inevitably into the other as the mind and soul are detached from outer sensations. This second trend simply emphasizes the initial stage of mysticism.

Although these mystics *speak* the language of mystical contemplation, they *live* highly ascetical lives exhibiting considerable moral, ethical, and even missionary zeal. Even though mysticism is "born of surrender to the divine initiative"; even though the overall mystical temperament, as mentioned previously, leans to antinomianism in its constant struggle against "false activity"; and even though some mystics allowed their hard-earned virtue to become marred by antinomian self-indulgence, John Wesley could still use the example of mystics like Madame Bourignon and Mon. de Renty as an effective weapon in his own battle against the antinomian concepts of grace.[30] Brother Lawrence's "practice of the presence of God," even amidst the mundane chores of the kitchen, must surely be a classic example of the ideal portrayal of mysticism as "an attitude of mind which moves towards the spiritual even in the common things of life."[31] Molinos, the archetypal quietist, nonetheless in his *Spiritual Guide* strongly exhorts one to mortify the senses. The mysticism of the Catholic Reformation as known and abridged by John Wesley, although infused with paradoxes, stresses first and foremost the ascetical means of purgation in the spiritual conflict against carnal lusts.

Another characteristic of this ascetical trend lies in the area of the intellect. Where the intellect is sacrificed, there is no check upon superstition. There are no mystical shortcuts, and perversion occurs when one tries to clutch at the fruits of mysticism before going through

---

[28] Underhill, *Mystic Way*, 68. Loyola's "mysticism of service" is presented in his *Spiritual Exercises* and perhaps best represents this trend.

[29] Contemplation is essential to mystical theology; nonetheless, it is a treacherous and equivocal word.

[30] Dunn Wilson, "The Influence of Mysticism on John Wesley" (Ph.D. dissertation presented at Leeds University, 1968); cf., for example, *Journal*, 1:15n (#3); and *Works*, 8:190f. All subsequent references to the *Works* are to the Jackson edition; to the *Letters*, the Telford edition; to the *Journals*, the Curnock edition; to the *Sermons*, the Sugden edition; and to the "new" *Works*, the Baker edition (Frank Baker, editor-in-chief).

[31] Inge, *English Mystics*, 13.

the toilsome preparation of the will and the intellect. These mystics, therefore, by emphasizing the first stage of mysticism, stood a better chance of resisting (although frequently without complete success) the more antirational tendencies of a purely negative path (*via negativa*). In addition, they were generally intellectually and morally strong.

William James tells us that in those mystics whose natural character is passive and whose intellect is feeble, mysticism often leads to an over-abstraction in the practical life.[32] On the other hand, in those natively strong in mind and character, the opposite is often true. Some of the greatest mystics of this period, for example, carried the experience of mystical union as far as it has ever been carried, but still revealed an indomitable spirit and matchless energy. It has been said of Loyola that his mystical experiences made him "one of the most powerfully practical human engines that ever lived."[33] Clearly, the dangers of mysticism are subtle and strong, but the rewards can be great indeed. True, much in mysticism can be abnormal, even pathological, and many mystical movements have overemphasized the nonessential ecstasies, glorifying abstractions to the degree that mystical phenomena mean nothing less than "supernatural suspensions of physical laws."[34] Yet the fact remains that mystical experiences frequently made the mystics of the Catholic Reformation even "more energetic in the lines which their inspiration favored."[35] Schmidt writes that the role of Romanic mysticism as the spiritual bond of unity in Europe in the seventeenth and eighteenth centuries is important and must be conceived in a new way.[36] Therefore, since so much emphasis is placed on the Catholic Reformation and since much of the remaining material can be understood accurately only in the light of its development, it is imperative to outline the movement in brief (especially its mystical thread).[37]

---

[32] James, *Varieties*, 414.

[33] Ibid.

[34] Ibid., 415.

[35] Ibid.

[36] M. Schmidt, *John Wesley: A Theological Biography*, trans. Norman P. Goldhawk (London: Epworth, 1962), 48n (#9); cf. Schmidt's contribution to *History of the Ecumenical Movement*, eds. Ruth Rouse and Stephen Neill (London: SPCK, 1954), "The Ecumenical Movement in Continental Europe in the Seventeenth and Eighteenth Centuries"; and John Kirk, *Mother of the Wesleys* (London: Jarrold and Sons, 1866).

[37] *The Oxford Dictionary of the Christian Church*, 348. Cf. H. Daniel-Rops, *The Catholic Reformation* (London: Dent, 1962) where the Catholic Reformation is described as a "Renaissance" where the clergy were limited to their own parishes, where preaching could now be heard in one's native tongue, and where seminaries were being established.

The Catholic Reformation

Generally speaking, the Catholic Reformation was not just a negative reaction against Protestantism but the revival of the Roman Catholic Church in Europe from the first half of the sixteenth century to the end of the Thirty Years' War (1648). Although stimulated by Protestant opposition, it was also an internal reform movement which had begun almost simultaneously with the Lutheran schism. One Catholic Reformation scholar states that "the two reforming movements may be regarded with some justification as streams proceeding in reverse directions but from the same source."[38] The new Orders of the 1520s, however—the Capuchins, the Theatines (the Order of Lorenzo Scupoli, one of Susanna Wesley's favorite authors) and the Barnabites—are usually considered to be the earliest organic signs of the Catholic Reformation. Then about twenty years later the movement really began to take effect under the leadership of the Jesuit and Carmelite Orders and it was here that the Catholic church experienced the revival of mysticism. Inge observes that the history of mysticism has always embodied the spirit of reformation and revival. As religion "tends to formalize its symbols of our consciousness of the beyond, mysticism brings a revival of the spiritual in the midst of formalism."[39] It was only natural then that post-Reformation Catholicism should flourish with mystics.

Spanish Spirituality. The Catholic revival of mysticism after the Reformation first centered in Spain. Ignatius Loyola (c. 1491–1556), the epitome of the Catholic Reformation and the founder of the Society of Jesus, was himself an ecstatic mystic who established a scheme of spirituality which produced a number of mystics.[40] A great deal of speculation has linked Wesley and Loyola. Bishop Kelley writes that only because Wesley was so thoroughly Protestant in a land where there were nothing but Protestants did he "barely escape meeting Loyola with the *Exercises*."[41] Perhaps even closer to the truth is the suggestion that

---

[38] Friedrich Richter, *Martin Luther and Ignatius Loyola* (Westminster: Newman, 1960), depicts Luther as "reformer" and Loyola as "restorer" side-by-side.

[39] Inge, *Mysticism*, 6.

[40] Loyola's *Spiritual Exercises,* for example, inspired Alphonsus Rodriguez (1533–1617) whose mystical *Treatise on Humility* Wesley read in 1733.

[41] M. Piette, *John Wesley in the Evolution of Protestantism* (London: Sheed and Ward, 1937), x. Cf. W. H. Fitchett's *Wesley and His Century* (London: Smith, Elder, 1906), 302, 335, where he compares Wesley and Loyola. Both were enthusiastic and fanatical but created imperishable institutions. "Loyola at Oxford would have headed secession and

Wesley combined the genius of Luther and Loyola, the Reformed doctrine of grace with the piety and organizational strength of the Roman Catholic saint. On August 16, 1742, John read the life of Loyola.[42] At that time he thought Loyola to be "one of the greatest men to support so bad a cause, but he was no enthusiast. In the interest of his Church he acted consistently in all things."[43] Wesley on several occasions was called a Jesuit, just as many of the Methodist leaders were characterized as "sons of Loyola" and "bedlam popes," but he was always quick to deny the charge.[44] One interesting anecdote describes a man shouting out in the middle of one of Wesley's sermons, "Aye, he is a Jesuit; that's plain," to which a Roman priest in the audience replied, "No, he is not; I would to God he was."[45]

Loyola's mysticism of service, which focused on perfect obedience to the will of God, probably had a considerable influence on John of Avila (1500–1569), the first mystic of the period to be abridged by Wesley.[46] John of Avila was an effective preacher whose early association with the Jesuits did much to foster their work in Spain. His best known works are *Audi Filia*, a treatise on perfection, and his spiritual letters, extracts from the latter being included in Wesley's *Christian Library*. Largely through John of Avila, the spirit of the Catholic Reformation soon spread from the Jesuits to the Carmelites, considered by many to be responsible for the finest expressions of post-Reformation mysticism.[47] John of Avila was the trusted counselor of St.

Wesley at Rome would have become the general of a society devoted to the interest and honor of the Church." Cf. also H. B. Workman, *The Place of Methodism in the Catholic Church*, rev. ed. (London, Epworth, 1909), 74f. Workman compares the two on the surrender of the will.

[42] Dominick Bouhours, *The Life of Ignatius Loyola* (London: Henry Hills, 1686; trans. into English at London, 1686). He may have borrowed this biography from Charles Wesley as a copy is still among Charles' books in the Manchester archives. Also the marks and marginal notes look more like John's, and they emphasize Loyola's spiritual struggle between God and the world (p. 11), his extreme mortification (pp. 13, 22), his devotion to God (p. 22), and the high degree of perfection that he reached in such a short time (p. 26).

[43] *Journal*, 3:40.

[44] Lyles, *Methodism Mocked—The Satiric Reaction to Methodism in the Eighteenth Century* (London: Epworth, 1960), 88. Cf. *Works*, 9:58 and Wesley's letter, December 1751 (*Letters*, 3:295–331), to Bishop Lavington where he denies the charge.

[45] *Journal*, 3:353.

[46] Both Loyola and Avila have been associated with the Alumbrados or "Illuminati."

[47] It is good to remember here that the Jesuits are known as an "active" Order and the Carmelites as a "contemplative" Order.

Teresa of Avila (1542–1582) who persuaded the disgruntled John of the Cross (1542–1591) not to leave the sagging Carmelites but to help in introducing her reform among the friars of the Order as she had done among the nuns. Although Wesley never mentions Teresa or John of the Cross and probably never read them, it was their brand of mysticism that deeply affected the mystics of the Catholic Reformation and that Wesley relied upon so heavily for extract material.

Both Teresa and John of the Cross set out to enforce the principles of the Catholic Reformation with a carefully planned scheme of spiritual ascent. Both faced strong opposition and a great deal of their mystical doctrine no doubt arose out of the personal experience of suffering. Dunn Wilson, who relies a great deal on Teresa in his examination of the mystical influences on Wesley, tells us that Teresa taught that "when conformity to Christ is achieved, the human will becomes 'quiet' and is truly 'at rest' "[48] Likewise, John of the Cross "describes the soul's journey through the dark night of sense and faith until it reaches a passive state of rest."[49] Inge elaborates on this, adding that Teresa's mystical theology (unlike Loyola's *active* mysticism) stresses complete conformity to the will of God as the human will becomes more and more passive. Similarly, John of the Cross leads one through the successive nights of sense, faith (or darkness), memory and will until the soul eventually sinks into "a holy inertia and oblivion," actually becoming one with God through participation.[50]

It is almost certain that John of Avila also influenced a lesser-known Spanish mystic, Gregory Lopez (1542–1596). Whereas John of Avila was diverted from his preparation for missionary work in Mexico, Lopez carried through with the same plan, actually settling in the New World and spending his life among the natives there.[51] Lopez was a man of extraordinary self-denial and obedience to God, and Wesley would be quick to recognize his value as evidence for perfection in this life.

The Movement Spreads

Since mysticism is so highly contagious it was inevitable that it should spread to other countries. It was the Carmelites more than the Jesuits, however, who were responsible for the spread. The formalistic

---

[48] Wilson, "Influence of Mysticism," 152n (#3).

[49] Ibid.

[50] Inge, *Mysticism*, 213ff., especially 222, 224.

[51] Wesley included an extract of Lopez' *Life* in John Wesley, *The Christian Library*, 50 vols. (Bristol, Eng.: William Pine, 1749–1756).

mysticism of Loyola's *Exercises,* which some suggest might have been promoted by Rome to stem the tide of Protestantism, was strongly suspected outside of Spain. France in particular disliked the anthropocentric meditation of the Jesuits but readily embraced the theocentric contemplation of Francis of Sales (1567–1622). Francis, depending largely on the mystical systems of Teresa and John of the Cross (although the Spanish mystics demonstrated a greater devotion to the person of Christ), made sanctity available to the ordinary person. Flew writes that "the Reformation brought the idea of perfection out into the open" making it attainable in ordinary life, and nowhere is this "new conception of the ideal more immediately apparent than in the writings of St. François de Sales."[52] By carefully blending the mysticism of the Jesuits and Carmelites, Sales sought "to soften and polish Spanish mysticism into a graceful and winning pietism" capable of refining and elevating the common person.[53] Wesley read Sales' mystical treatise, *Introduction to the Devout Life,* in 1733 and again the following year. Unfortunately, he never read the *Life* of Sales or any of the remaining works. It is apparent that Francis of Sales had many of the qualities most admired by John Wesley and had he known him better he would undoubtedly have abridged at least some of his works.[54] The "devout life," for example, meant perfection.[55] In another treatise (on the love of God) Sales compares the mystical path to perfection to Solomon's temple: the three courts represent the progressive modes of reasoning, first by the experience of sense, then by the human sciences, and finally by faith. The temple sanctuary then represents the complete submission of the mind to the will of God.[56]

Before we go on to the Jansenist and Quietist controversies, we should mention the influence of a lay brother and a mystic, Nicolas Herman (1605–1691), better known as Brother Lawrence of the Resurrection. After entering the Carmelite monastery at Paris in 1649,

---

[52] R. Newton Flew, *The Idea of Perfection in Christian Theology* (London: Humphrey Milford, 1934), 258.

[53] Inge, *Mysticism,* 230.

[54] Although Wesley did not read Sales' *Life* (cf. *Letters,* 3:329), Wilson provides some interesting facts which would have deeply impressed Wesley. Sales, like Wesley, experienced spiritual depression, he was frequently slandered, he was an exceptional preacher with the gift of speaking to the common people, he urged religious people to leave their seclusions and visit and sustain the poor, and he gave spiritual instruction at meetings inaugurated for women. Wilson, "Influence of Mysticism," 154 (#1).

[55] *Devout Life,* i.c. 3.

[56] Flew, *Perfection,* 259. From the *Treatise on the Love of God* by Francis of Sales.

he was given the difficult task of managing the kitchen. Brother Lawrence, however, transformed life among the mundane chores of the kitchen into the constant practice of the presence of God. His maxims soon became known among his contemporaries and were highly appreciated. Wesley included extracts from some of his "conversations" and letters in *The Christian Library*.

Thus far we have encountered only three of the Catholic Reformation mystics abridged by Wesley: the somewhat lesser-known John of Avila, Gregory Lopez, and Brother Lawrence. Although the mystics of the sixteenth century were frequently slandered, suspected, or even hauled before the Inquisition and imprisoned, they were generally highly acclaimed and eventually became *Saint* Francis of Sales, *Saint* Ignatius, *Blessed* John of Avila, *Saint* Teresa, and *Saint* John of the Cross. Among the seventeenth-century Catholic Reformation mystics, however, those who would have been canonized a century earlier now came under strong suspicion. As mysticism began to rival the church and sacrament the mystics were persecuted. Is it not strange, then, that six of the nine Catholic Reformation mystical works selected by Wesley for publication were from these seventeenth-century "outcasts"?[57] These six, one way or another, can be associated with either of two contrasting movements, Jansenism or Quietism.

Jansenism. This movement (said by some to have inaugurated French spirituality) takes its name from Cornelius Jansen (1585–1638) who migrated to Paris in 1604 where he met Jean du Vergier (1581–1643), after 1620 the abbot of Saint-Cyran. Having become friends, Jansen and Cyran were soon attracted to the writings of St. Augustine, and together they studied Augustine continually for five years (Jansen read the whole of Augustine ten times). Eventually these friends judged the prevailing scholasticism and many of the theologians of the Catholic Reformation, namely, the Jesuits, incompatible with Augustine, and a controversy developed.[58] Jansen conceived an elaborate plan of attack which culminated in his *Augustinus* (begun in 1628 and published posthumously in 1640), a highly theological treatise which sought to propagate a type of theological pessimism, emphasizing to an extreme human corruption alongside the nature and efficacy of grace.

---

[57] Wesley's high church sympathies may have attracted him more to the "outcast." There would be obvious parallels in his own experience.

[58] According to Wesley's *Ecclesiastical History*, 4 vols (J. Paramore, 1781), all other controversies against Rome were only light blasts next to this hurricane; 4:52ff.

Saint-Cyran (frequently portrayed as overbearing) quickly emerged as the real leader of the Jansenists. The movement, severely persecuted by Rome (and by the Jesuits in particular), was riddled with a strange mixture of mysticism and quasimysticism.[59] Wesley's *Ecclesiastical History* mentions the mystical tendencies in Saint-Cyran. His prayers, for example, were criticized as consisting not in distinct ideas but blind impulses. Cyran was also said to have thought "his being the residence of deity." The Jansenist notions of repentance as consisting chiefly of voluntary suffering and the expiation of original guilt by acts of mortification were also criticized in the *Ecclesiastical History* as being "fanatical," although one must remember that this does not necessarily reflect Wesley's personal opinion.[60]

The development of Jansenism, however, has many interesting crosscurrents. In 1618 Francis of Sales preached in Paris emphasizing the need for Christian concern in the care of the sick and the poor. This preaching is known to have prepared the way for two active Orders, the Lazarist Fathers (now called the Vincentians) and the Sisters of Charity, both founded by the "secular" priest Vincent de Paul (1580–1660) and devoted entirely to works of charity.[61] In 1619 Angélique Arnauld (1591–1661), the abbess of the Cistercian Convent at Port-Royal fell under the influence of Sales, but being refused permission to join the Visitation nuns (conceived by Sales but entrusted to Vincent de Paul) she returned to Port-Royal. Nonetheless Vincent and Angélique were close friends; therefore, when Saint-Cyran visited Port-Royal in 1622 the stage was set. Vincent and Saint-Cyran soon began to pool their resources; they took their meals together, and obliged one another in various other ways.[62] Vincent thought Cyran to be "one of the most virtuous men I ever met." Likewise, the Abbess Angélique and Cyran had a great deal in common, especially a pronounced antipathy toward Jesuits. Consequently, Port-Royal soon became the focal point for the Jansenist movement. Unfortunately, the story does not end there. Although Vincent always remained reasonably friendly toward Cyran,

---

[59] The bulls *Cum Occasione* (1653) and *Unigenitus* (1713) condemned the Jansenists. In 1709 Louis XIV (again urged by Jesuits) completely destroyed Port-Royal.

[60] Wesley, *Ecclesiastical History,* 4:51ff. Most of these volumes were taken directly from a work by a man named Mosheim; in the Preface, Wesley writes that Mosheim had "little knowledge of inward religion and he therefore condemns the mystics in a lump." Wesley also omitted a great deal of the criticism against the mystics in these volumes.

[61] The Sisters of Charity are now the largest Order in Catholicism, numbering 45,000; 13,000 in the British Isles.

[62] Mary Purcell, *The World of Monsieur Vincent* (London: Harvill, 1963), 154.

after 1635 they began to see less and less of one another.[63] Cyran grew more and more bitter in his polemic against the Jesuits and eventually Vincent sensed that he was going too far in his attack. Vincent's affection grew cold, and later he became one of the most uncompromising opponents of Jansenism.[64] Cyran and Vincent, therefore, continued to exercise tremendous influence but in different directions.

Vincent exerted considerable influence over mystics like the Cardinal de Retz (1614–1679), Jean-Jacques Olier (1608–1657) and a French marquis, Gaston Jean Baptiste de Renty (1611–1649). De Renty, one of Vincent's helpers, had perhaps the strongest continuous influence of any mystic on Wesley. Mon. de Renty was the first mystic life to be published by Wesley (1741) and is included in the first edition of his own works. Mon. de Renty, like Lopez, would provide an excellent illustration for perfection in this life. It is interesting to note that Sales, Vincent, Retz, Olier, and de Renty all appear in Augustin Léger's impressive (but still far from complete) list of mystics comprising Wesley's favorite masters.[65]

In the meantime, Saint-Cyran deeply impressed quasimystics like Antoine Arnauld (Angélique's younger brother), Blaise Pascal (1623–1662), and Pasquier Quesnel (1634–1719). Orcibal singles out both Pascal and Quesnel as two of Wesley's favorite authors during the period from 1725 to 1735.[66]

Wesley came to know these works in various ways and with various reactions. Knox claims that Wesley had "the mind of a Jesuit and the morals of a Jansenist."[67] Wesley was introduced to Saint-Cyran, for example, by a Roman Catholic, Miss Freeman Shepherd, and Orcibal adds that in spite of the predestinarianism Wesley held Saint-Cyran and the Jansenists in high esteem. In support of this, Wesley condemned the papal suppression of "this zeal for genuine piety."[68] On January 11, 1750, Wesley wrote that the Abbé Paris phenomena (convulsions at the grave of Francis of Paris, a Jansenist deacon, that were growing more

---

[63] Ibid.

[64] Vincent was present at Cyran's inquiry and testified against him, but he also prevented his execution. Ibid., 177, 181.

[65] M. Augustin Léger, *La Jeunesse de Wesley*, 184, cited in *Sermons*, 1:279n.

[66] Jean Orcibal, "The Theological Originality of John Wesley, and Continental Spirituality," *A History of the Methodist Church in Great Britain*, ed. by R. Davies and G. Rupp (London: Epworth, 1965), 1:93. Quesnel is important as the late seventeenth-, early eighteenth-century leader of Jansenism.

[67] Knox, *Enthusiasm*, 493.

[68] Wesley, *Ecclesiastical History*, 4:44ff.

and more pronounced; some endured sword thrusts and even crucifixion) were not popery since the Abbé "lived and died in open
opposition to the grossest errors of Popery and in particular to that
diabolical Bull Unigenitus, which destroys the foundations of Christianity."[69] This bull was issued by Pope Clement XI at the instigation of the
Jesuits, and had as its object the overthrow of Jansenism.

Wesley demonstrated considerable interest in Saint-Cyran and
Quesnel but his favorite Jansenist was the most mystical of the Port-
Royal apologists, Blaise Pascal.[70] Saint-Cyran was imprisoned in 1638
where he remained until his death in 1643. Antoine Arnauld was
condemned by the Sorbonne in 1655. Pascal, however, continued to
fight against the Jesuits, and, according to some, an invalid obsessed by
original sin, published his *lettres provinciales* which attacked the Jesuit
theory of grace and the immoral character of their casuistry. His well-
known *Pensées* (selections from his notes published posthumously) was
abridged by Wesley for publication in *The Christian Library* and was a
favorite among the devotional works in the Epworth rectory.

Quietism.   If Wesley was impressed by the Jansenists, he was
equally impressed by the contrasting Quietists. Knox tells us that the
Quietists put the Jansenists' theory into practice.[71] Whereas the
Jansenists emphasized theology, the Quietists emphasized experience.
Both the Jansenists and the Quietists had affinities with the Protestant
and Catholic Reformations, but not the same affinities. Both disliked the
Jesuits but for entirely different reasons. Jansenism emphasized a
theology of grace while Quietism emphasized the experience of faith. It
is a serious mistake, however, to equate the mystical concept of grace
and faith with Reformation terminology. The Quietists, for example,
emphasized faith, not so much over and against works (as in
Reformation thought), but in contrast with the rival claims of the active
life (sensible devotion and consolation in prayer) as opposed to the
contemplative life. Many have studied Quietism only in the light of the
"faith against works" controversy, but to say, for example, that Quietism
was reacting against penance as having *atoning* merit "is to convict
yourself of having read the Quietists without taking the trouble to
master their vocabulary, or for that matter, the rudiments of Catholic

---

[69] Wesley, *Works*, 2:171.

[70] Wesley published extracts from the quasimystics Saint-Cyran (*Letters to Andilly*),
Quesnel (*Reflexions Morales Sur Les Evangiles*), and Pascal (*Thoughts on Religion*).

[71] Knox, *Enthusiasm*, 232.

theology."[72] Few Catholics have taught that penance furnishes a justification for past sins. Likewise, Quietism never doubted for a moment the value of suffering in spiritual discipline. The Quietists simply said "that the sufferings which God inflicts upon the soul when it gives itself up to contemplation have a much higher satisfactory value than the self-imposed penances of the Christian who remains in the common way of prayer."[73] The Quietist polemic was to a large extent underscoring the difference between the anthropocentric *meditation* which asked, "What is God for me?"—(Loyola's formalized meditation and to a lesser extent Pascal's teaching on *assurance*); and the theocentric *contemplation* which asked, "What is God in himself?" (the Quietist path to *perfection*).[74]

The Quietist train of thought (unlike the more spontaneous nature of Jansenism) has deep roots. Some traces can be found in the fifth and sixth centuries from which the torch was passed on to the Catholic Reformation through the medieval "heretics." The term itself was apparently first used in the fourteenth century of the Hesychastai (from the Greek word for "quiet"), the mystical monks of Mt. Athos who taught that one, by an elaborate system of ascetics involving the perfect quiet of body and mind, could arrive at the vision of the "uncreated light of the Godhead."[75] Traces reappear in John of Avila and the Alumbrados (also known as the *Illuminati* or the "enlightened") whose contemplation tended to dispense with "mental images" altogether.[76] From the Alumbrados, Quietism spread eventually into France through the mysticism of Teresa, John of the Cross, and particularly Juan Falconi's *Alfabetto et Lettera* which prepared the way for the great seventeenth-century unveiling of Quietism in Miguel de Molinos (1640–1697).

The Spanish mystic Molinos, born at Muniesa near Saragossa, went to Rome in 1663 when Italy was ripe for mysticism, and soon rose in prominence as a confessor and director. In 1675 he published his *Spiritual Guide*, the textbook for Quietism abridged by Wesley and included in *The Christian Library*. Here Molinos emphasized the

---

[72] Ibid., 237.

[73] Ibid.

[74] Ibid., 248f. From the Quietist point of view, Molinos speaks of "acquired contemplation," Fénelon of "disinterested love," and Malaval criticizes those who make long speeches to God but never listen to hear God speak.

[75] *Oxford Dictionary*, 633.

[76] In 1527, while a student at Salamanca, Loyola was accused of Illuminati associations. These unorganized confraternities were condemned by the Inquisition in 1623.

advantage of "pure faith" (contemplation) over the discursive thoughts of meditation. Perfection is not to be found in meditation. In fact, "he who uses images, figures, ideas or conceptions of his own in prayer *does not worship God in Spirit and Truth.*"[77]

Soon after the publication of *Spiritual Guide*, Molinos was accused of error by the Jesuits and the Dominicans but his accusers were silenced. As he grew more and more extreme, however—especially in his private letters, which are said to have taught the total annihilation of the will—his doctrines began to have an adverse effect on many of his followers. Inge warns against this tendency among mystics. Although they rarely imply deification, they frequently imply the loss of personality, an objection which Wesley raised in his own criticism of mysticism.[78] Eventually ecclesiastical discipline completely broke down among the nuns whom he directed (they refused to recite their office, refused confession, discarded their rosaries and holy pictures, and caused general disturbances in their houses).

In 1685 the storm broke when he was imprisoned. Nonetheless, Molinos made a tremendous impact on Europe. *Spiritual Guide* (apparently not so extreme as his private correspondence) encouraged one to abandon self to the will of God: One should choose little for oneself, remaining indifferent to hardship; one should be like wax in the hand of one's director (again it is said that his private direction implied that all external observances, even resisting temptation, were hindrances). Although Molinos did not teach the extreme spiritual "prayer of quiet" or "infused contemplation" where all of one's faculties were held in divine suspense as supernatural grace acted directly upon the soul, he did emphasize that prayer should never express one's own will. This, at least in his *Guide*, was known as the "prayer of simple regard" or "acquired contemplation" inasmuch as it was reached by the normal development of the natural faculties.

Quietism made a lasting impression upon the seventeenth century. Inge suggests that Rome first encouraged Quietistic mysticism to counterbalance the tide of Protestantism, but this is certainly a mistake.[79] It seems more likely that Rome promoted the activistic mysticism of Loyola and that Quietism (like Teresa and John of the Cross a century earlier) was reacting against the mental gymnastics of a

---

[77] Knox, *Enthusiasm*, 264. It is interesting to note that whereas the Reformers condemned *physical* images, Quietism condemned *mental* ones.

[78] Inge, *Mysticism*, 30.

[79] Ibid., 242.

formalistic meditation (the peculiar glory of the Jesuits) that was stifling to the contemplative spirit of freedom. It was this freedom which captivated the seventeenth century, and the strength of its influence can be seen in the severity of efforts to stamp it out.

The last three Catholic Reformation mystics abridged by Wesley number among the French and Flemish Quietists—Madame Guyon (1648–1717), François Fénelon (1651–1715) and Antoinette Bourignon (1616–1680). Quietism entered France largely through the Barnabite friar F. Lacombe's influence on Madame Guyon, his most famous disciple. Wesley describes her as a woman of considerable piety and devotion but whose lack of prudence made her vulnerable to slander. Characterized by a neurotic youth and an unhappy marriage to an invalid husband twenty-two years older than herself, Madame Guyon was easy prey for the mysticism of Molinos and quickly exchanged meditation for the "prayer of simple regard." After the death of her husband in 1676 she endeavored to propagate her mystical beliefs. In 1681 she unwisely began a five-year journey through France in the company of Lacombe, and in 1687, suspected of heresy and immorality, they were arrested. Lacombe remained in prison until 1699 and eventually died insane, but Guyon was freed through the efforts of Madame de Maintenon. Madame Guyon wrote prolifically, producing for example her *Moyen Court, Les Torrents Spirituels,* and an autobiography that was abridged and published by Wesley in 1776.[80]

Unfortunately, after her first release from prison her trials were not yet over. One of the great French preachers, Jacques Bossuet, suspicious of her illuminism, began another attack. This time Guyon had a worthy champion in Fénelon, with whom she had begun to correspond in 1688. Fénelon, a Quietist of high caliber who exercised a considerable influence on Wesley, was strangely drawn to the unstable Guyon. For several years he wrote in her defense, but in spite of his efforts she was again condemned (and arrested) by the Thirty-Four Articles of the Conference of Issy which Fénelon signed (although he continued to defend her).[81]

Guyon and Fénelon both described the path to perfection through "pure love," Fénelon coining the frequently misunderstood term "disinterested love." In order to give God the complete right of spiritual

---

[80]*Les Torrents Spirituels* perhaps best illustrates Guyon's mysticism as it describes the three classes of the soul: (1) the way of meditation and works; (2) the way of sight; and (3) the passive way of "faith" accessible only to the *elite*.

[81]The same year he became the archbishop of Cambrai.

initiative, this fifth stage of contemplation virtually did away with human effort as such. For example, Fénelon's *Explication des Maximes des Saints* (condemned in 1699) emphasized self-love as the root of all evil and insisted that the Christian's ascent toward union with God must be made by the stages of love where resignation becomes indifference, and self (even one's own salvation) becomes less and less important. "Pure love" is all in all. Horrified by consolation, Fénelon taught that one loves God for what God *is,* not for what God *grants.* Wesley included extracts from some of the Frenchman's influential letters in *The Christian Library.* Wesley also published an extract from *Les Moeurs des Chretiens* (1682) of Claude Fleury (1640–1725). Fleury, another semi-mystic, came under the patronage of Fénelon and was accused of Quietism, but he was generously saved by Fénelon's arch-rival, Bossuet.

The last Catholic Reformation mystic mentioned in this brief survey and of particular interest to us here is Antoinette Bourignon. A paradoxical figure described by Knox as a "Jansenist who was also a Pelagian," she can best (or paradoxically) be associated with Quietism. After several unsuccessful ventures at Liège she was more or less estranged from organized Christianity. Eventually, however, she founded a small colony of believers on the island of Norstrand where, in spite of persecution, Bourignonism flourished. Her writings (Wesley published an extract from her *Treatise on Solid Virtue*), circulated by the indefatigable Protestant mystic Pierre Poiret, made an amazing impact on Europe. Count Marsay, for example, another mystic read by Wesley, adopted Bourignonism; and its influence in Scotland was felt in the early part of the eighteenth century.[82]

To summarize, Quietism was far from "quiet" (much of its persecution arose out of its refusal to remain quiet), although it did lean toward unchristian apathy. Undoubtedly, many mystics were Quietists, but it is an open question whether all Quietists were mystics. Ruysbroeck was known to be critical of the "natural repose." Bossuet, misunderstanding Quietism for "infused contemplation," called Quietism "a morbid growth on the healthy body of mysticism."[83] Evelyn Underhill calls Quietism an "abortive child," a blind alley leading off from mystical theology.[84] Brash writes that the Quietism at Fetter Lane

---

[82] *Journal,* 6:71. Incidentally, Wesley states that he admires Marsay's piety but "sees in him a reflection of the 'enthusiasm' and 'spiritual mysticism' of the Middle Ages."

[83] Knox, *Enthusiasm,* 239ff.

[84] Underhill, *Mystic Way,* 59.

was only a caricature of mysticism.[85] He asserts that the great mystics have always been nourished by the means of grace and have shown a noble standard of life. This perhaps pinpoints a part of the paradox in Quietism. Knox states that the Quietists frequently spoke out against virtue as such, but were in fact all virtuous.[86] Perhaps they simply overstated their case in an attempt to ensure complete freedom in the pursuit of pure love.

The writings of Abbé Bremond support this moderate position in their description of Quietism as "mysticism being given a bad name by those disliking it."[87] He saw nothing in Madame Guyon which had not passed without question in the sixteenth century. Fénelon's "disinterested love" was common doctrine with men like Cardinal Pierre de Bérulle; and Molinos' "acquired contemplation" had been the mainspring of sixteenth-century spirituality.[88] Nonetheless, orthodox mysticism has never pedantically insisted on the Quietist "fear of action." Perhaps, therefore, it is more accurate to interpret Quietism as "ultramysticism." Knox states that Quietism follows out (but exaggerates) the lines of orthodox mysticism.[89] It might, then, be suggested that Quietism's acute mental and spiritual sufferings, which begin *after* the soul's surrender to God and its suspicion of consolation (so common among mystics), simply degenerated into an extreme position of complete indifference.

John Wesley, nonetheless, recommended and published many of the Quietist writings as they expressed a growing mystical experience that relentlessly pursued the goal of Christian perfection. Later, plagued by the problems of backsliding societies, Wesley would draw upon innumerable sources which demonstrated genuine piety and the necessity for perseverance in the overall Christian experience.

This brief study has not attempted to mention all of the Catholic Reformation mystics known by Wesley. There were several like the Benedictine Juan de Castaniza, Magdalen de Pazzi, and even the semi-mystic Malebranche, who have not been mentioned.[90] This section has

---

[85] See below, the "Moravian stillness controversy."

[86] Knox, *Enthusiasm*, 280. None of the immorality charges against Molinos or Guyon were substantiated.

[87] Ibid., 40n.

[88] Ibid.

[89] Ibid., 237ff.

[90] Wesley admired Castaniza's insight into the true significance of sanctification (*Works*, 7:204). Castaniza often appeared bound with Scupoli and has been confused with him. Wesley also admired the piety of the Carmelite divine, Magdalen de Pazzi (*Journal*,

simply attempted to provide a suitable context for some of the most significant mystics encountered by Wesley. Schmidt groups the mystics of the Catholic Reformation under the heading of "Romanic mystics." He concludes that the Romanic mystics introduced Wesley to a particular type of *spiritual culture* found in Spain and France and mediated to the pietism of the Netherlands and Germany through Pierre Poiret.[91] This same "spiritual culture" was mediated to the eighteenth-century religious scene by none other than John Wesley.

Only one or two concluding remarks about this phase of Catholic mysticism are needed before the actual analysis of mysticism in John Wesley's life begins. By and large these mystical experiences were self-authorizing and self-authenticating, and it is useless for rationalism to grumble about this. Anyone has a right to live by that force which seemingly motivates him or her best. Again, this mysticism is in general theocentric rather than Christocentric; it is monistic but not pantheistic. Finally, and perhaps most significantly, it would be wise to underscore one characteristic mentioned earlier and of particular importance to John Wesley: these mystics are especially emphatic about progress in love. Perfect love is the goal of all religion. Union involves both the shifting *moi* of Fénelon and the achievement of the mystical *ideal*. In essence, the *moi progressus ad infinitum* to the *ideal* of perfection. "Be ye perfect" for the mystic is both a command and a promise.

With these characteristics now firmly established, it is time to continue our study of mysticism in the Wesleyan tradition as we turn to the life of Wesley himself.

4:540). She died in Florence in 1607 and was canonized by Clement IX in 1669. Malebranche, a French philosopher associated with "occasionalism" and attacked by the Jansenist leader Antoine Arnauld and Fénelon, greatly influenced John Norris.

[91] Schmidt, *Theological Biography,* 13ff. Schmidt also emphasizes the significance of the Romanic mystics for England, but he implies that in England "their sensitive introspection hardens into a scrupulous, rationalistic, and empirical analysis of the individual ego."

2

eARly mystic influences on john wesley

Much of John Wesley's attitude towards mysticism seems, at least on the surface, to be psychoneurotic. It can be demonstrated that although he was frequently disillusioned with mysticism, even to the point of despair, he was nonetheless almost irresistibly drawn to the mystics. Admittedly, the answer to this puzzle will be found in part in the enigmatic nature of mysticism itself, but the complete answer must first take into account Wesley's emotional, intellectual, and spiritual development as well. Following the trend in much of modern psychology, the origin of a great deal of Wesley's frustration and instability in relation to mysticism must be traced to his home environment, first through his years as a student at Christ Church, Oxford, and then culminating in his religious conversion.

THE HOME ENVIRONMENT

It is fairly safe to assume that by the time John entered Oxford he rarely, if ever, just stumbled into anything. His methodical life was motivated by the seeds of impulse sown long before, and by 1720 the areas of thought which would influence him most were fairly well established. For this reason one cannot pass too quickly the impressions of childhood and adolescence. There is not sufficient time or space to develop this theme in great detail, but a few of the issues relevant to mysticism in Wesley's life and thought should be understood.

Family Piety

Piety and even mystical piety was impressed upon young John at an early age, but it is difficult to say just how early this began to register. In spite of Tyerman's well-known description of Wesley's rather "sordid" early life, Piette claims that "an anxiety for the inner life is an essential characteristic of his youth."[1] At any rate, John tells us that little of all that he had been taught concerning inward obedience or holiness was remembered upon entering Charterhouse. Yet the fact remains that Susanna saw a spark of piety in John and vowed to take special care with his early training.[2]

The exact method of his overall training is an interesting story in itself because of its rigid discipline.[3] For Susanna, self-will was the root of all sin and the subjection of the will was therefore essential for all aspects of education.[4] Even more important for us here, however, is the *purpose* of the more spiritual or devotional training, which was most certainly to promote a genuine sense of piety. Piety was important to the Wesleys. Perhaps the only real common denominator found in all of the men and women of religion that Wesley admired was a sense of vital piety leading to a wholehearted devotion to God. At the Epworth rectory this deep appreciation for piety was first instilled in John.[5] Various sources are available to those who wish to explore this further.[6] Susanna obviously had a tremendous influence on John, and his earliest letters reveal the weight of this influence which continued until her death in 1742. An example can be seen in the words of one of her earliest extant letters to John, that of February 23, 1725: "And now in good earnest resolve to make religion the business of your life . . . I heartily wish you would now enter upon a strict examination of yourself, that you may know whether you have a reasonable hope of salvation by Christ Jesus." The date of this letter, in light of Wesley's religious conversion, should be carefully noted.

Susanna's remarkable piety, however, should not allow one to forget completely the other members of the Wesley family. To be sure,

---

[1] Piette, *Evolution of Protestantism*, 212f.

[2] *Journal* 1:465. Wesley attended Charterhouse, a London boarding school for boys from 1714–1720.

[3] C. E. Vulliamy, *John Wesley* (London: Geoffrey Bles, 1931), 6; Maldwyn Edwards' *Family Circle* (London: Epworth, 1949). Here Edwards has a lengthy discussion of the training habits in the Epworth rectory, 57–86.

[4] Schmidt, *Theological Biography*, 60. This is an echo of Romanic mysticism.

[5] The works in *The Christian Library* make this abundantly clear. Even the mystics are arranged not because they were mystics but because they were Christians of great piety.

[6] Two significant books have been published on Susanna Wesley written by John Newton, *Susanna Wesley and the Puritan Tradition in Methodism* (London: Epworth, 1968), and Rebecca Harmond, *Susanna, Mother of the Wesleys* (Abingdon, 1968). Cf. also John Kirk, *Mother of the Wesleys*.

all of the Wesleys were not only "more or less critical, independent in opinion, and self-willed,"[7] but they also stood out as Christians with a deep sense of piety. Samuel Wesley, for example, was in many ways an admirable man, deeply pious though severely controlled.

High Church and Puritan

John Wesley's heritage of piety has at least two (more or less) non-mystical branches—high church and Puritan. Edwards tells us that all of the Wesleys were high church "in the current acceptation of the term" but to varying degrees.[8] Samuel was a high churchman but a strong Loyalist, and all three of his principal works were dedicated to royalty.[9] Susanna was high church and had strong Jacobite sympathies, accepting the accession of William and Mary *de facto* but not *de jure*.[10] Samuel, Jr., was a high churchman but he alone (except perhaps Jeffery, the family ghost) carried his Jacobite sympathies so far as to identify himself with the Stuart cause in his political creed.[11] With this background, it is not surprising that John, too, was high church and with his father developed an intense sense of loyalty to the Crown (but a real distaste for Roman Catholicism).[12] At this point, Orcibal's statement is worth mentioning, that Wesley could have been drawn to the mystics by his high church convictions. He claims that the non-juror persecution attracted him to this type of mortification.[13]

In support of this, V. H. H. Green informs us that high churchmanship "tapered off into unexpected points. It harbingered an interest in mystical theology and the possibility of reconciliation with non-Papalist but essentially Catholic churches."[14] Furthermore, when Wesley entered Oxford, the patristic scholar, John Grabe, epitomized the high church tradition at the university and "showed that founded as it might be on patristic theology, it had yet components which brought it into touch with German pietism and post-Reformation Catholic

---

[7] *Journal,* 1:197.

[8] Edwards, *Family Circle,* 115.

[9] Ibid., 23.

[10] Ibid., 47.

[11] Ibid., 115.

[12] V. H. H. Green, *The Young Mr. Wesley* (London: Edward Arnold, 1961), 78.

[13] Orcibal, "Theological Originality," 90. It is interesting to note that Wesley took almost all of his mystical "Extracts" from those mystics under persecution during the second half of the Catholic Reformation.

[14] V. Green, *Young Wesley,* 273.

devotional literature."[15] This devotional literature, of course, came largely from the mystics.

The continuity of the Puritan thread is much clearer and provides a point of transition into Wesley's mystical heritage. The Puritans had an unmistakable concern for the practical application of the Gospel to the believer's daily life. John Newton writes that Susanna's "Puritan home and upbringing set a stamp upon her which exercised a formative influence on her piety and devotion and the way in which she managed her own household at Epworth."[16] The Puritans sought to purify the church from all unscriptural forms of public worship. In their fundamental appeal to Scripture they also looked to reason and experience embodying a "conception of the Christian life in terms of disciplined living, moral rigorism, and Christianity in earnest."[17] Influences from all of these last elements can be clearly detected in both Susanna and John. First they can be seen in her as she stressed moral virtue and the place of reason in religion in the devotional training of her family. Likewise, it is good to remember at this point that John was by nature a moralist and a lover of reason.[18] One anecdote illustrating the latter trait describes John as unwilling to attend to even the barest necessities of life if he could not find a good reason for it.

A Mystical Heritage

Schmidt writes that John Wesley's household at the same time "drew its sustenance from the Puritan culture of family life and from the nurture of individual souls found in Romanic mysticism."[19] Susanna is called "at once a mystic and superbly practical housewife and mother."[20] Dunn Wilson writes that "most Puritans display an interest in the mystical tradition."[21] Perhaps it is best, then, to lead into our discussion of Wesley's mystical heritage with a question: What is the appeal in

[15] Ibid.

[16] Newton, *Susanna Wesley,* 43.

[17] Ibid., 16.

[18] Alexander Knox's "Remarks" in Southey's *The Life of Wesley,* 2 vols. (London: Longman, Brown, Green, Longmans, and Roberts, 1858), 2:293ff.

[19] Schmidt, *Theological Biography,* 63.

[20] Newton, *Susanna Wesley,* 43.

[21] Wilson, "Influence of Mysticism," 182; cf. also G. F. Nuttall, *The Holy Spirit in Puritan Faith and Experience* (Oxford: B. Blackwell, 1946), where he suggests that Quakerism is Puritanism taken to its extreme; cf. also V. de Sola Pinto, *Peter Sterry: Puritan, Platonist, Mystic* (Cambridge [Eng.]: University Press, 1934).

mysticism for Puritanism? To put it another way, to what extent can Puritanism be called mystical?

First of all, the Puritans admired the mystical piety which aimed at holiness and perfection. Most Puritans would heartily concur with Wesley's statement in his *Ecclesiastical History* where he describes the contribution of the mystics in this manner:

> In the Church prior to the Reformation the only sparks of piety were among the mystics. As a sect they renounced the subtilty of the schools, the vain contentions of the learned, with all the acts and ceremonies of external worship (an empire of superstition). These mystics encouraged followers to aim at nothing but internal sanctity of heart and communion with God, the source of holiness and perfection.[22]

Wesley goes on to say that although these mystics were not entirely free from reigning superstition, they were loved and respected by those (like the Puritans) who had a serious sense of religion.[23] Apart from the Puritan admiration for mystical piety, there is also a considerable overlap between the Puritan emphasis on mortification and the initial stage in mysticism. As in the high church tradition, both Puritanism and mysticism strongly emphasized self-denial, renunciation of the world, and the various other spiritual exercises.[24] One might ask, then, whether there is a Puritan mysticism. Gordon Wakefield asks the same question in his book *Puritan Devotion*.[25] He concludes that although some fringe Puritans "followed closely the teaching of Dionysius the Areopagite and the *Theologia Germanica*," Puritanism in the main seeks no mystical absorption and follows no "inner light."[26] Although there is in Puritanism "an intense desire for immediacy of communion with God" it is basically a Christocentric mediated *com*-union focused on justi-

---

[22] Wesley, *Ecclesiastical History* (printed by J. Paramore, 1781), 3:63.

[23] Ibid.

[24] A great deal has been written with respect to Puritan mortification and the ascetical elements of purgation. Both H. B. Workman and R. C. Monk (*Wesley, His Puritan Heritage* [London: Epworth, 1966], 250) seem to think that Wesley's Puritan heritage enabled him to place asceticism in its proper perspective, that is, as a means to an end. Todd (*John Wesley and the Catholic Church* [London: Hodder and Stoughton, 1958], 43ff.) claims, on the other hand, that the mystics make asceticism a means to an end in spite of Puritanism. It is doubtful, however, that either would see mortification or asceticism as an end in itself.

[25] Gordon S. Wakefield, *Puritan Devotion—Its Place in the Development of Christian Piety* (London: Epworth, 1957), 101–08.

[26] Ibid., 102, 108.

fication as a beginning, not a theocentric unmediated *union* focused on sanctification as an end.[27]

These words from Wesley's preface to the Puritan extracts shed even more light: "The Puritans uproot antinomianism as they demonstrate the necessity of 'legal repentance' which is prior to faith. They hold an 'imperfect view of sanctification or holiness' but nonetheless provide a suitable antidote for the mystic misunderstanding of justification."[28] It should become more and more apparent that the Puritan Wesleys both knew and understood the mystic writers.

Schmidt makes a great deal of the importance of Susanna's inheritance of the Romanic mystical tradition.[29] He writes that she "lived in the Romanic mysticism whose influence had been growing in England since the early days of Elizabeth."[30] We know that Susanna's father, Samuel Annesley, had at least some acquaintance with mysticism. He knew Gregory of Nyssa and referred to him when writing on "what it is to love God with the whole heart."[31] He knew Francis of Sales and appealed to him when arguing for "the love of God as a gift of the Spirit."[32] He also knew St. Teresa as he referred in one of his sermons to her maxim, "all that is not God is nothing."[33] Although there is no evidence that her father influenced Susanna in this direction, her own emphasis "on the will, on humility, and on the outworking of prayer in love to neighbor,"[34] are all strongly reminiscent of the mysticism of St. Teresa and *The Interior Castle*. It is also known that the quasimystic Blaise Pascal helped to rescue her from skepticism, and Orcibal claims that she knew Pascal's *Pensées* practically by heart.[35] Pascal recom-

---

[27] Ibid., 101ff.

[28] *The Christian Library* 7:"Preface," paragraphs #4 and #8.

[29] Schmidt, *Theological Biography*, 1:52n (#1). Schmidt states here that Leger's book on Wesley's youth stresses this somewhat one-sidedly. Schmidt then suggests (although it is by no means apparent to me) that the letter of October 25, 1932 (*Proceedings of the Wesley Historical Society* XVIII, 1931/2, pp. 169–72), proves that Wesley was heir to the Romanic mystical tradition.

[30] Ibid., 48f.

[31] *A Supplement to the Morning-Exercise at Cripplegate*, ed. Samuel Annesley, 2d ed. (1776), 4–5; quoted in Newton, *Susanna Wesley*, 31.

[32] Ibid., 12. Quoted in Newton, *Susanna Wesley*, 190.

[33] Newton, Ibid., 136.

[34] Ibid.

[35] Orcibal, "Theological Originality," 86. A French edition of *Pensées* is in Wesley's personal library. The English translation was abridged for *The Christian Library*, vol. 23. It is interesting to note that mysticism in philosophy is charged against skepticism (Inge, *Mysticism*, 19) and that Susanna, although never disparaging reason, does react against the extreme rationalism of her day. Cf. her letter to John, August 18, 1725.

mended a rigorous mortification to enable one to endure pain and suffering with joy and satisfaction.[36] Although there is some evidence that Susanna must have disliked his glorification of spiritual trials to the extent of welcoming temptation, she undoubtedly admired his great piety and she quotes him both in her theological writings and her private correspondence.[37]

Furthermore, it is certain that the mystic Lorenzo Scupoli and his *Pugna Spiritualis* or *Spiritual Combat* (known through Castaniza's translation) held a central place in Susanna's devotion.[38] It is through Scupoli, an Italian Theatine monk, that we find the strongest evidence for what Schmidt calls an "intellectualist and voluntary mysticism."[39] Primarily addressing the *understanding* and the *will* (thus his *intellectual* and *voluntary* mysticism), Scupoli argues that we must hate ourselves, renounce our own ego, and turn with wholehearted love to God.[40] Although feeling and emotion may follow, Scupoli (like Pascal in many ways) finds the *virtus Patientiae* the essential factor in Christian obedience, that is, the readiness to accept suffering and temptation as "grist for the mill of perfection."[41]

Schmidt writes that Susanna heard in this particular type of mysticism the summons to continue the struggle for Christian perfection and to withdraw from the things of the world, for the love of God alone is efficacious and all-powerful.[42] This was to have a profound influence on both Susanna and John.[43] Susanna also knew and recommended à Kempis, the Cambridge Platonists More and Norris, and the Scottish mystic Henry Scougal, author of the influential *The Life of God in the Soul of Man*. Schmidt concludes that Susanna was deeply affected by the various mystics, and through her their influence passed

---

[36] Remember that the Jansenists had a strong tendency to reject creation.

[37] Susanna objected to Scupoli on this same issue; she frequently quoted these words from the Lord's Prayer, "lead me not into temptation."

[38] Newton, *Susanna Wesley*, 137. Newton writes that Susanna may have been "predisposed" toward the *Spiritual Combat* by her father's typically Puritan conception of the Christian life as a holy war.

[39] Schmidt, *Theological Biography*, 48f.

[40] Ibid.

[41] Newton, *Susanna Wesley*, 137.

[42] Schmidt, *Theological Biography*, 48f.

[43] In their struggle for perfection Susanna and John sought to abandon all affection for the world. At the time of her death she reproached herself for having loved her son too much and thereby having clung too closely to earthly things. John almost stoically tells his sister that the death of her children has given her more time for God. He tells Charles' wife, Sarah, that her smallpox scars will discourage vanity. He writes Adam Clarke, surprised at the degree of bereavement upon the death of his child.

to her large family, especially John.[44] Schmidt then exhorts one not to overlook the fact that certain essential characteristics of John's own system are contained in these mystics, and "questions are apparent with which he was constantly concerned in his maturity."[45] We shall see.

There can be little doubt that Susanna had the greatest devotional influence on John, but the evidence is not yet complete. A few words about Samuel are now appropriate. It is well known that Samuel had the dull obstinacy of a rigid formalist more prone to political and ecclesiastical quarrels than internal religion. His words on his deathbed to John concerning the inward witness as "the strongest proof of Christianity" are said by some to be spoken out of regret for his own lack of an interior spiritual life. This may or may not be true. Samuel's life at Epworth was not an easy one and hardly conducive to spiritual indulgence, but the fact remains that he, too, knew the mystics. Thomas à Kempis, the springboard to mysticism, was his "old friend and companion," and he frequently referred to Mon. de Renty and Pascal. Considerable evidence points to the influence of Samuel on John. In one letter dated July 14, 1725 (again the date is significant), he cautions John against the "peril of levity" (paraphrasing Ecclesiastes 7:16–18 and quoting Ecclesiastes 11:9; 12:14) stating that mortification is still an indispensable Christian duty. There can be little doubt, therefore, that all of the Wesleys contributed to an atmosphere that was at once Puritan, high church, and mystical.

In a moment we will summarize our divergent thoughts in this section relative to mysticism, but first we should point out that if Wesley was by nature a moralist, he also had a natural disposition to solitude and contemplation which he persistently had to resist.[46] "Having from infancy loved silence and obscurity," this was his natural temper.[47] Curnock writes that John "had not the making of a recluse," but weigh this against John's own testimony and the evidence seems to lean the other way.[48] Wesley's *Works* reveal his love for the solitary life and that he was frequently tempted to withdraw. While at Oxford he is said to have lived almost like a hermit and "saw not how a busy man could be saved."[49] Even later in life John was envious of the solitary life. A

---

[44] Schmidt, *Theological Biography,* 58.
[45] Ibid.
[46] Knox, *Enthusiasm,* 433.
[47] *Letters,* November 30, 1769, 5:163.
[48] *Journal,* 1:19.
[49] *Letters,* 6:128, 232–33, 292; 7:89.

sentence in one of Charles' shorthand notes makes it probable, if not certain, that John was tempted to return to a "cloistered life" while on a visit to Oxford on February 2, 1751.[50] More than thirty years later (November 15, 1781) he is still displaying an inborn affection for solitude.[51] This characteristic is described by one author as the primary ingredient in Wesley's mysticism.[52]

An Impasse

Before the overall perspective of this chapter is lost, a summary of the effect of these influences should be given. It is not too difficult to appreciate Wesley's inconsistency with regard to mysticism as a whole once one understands the nature of mysticism itself and the problem of overlap and contradiction among the forces which influenced his early life. Again, he has been called a rigorist, a moralist, a legalist, and a lover of reason, but at the same time a stoic, an ascetic, a mystic, and a lover of solitude and contemplation. The more perceptive student might well ask whether this is possible. Coleridge writes that everyone is born either a Platonist or an Aristotelian, a mystic or a legalist. Inge adds that it is doubtful that anyone could be fully committed to the two simultaneously. John Wesley is the classic illustration; no one has been influenced more from both directions. Perhaps no one has tried harder to be both legalist and mystic. But, when the balance is weighed, although the Wesley family knew and appreciated the mystic writers and even though John's natural disposition was prone to solitude and contemplation, an impasse is reached. For various reasons, the eighteenth-century stage (the "Age of Reason") was poorly set for mysticism, and John was a natural-born moralist nurtured in a home where both reason and experience were the rules of thumb. Consequently, it is no real surprise when Workman, Monk, and Brazier Green all agree that Wesley's home environment ultimately kept him from sinking wholly into mysticism.[53]

---

[50] *Journal*, Editor's note #1, 3:513f.

[51] T. R. Jeffery, *John Wesley's Religious Quest*, (New York: Vantage, 1960), all of chapter 18.

[52] Inge, *Mysticism*, 52ff.; perhaps Pascal and some of the Jansenists come the closest. Pascal, to an extent, was both moralist and mystic.

[53] Brazier Green, *John Wesley and William Law*. (London: Epworth, 1945), 84ff. Green recognizes that Wesley's Puritan heritage first attracted him to mysticism, but ultimately the mystical misunderstanding of justification and the tendency toward Antinomianism which (in some cases) undermined piety and Christian morality caused the inevitable break.

The fact is that by the time Wesley began to develop an interest of his own in religion his mind was set in one direction, and his heritage, although introducing him to the mystical tradition, had made it impossible for him to give himself completely to mysticism. Although the mystic piety (and at first even the novelty of mystical contemplation) was to have an almost hypnotic appeal for John Wesley and, as we shall see, drew him dangerously close to the mystic way, the fact remains that one who was by nature a severe moralist and to whom duty, the stern daughter of the voice of God, was all in all could never, *try as he may,* give himself entirely to mysticism. From the time that he entered Oxford, however, it was to take him nearly eighteen years to learn this basic truth.

The above, however, should not lead one to believe that we have eliminated our task and that Wesley was not influenced by the mystics at all. Indeed, he was and throughout his life. In spite of the fact that Wesley was never a mystic in the sense of the mystics that he knew and abridged, he nonetheless combined high church, Puritan, and mystical casuistry to fill a void in Protestantism left by the removal of spiritual direction to set ethical and moral traditions within the Roman Catholic Church.[54] This is the story that continues as Wesley leaves for Oxford in 1720.

A STUDENT AT CHRIST CHURCH

The next two sections deal with the period between John's entrance into Christ Church College, Oxford, on June 24, 1720, and his ordination to Deacon's Orders on September 19, 1725. During this time Wesley completed the requirements for his B.A. degree (1724) and began the requirements for his M.A. degree (completed in 1727). Even more important, the soil was being prepared for a religious conversion which was to launch his unpredictable mystical career in the spring of 1725.

V. H. H. Green writes that John Wesley went up to Oxford "an earnest, high-minded young man, to one of the most diversified societies in existence."[55] Wesley quickly acquired an affection for the university which lasted throughout his life. Unfortunately, little material is

---

[54] Robert C. Monk, *John Wesley, His Puritan Heritage,* (London: Epworth, 1966), 244ff. Cf. Piette, *Evolution of Protestantism,* on this important point. Cf. also Alexander Knox's "Remarks," in Southey's *Wesley,* 2:293ff.

[55] V. Green, *Young Wesley,* 61.

available from this earlier period covering his intellectual development: there are few pre-1725 extant letters, and Wesley does not begin his Diary until April 5, 1725. We do know, however, that if John was *homo unius libri* later in life (according to some a debatable point) he was certainly more of an eclectic here. He read widely and no doubt rapidly, developing mental reflexes which were to become even more strongly pronounced. Hutton, for example, describes Wesley as a "level-headed Briton, with a mind as exact as a calculating machine."[56] Some are dubious about that, but the fact remains that Wesley's earliest Oxford training concentrated to a great degree on logic. He regarded Aldrich's *Compendium Artis Logicae* with profound reverence.[57]

It was probably during this period that he was attracted to a method of debate which has caused so many students of Wesley considerable trouble, especially where his attitude toward mysticism was concerned. Wesley frequently used the modes of argument known as *argumentum ad hominem* or *reductio ad absurdum* where by appealing to opponents' prejudice he could use their own argument against them and then, if need be, reduce it to the absurd. This may have been a legitimate form of debate, but it has been confusing for the historian. It frequently gave Wesley the appearance of self-contradiction, but when his works are examined more closely a curious consistency is revealed. Later on, for example, we find Wesley using Thomas à Kempis among the Catholics in Ireland; he uses Fénelon's *Simplicity* against mystical refinement in religion; Madame Bourignon is used against the mystical antinomian concept of grace; Gregory Lopez is used against Madame Guyon; Anna Maria Van Schurmann against William Law; and even the *Mystical Divinity* of Dionysius against the Moravian "Stillness" at Fetter Lane.[58] For this reason the uninformed reader can easily misinterpret Wesley's own words, and since we are primarily concerned with Wesley's own words (especially from this point on) a word of caution is provided here.

Wesley's earliest academic training at Oxford not only strengthened his analytical prowess, but also accentuated his intellectual impetuosity. Charles Wesley claimed that John could never keep a secret.[59] Alexander

---

[56] J. E. Hutton, *History of the Moravian Church*, (London: Moravian Pub., 1923) 300. Wesley is here being contrasted with Zinzendorf.

[57] V. Green, *Young Wesley*, 130. Wesley published a translation in 1750 entitled *A Compendium of Logick;* cf. *Journal*, 3:459.

[58] The last example (being *reductio ad absurdum* and the others *ad hominem*) backfired when some in the society failed to see the absurdity of the argument.

[59] J. H. Overton, *John Wesley* (New York: Houghton, Mifflin, 1891), 191.

Knox, a friend of Wesley in his old age, writes that "his habits of reflection bore no proportion to his quickness of apprehension, nor could he endure delay either in reasoning or in acting. From uncertain and scanty premises he rapidly formed the most confident and comprehensive conclusions, mistaking logic for philosophy in matter of theory, and appearances for realities in matters of fact and experience.[60] Piette claims that it is necessary to defend Wesley against himself, as anyone so prone to "prompt effusions" is prone to exaggerate.[61] Wesley often wrote on impulse and in the interest of time frequently published half-digested ideas that prompted some to suspect him of religious exhibitionism. Those who know John Wesley best, however, know that if there was anomaly of mind there was certainly no anomaly of heart.

As for John's attitude toward mysticism at this time, Bishop William Cannon writes that it is interesting to speculate whether or not Wesley became a mystic between June 24, 1720, and May 24, 1738.[62] Although he undoubtedly had at least a casual acquaintance with several of the mystical treatises influential in the Epworth rectory, there is no reason to suspect that John was any more than neutral with respect to mysticism until the spring of 1725. This is not to imply that Wesley was neutral toward religion in general, however. His parents were undoubtedly sending him spiritual advice from home. Also one interesting anecdote suggests that Wesley began to consider the condition of his soul as early as 1721. Reynolds mentions that impression made upon John by an encounter with a poor but saintly college porter who demonstrated beauty of contentment in the midst of hardship, a lesson he would later learn from the mystics and ultimately associate with perfection.[63] Generally speaking, however, although he had a "kindliness for religion," and even though he said his prayers and read the Scriptures, he tells us that during his undergraduate days he "was continually sinning against that little light that he had and without so much as a notion of inward holiness."[64]

---

[60] Southey, *Wesley,* 307.

[61] Ibid., 295f.

[62] William R. Cannon, *The Theology of John Wesley* (New York: Abingdon-Cokesbury, 1946), 61.

[63] John Reynolds, *Anecdotes of Wesley* (Leeds: 1828), 8. Quoted in Luke Tyerman, *The Life and Times of the Rev. John Wesley* 3 vols. (London: Hodder and Stoughton, 1890), 1:24.

[64] *Journal,* 1:466.

A RELIGIOUS CONVERSION.[65]

Some time around the turn of the year 1725, no doubt still plagued by those "transient fits of repentance" so characteristic of his undergraduate days, John's attitude toward religion began to change.[66] On February 23 his mother wrote, "The alteration of your temper has occasioned me much speculation ... resolve to make religion the business of your life."[67] Many things then began to happen almost simultaneously, and it is difficult to know the exact sequence. On March 13 John received word from his father pressing him to enter Orders as soon as possible and to prepare himself for ordination through prayer and religious study. Then the following events took place in fairly rapid succession: (1) He met his first "religious friend"; (2) he was introduced to Jeremy Taylor's *Rules for Holy Living*, and Thomas à Kempis' *Imitation of Christ*; and (3) these brought about the alteration of the whole form of his conversation and set him in earnest upon a new life.[68]

A Religious Friend

Although Wesley's parents exercised a continual influence on his spiritual growth, Nehemiah Curnock is correct to insist that it was someone else who kindled John's enthusiasm for the devotional literature which influenced him so strongly at this time. Susanna, when questioned by John, was forced to admit that she knew little or nothing about Jeremy Taylor, other than that he was generally highly esteemed, and that she had not read à Kempis for some time. The responsibility must, then, surely fall to Varanese, Wesley's first religious friend. One need hardly say that the identity of Varanese has been discussed at length. Although traditionally Varanese was thought to be the fashionable pseudonym for Betty Kirkham, "it can now be stated categorically that Varanese was Sally Kirkham," Betty's sister.[69] More important than the identification of this friend, however, is the role that she played in

---

[65] Whether or not this was a *Christian* conversion is a many-sided question. This somewhat exaggerated problem will be discussed under the "Aldersgate" heading to follow. For the moment it is best to see this "religious conversion" and "Aldersgate" as one continuing experience.

[66] *Journal*, 1:467.

[67] Tyerman, *John Wesley*, 1:32.

[68] *Journal*, 1:467.

[69] *Proceedings of the Wesley Historical Society*, VIII:147–48; cf. Augustin Léger, *La Jeunesse de Wesley;* Grace Harrison, *Son to Susanna* (Nashville: Cokesbury, 1938), 40–41; and V. Green, *Young Wesley*, 207n (#3).

John's religious development. It is significant that Curnock reminds us in a note to the *Journal* that Wesley's indebtedness to his friends is territory virtually unquarried. Wesley, throughout his life, emphasized the importance of a Christian friend for the sake of discipline or encouragement and according to his Diary, begun on April 5, 1725 (which roughly coincides with his religious conversion), he spent considerable time in Stanton where Sally's father was the parish priest.[70]

Interestingly enough, Wesley's introduction to a great deal of the influential devotional literature in his life seems to correspond with his visits to Stanton.[71] There can be little doubt that this is where John developed an interest in Taylor and à Kempis. According to Wesley's *Plain Account of Christian Perfection* and his letter to John Newton dated May 14, 1765, Taylor was read first and à Kempis was read soon afterward.[72] Here again debate has risen, this time over the exact order of their appearance. But if we can take Wesley at his word (he never contradicts the above order although for some reason Taylor is omitted from the Journal review for May 24, 1738), then this is the sequence.[73] Again, however, even more important is the fact that Sally had started John Wesley along the way to mysticism, which can be demonstrated by a rapid glance at the nature of the books which she recommended.

Jeremy Taylor[74]

While it seems fairly obvious that Jeremy Taylor was no mystic in the sense that John Wesley was to understand the term, it has been pointed out that Taylor had some mystical characteristics. Although there are some who deny any mystical element in Taylor,[75] D. Dunn Wilson points out convincingly that Taylor was also "concerned with

---

[70] E.g., *Letters,* 7:54.

[71] E.g., *Diary,* April 15, 1725; "saw Varanese, Kempis"; later after a visit to Stanton he reads Law's *Christian Perfection* for the first time.

[72] *Works,* Jackson ed., 14 vols. (Grand Rapids: Zondervan, n.d.), 11:366, "1725 met with Taylor; 1726 met with à Kempis."

[73] The number of scholars (e.g., Curnock, Simon, Brigden, etc.) who place à Kempis before Taylor is surprising. Glasson, *Proceedings of the Wesley Historical Society,* XXXVI:105f. argues for Taylor. Perhaps placing à Kempis (a general treatise) before Taylor (the specific application) shows more of an appreciation for deductive reasoning than for scholarship. John L. Peters, *Christian Perfection and American Methodism* (New York: Abingdon, 1956), 19, has the correct order.

[74] Taylor's influence, once neglected, can now be studied in considerable detail in studies by Piette, Jeffery, and Wilson (see bibliography).

[75] E.g., H. Trevor Hughes, *The Piety of Jeremy Taylor* (London: Macmillan, 1960), 160ff.

establishing a union between the believer and God in a Christian mystical relationship."[76] Taylor states that "God dwells in our heart by faith . . . so that we are also cabinets of the mysterious Trinity."[77] Wilson also suggests that Taylor, in true mystical fashion, has his own *scala perfectionis* by which the Christian climbs up to God.[78] Taylor seems to teach that through humility, self-renunciation, self-examination, scrupulous employment of time, purity of intention, and other similar rules of mortification, the Christian can strip away the worldly passions and that love can then grow step by step.[79]

The question now is this: How did these rules affect John? The answer is simple: Some he disliked, some he misunderstood, and some he put into practice. Wesley writes, "I have heard one I take to be a person of good judgement [i.e., Sally Kirkham] say that she would advise no one very young to read Taylor . . . he almost put her out of her senses . . . because he seemed to exclude all from being in a way of salvation who did not come up to his rules, some of which are altogether impracticable."[80] That John too objected to some parts can be seen in the revealing correspondence with his mother.[81] On June 18 he writes that if Taylor's conception of humility (as despising oneself and always thinking of oneself as worse than others) and repentance (where forgiveness cannot be perceived) are essential to salvation then "who can be saved?" Susanna's reply is interesting. She writes that Taylor seeks in humility a *habitual disposition* which is far more comprehensive than John's narrow understanding.[82] Susanna understood humility (thinking meanly of oneself) in contrast with God, and John understood humility in comparison with those around him. Susanna writes that one who realizes one's unworthiness before God will also realize (without thinking) one's unworthiness before others.

Nonetheless, it could be said that Jeremy Taylor provided the preamble for Wesley's attraction to the mystical ladder of perfection. D. Dunn Wilson suggests that ultimately, however, Taylor was not mystical enough for Wesley's changing taste.[83] Taylor's emphasis upon inward holiness (especially where it pertained to the extension of God's laws

[76] Wilson, "Influence of Mysticism," 62.

[77] *Holy Living,* Jeremy Taylor, *The Whole Works* (London: 1847–54, 10 vols.), 1:iii.

[78] Wilson, "Influence of Mysticism," 61–63.

[79] *Holy Living,* 1:iii.

[80] *Letters,* 1:17, 18, 19, 20.

[81] Ibid.: John's, June 18, July 29; and Susanna's replies, July 21, August 18, 1725.

[82] Tyerman, *John Wesley,* 1:39–40.

[83] Wilson, "Influence of Mysticism," 75.

over one's thought as well as one's words and actions) was soon to gain additional impetus through the even stronger influence of Thomas à Kempis, Wesley's springboard into the esoteric world of mysticism.

Thomas à Kempis

Every review of Wesley's religious awakening must emphasize the important contribution of devotional literature. Undoubtedly Taylor, à Kempis, and eventually William Law number among the most influential (abridged by Wesley). In fact, abridgments of à Kempis and Law (including his later works) are included in the first edition of Wesley's own works.[84] Taylor, who apparently failed to hold the more permanent influence of à Kempis and Law, is included in *The Christian Library*.

It is interesting that à Kempis and Law (i.e., his earlier *Christian Perfection* and *Serious Call*) follow an almost identical vein in the pursuit of Christian holiness. Since Law will be closely examined elsewhere, however, we will concentrate more on the earlier, if not more important, influence of à Kempis.[85] Eric Baker implies that Taylor and à Kempis prepared Wesley for the influence of Law. More accurately, however, it seems apparent that Wesley was drawn to all three for much the same reason—their strongly disciplined ethical piety. This ethical piety was conditioning Wesley for the impact of the mystical writers, and, though he was probably unaware of the mystical thread at this time, the foundation was being laid. Let us review the sequence. Taylor had convinced John that there was no medium in religion; his entire life must be given to God or to the Devil.[86] Then à Kempis, and later Law, further convinced him of the nature and extent of inward religion. True religion was seated in the heart; therefore, one must give not just one's *life,* but one's *heart* to God. For Wesley, "simplicity of intention and

---

[84] The 1771 Pine Edition of John Wesley, *Works,* 32 vols. (Bristol, Eng., 1771) includes "Extracts" not only from à Kempis and Law but from the Roman Catholic mystic de Renty as well as Scougal, Norris, Francke, and Haliburton. Since Benson and Jackson omit these Extracts without a word, many Wesley scholars are not aware of this significant fact.

[85] Cf. B. Green, *John Wesley and William Law,* and Eric Baker, *Herald of the Evangelical Revival* (London, Epworth, 1948) for the detailed examination of Wesley and Law. Law will also figure prominently in chapter 4 below when examining the correspondence with him just prior to Aldersgate.

[86] *Works,* 11:366.

purity of affection" (so essential to Romanic mysticism) became the "wings of the soul."[87]

Thomas à Kempis' *Christian Pattern* or *Treatise on the Imitation of Christ* was no doubt familiar to Wesley long before Varanese encouraged him to study it carefully. He wrote his mother that he had seen it many times before but that he had never examined it closely. Piette's statement that Susanna read it "constantly" is a slight exaggeration, but it has been stated that it was Samuel's "friend and old companion." Furthermore, Dr. John King, master of Charterhouse, is said to have always carried about with him a copy of *The Imitation of Christ*.[88]

Although *The Imitation of Christ* has been called the "flower of Christian mysticism," Inge insists that it is not, properly speaking, a mystical treatise. There are several distinguishing characteristics in mysticism that are apparently not present in à Kempis. The most important is the mystical emphasis on the possibility of essential unity between God and humankind. The *Imitation*, although stressing an immediate contact between God and humankind, emphasizes human depravity, ever prone to evil and ever in need of grace.[89] Likewise, whereas mysticism emphasizes the Incarnation, *The Imitation* stresses the Cross.[90] *Imitatio Christi* is more of an ascetical attempt to imitate the moral example of Jesus through the instruments of mortification (an *ethical* harmony of wills) than an attempt to become one (an essential unity of being) with God through mystical contemplation.

Having said this, however, many of the lines are not clearly drawn. There is a great deal of the mystic in à Kempis. It would be difficult to find a mystic who did not know *The Imitation* and many of the greatest mystics received their first religious inspiration from the work of à Kempis.[91] *The Imitation* was especially apt at awakening the complacent, and more often than not, it had an amazing effect on its reader. In his Journal, Wesley preserves a letter describing the effect of à Kempis

---

[87] Ibid.

[88] John Telford, *The Life of Wesley* (London: Epworth, 1924), 26.

[89] *Works* (Pine Ed., 1771), 8:90ff. "I am nothing, I can do nothing, *I have nothing that is good of myself,* but in all things I am defective, and ever tend to nothing" (italics mine). It occurs to me, however, that à Kempis (like the mystics) is still giving only lip service to the concept of grace.

[90] The Cross here, however, is not to be understood in the Reformed sense. It provides more of a pattern for Christian action than an atonement for sin. See chapter 5 below.

[91] Cf. for example the experiences of de Renty, Guyon, and Fletcher. Wesley writes that he rarely saw Fletcher without à Kempis before him.

on one of his Methodists.[92] *The Imitation* frequently served as a book for mystical initiation as it qualified its reader for even deeper things to come. À Kempis knew the esoteric mystic terminology and could convey this understanding to others serious-minded enough to respond to his call. He compelled those of principle to allow their faith to penetrate into every aspect of life. He placed the religious seeker within the stream of vital piety so vulnerable to the mystic appeal.

Although in 1725 à Kempis' mystical bias was more or less incidental as far as Wesley was consciously concerned, as time progressed he undoubtedly associated à Kempis with mysticism. Wesley's letters and Journal frequently place à Kempis in company with mystics like Sales, de Renty, Lopez, and many others.[93] The influential John Fletcher in his *Fourth Check to Antinomianism* refers to à Kempis as a mystic.[94] Furthermore, anyone who has read *Imitation* carefully must see the mystical implications in its pursuit of holiness and perfection. Wesley's extensive preface to his 1735 translation of à Kempis is revealing as to the mystical undertones of both the man and his treatise. Wesley depicts à Kempis as a deeply pious man who frequently appeared rapt from above and quite in ecstasy.[95] Born in 1380, he spent seventy-one years on Mt. Agnes, passing most of his time in fervent prayer, contemplation, and writing. He was cheerful and patient under affliction, having a gentleness in bearing and a kindness in excusing.[96] In the same preface he goes on to describe the treatise as having a plain and simple style which "comprehends all that relates to perfection." The fruitful seeds of meditation (he prepared for speaking by meditation) produce internal worship, the essence of which is love and which unites the soul to God. This all-important love implies "entire *humility,* absolute *self-renunciation,* unreserved *resignation* and the *union of our will to God* as makes the Christian one spirit with God." Wesley, further illustrating the mystical tendencies, goes on to list the various stages of

---

[92] *Journal,* 3:158f.

[93] E.g., *Letters,* 2:179. Several of Wesley's treatises also portray à Kempis in the company of mystics.

[94] J. Fletcher, *The Works of the Reverend John Fletcher,* ed. Joseph Benson, 9 vols. (London: John Mason, 1860), 2:17.

[95] *Works,* 14:198ff.; Wilson, "Influence of Mysticism," 59ff., notes that although à Kempis insists that "a man's worthiness is not to be estimated by the number of visions and comforts which he may have, these experiences of being 'rapt on high' are no illusion and a man ought still 'to go out of himself and stand in a sort of ecstasy of mind,'" *Christian Pattern,* 3:vii, 5; vi, 3; xxxi, 1.

[96] Ibid.

this perfect love: one must first hate sin, then resist sin, and then root sin out through the mortification of the passions, which completes the purgation of the soul. One then constantly practices all virtue to enlighten a fuller knowledge; finally, humility, patience, and love, manifested through hope and trust in God, ultimately unites the soul with God.[97] The parallels here with mysticism should be apparent, and they will be underscored once again as we measure their effect on Wesley's own doctrine of perfection. But we must first ask about the effect of this treatise on John in 1725 with respect to mysticism.

As with Taylor's *Rules,* John disliked, misunderstood, and put into practice various parts of *Imitation.* On May 28, 1725, he wrote to his mother concerning à Kempis:

> I can't think that when God sent us into the world He had irreversibly decreed that we should be perpetually miserable in it. If it be so, the very endeavour after happiness in this life is a sin; as it is acting in direct contradiction to the very design of our creation. What are become of all the innocent comforts and pleasures of life, if it is the intent of our Creator that we should never taste them?[98]

On June 8, no doubt a relief to John, Susanna replied to his letter, agreeing with his opinion, although she could not recollect the passage to which he referred. She stated that à Kempis was undoubtedly "an honest weak man, who had more zeal than knowledge"; then, sensing John's anxiety about his innocent pleasures, she applied this practical criterion: "What ever weakens your reason, impairs the tenderness of your conscience, obscures your sense of God, or takes off the relish of spiritual things . . . that thing is sin to you, however innocent it may be in itself." H. B. Workman gives one the impression that Wesley now put à Kempis aside for the "common sense" of his mother's rule, but, in fact quite the contrary is true. John's father, apparently not fully satisfied with Susanna's impressions, wrote John to set the matter straight. After conceding that à Kempis might have been somewhat one-sided, he reiterates the indispensable duty of mortification. "The world is a Syren, and we must have a care for her; and if the *young man* will *rejoice in his youth,* yet let him take care that his joys be innocent; and, in order to do this remember that *for all these things* God will bring him into judgment." Samuel adds that his "friend and old companion . . . may be read to great advantage." This letter must have had a powerful impact

---

[97] Ibid.

[98] *Letters,* 1:16.

on John.[99] Between 1725 and 1735 Wesley drew closer and closer to the monastic asceticism of à Kempis as he drew closer and closer to mysticism.

Wesley writes of à Kempis in his Journal, "Yet I had frequently much sensible comfort in reading him, such as I was an utter stranger to before."[100] Two points can be taken from this statement. First of all, à Kempis provided a preamble for Aldersgate, the "sensible comfort" providing a foretaste of the Aldersgate experience of assurance. It would not do to strain this point, but the relevance of this first consolation becomes apparent when one realizes that this was one of the major issues that would take Wesley out of the excessive mystical stream. Secondly, it was now long before Aldersgate, and before Wesley's evangelical conversion à Kempis would first direct him by another route involving a thirteen-year "mystical" adventure.

Thus the second point places à Kempis at the door of Wesley's mystical quest where he would become preoccupied (if not obsessed) with internal "works-righteousness" (prayer and meditation as opposed to external action) as the means of salvation. *Imitation* had reaffirmed the essential inwardness of the Christian faith. Holiness and perfection extended to one's inmost being and the *goal of perfection* (according to a résumé of Scupoli, Scougal, and Taylor in Schmidt) lay wholly beyond this world and in the mystical subjectivity of the individual.[101] One should also remember that à Kempis is primarily an ethical treatise; therefore, the means of reaching this goal were reinforced as well. Humility, for example, was especially important as pride was the first hindrance to holiness.[102] Wesley had learned to embrace anything that led away from pride, recognizing even the assistance of affliction in defeating it. On one occasion he wrote that the loss of his reputation was "fair exchange for the lowest degree of purity of heart."[103] Self-renunciation and resignation, in true mystical fashion, also cleansed the soul from impurity of desire.[104] Wesley had been conditioned for

---

[99]Those tempted to underestimate Samuel's influence on John might do well to remember the continuing influence of à Kempis on John when, except for this exhortation, he might easily have tossed him aside as too strict.

[100]*Journal*, 1:467.

[101]Schmidt, *Theological Biography*, 82ff.

[102]A. Stevens, *History of Methodism* (London: W. Tegg, 1864), Bk. 1:44. For Wesley "humility meant at this time the ascetic self-abnegation of the *Imitation*."

[103]Cf. *Imitation*, 1:ii, 1 (on humility), 1:xix, 1 (vs. pride), with the Oxford *Letters*, 1:96, 109, 119, etc.

[104]*Imitation*, 1:15; 2:9, 10, 11, 12; 3:12, 54, etc.

mysticism. *Imitation* had driven away complacency for good as it had stirred deeper things in his mind and life. At one point in his abridgment of à Kempis, Wesley even adds a word to increase the strength of his ethical stand: "For the kingdom of God is [righteousness and] peace, and joy in the Holy Ghost."[105]

The tools of monastic asceticism leading to pure love were the qualities in à Kempis that Wesley would embrace so heartily in mysticism. To summarize, therefore, John's temperament (spawned in the Puritan high church environment of the Epworth rectory), his religious friend, Taylor, and now à Kempis were all factors which developed his understanding of the ascetical practices so essential to the beginning of his mystical journey. *Imitation*'s "fly the tumultuousness of the world" suited John's natural inclinations and the exhortation to strip oneself of all selfishness that "thou mayst 'follow naked the naked Jesus'" made a lasting impression indeed. Wesley was now vulnerable to mysticism. Piette states that "Wesley did not look upon these exchanges of thought simply as a kind of intellectual sport," and indeed this was no mere mental jousting—Wesley was now in dead earnest about the condition of his soul.[106] John's private notebooks of the next few years reveal how scrupulously he put into practice the counsels of his favorite authors. By the time of his ordination, he had taken the advice of his mother and had made religion the "business of his life." And, as he would observe among so many of his own society members, those who took religion most seriously were those most susceptible to mysticism.

---

[105] *Works*, (Pine, 1771), 7:344; brackets denote the addition; cf. Romans 14:17.
[106] Piette, *Evolution of Protestantism*, 259.

3

wesley's mystical experiments: an initial acceptance

Thus far we have examined the various conditioning influences introducing Wesley to the mystic appeal. It is now time to record his degree of acceptance. The period from September 19, 1725, to December 22, 1737 (when John leaves Georgia for his return to England), marks the boundary of mysticism's freest reign in the life and thought of Wesley. Although things were beginning to unravel while he was in America, it is during this time that the mystical influences build to a climax, and it is here that mysticism makes its most consistent impression as Wesley launches out into several mystical experiments.[1]

1725–1735, A CRUCIAL DECADE

The probability is great (if not certain) that John's first real contact with mysticism (beyond that of à Kempis where asceticism tended to be the "all in all") came from the Roman Catholics. They were certainly the first to attract his attention after his religious conversion; this is not surprising since several of them were well known at the Epworth rectory. If Wesley's abridgments are any indication, the Catholic mystics were his favorite by far. His earliest mystical source selected for publication came from the fourth-century desert father, Macarius.[2] Wesley read many of the early mystical fathers. Léger, Schmidt, Orcibal,

---

[1] There would be four such experiments: 1725–1727 at Oxford (except for a few months at Wroot); 1727–1729 at Wroot; 1729–1735 with the Holy Club; and 1736–1737 in Georgia.

[2] See *The Christian Library*, vol. 1, for the extract from Macarius.

Wilson, and a host of others demonstrate effectively the extent to which John explored the various Romanic mystical works from almost every age of the church. Likewise, several comparisons have been drawn between Wesley and the Catholic saints merely tinged with mysticism. For example, there were "many laudable and lovable things" in Wesley that reminded Piette of St. Francis, the founder of his own Order.[3] Workman, calling Wesley an eighteenth-century St. Francis, goes so far as to draw up an interesting list of similarities between Wesley and that honored saint.[4]

One Roman Catholic even argues that the treasures of spirituality have always been in Catholic custody and that Methodism in Wesley's day strongly suggested "a Catholic confraternity." He then adds that a Catholic Wesley would have founded a religious Order.[5] In fact, John Todd, a Catholic layman, who has written a book on Wesley and the Catholic Church, actually prays to God through Wesley as he would through a Catholic saint.[6] Furthermore, since some have noted that Wesley published (or republished) very little medieval work, it should also be mentioned that he paid little attention to any of the great reformers. A few would argue that Wesley considered these too antinomian on one side and too predestinarian on the other. Piette sees Wesley as a reformer of the Reformation, a sort of "one-man Counter Reformation" striking out at the immorality produced by the Lutheran-Calvinist doctrine of grace. Piette's Roman Catholic bias no doubt distorts the issue, but the fact remains that it is precisely the Catholic Reformation which provides almost all of the mystical material edited by Wesley. Wilson writes that "it is ironical that one of the greatest

---

[3] Piette, *Evolution of Protestantism,* ix.

[4] Workman, *Place of Methodism,* 65–72; both received the call of God to complete self-surrender, held the love of God as the central truth and rule of life, imitated Christ (one, his poverty; the other, his sinless perfection), revived personal religion, saw the world as their parish, and experienced incessant joy (perfection and joy were more or less synonymous for both). Their methods were also similar. Both used colloquial and simple sermons, preached in the fields, used hymns and music, renounced all pomp and splendor, and experienced similar persecution. However, one should not allow these similarities to obscure the differences.

[5] Piette, *Evolution of Protestantism,* x.

[6] Since it will be demonstrated later that Wesley was certainly no papist, it would be misleading to take it *too* seriously, but (for what it is worth) Neville Ward tells us that a rosary which supposedly belonged to Wesley (and that he used) has been preserved at the Leys School, Cambridge. J. Neville Ward, *The Use of Praying* (London: Epworth, 1967), 117.

Protestant leaders of all time should have turned to the Counter Reformation for his stable spiritual food."[7]

Oxford: 1725–1727

From the viewpoint of those who prefer to see Christianity as a life-long adventure, the race was on (as far as John Wesley was concerned). Outler is insistent that Wesley's radical change in the spring of 1725 was "a conversion if ever there was one."[8] Taylor (who according to Orcibal was also strongly influenced by the seventeenth-century mystics) and à Kempis had impressed upon John that "faith is either in dead earnest or just dead." Furthermore, Wesley's previous casual acquaintance with Roman Catholic mysticism would now be accentuated by his determined intention to give his *all* to God. Wilson adds that "in his search of self-discipline, Wesley had stumbled into mysticism."[9] Wesley's renewed enthusiasm for religion and his growing affection for mysticism, however, is not an easy picture to portray. These next few years would be packed with intense struggle, and it was, in fact, this terrific struggle which drew him (at least in part) irresistibly to like-minded mystics who struggled in much the same way. Mysticism, however, instead of decreasing his anxiety, increased his frustration. Wesley's struggle for holiness would now be exaggerated even more by the squabble among mystics as to whether the pursuit of holiness lay more in bodily austerity (Jesuit and Jansenist) or in the inward temper (Carmelite and Quietist). Perhaps this was a more subtle side to J. H. Rigg's suggestion that Wesley "oscillated between ritualism and mysticism."[10]

At any rate, Wesley, after his ordination in September 1725, was obsessed by the notion of moral imperfection, and he was continually dissatisfied with his efforts in the pursuit of holiness. Consequently, it was during this period of Wesley's life that the more ascetical side of his character gained ascendancy. On July 3, 1726, John wrote a memorandum in his Diary commending self-denial: "As we would willingly suffer a little pain, or forego some pleasure for others we really love, so if we sincerely love God we should readily do this for Him. For this reason

[7] Wilson, "Influence of Mysticism," 152–72; his section on the mysticism of the Counter Reformation; cf. H.O. Evennett, *The Spirit of the Counter-Reformation* (London, 1968), and Pierre Janelle's chapter, "Piety and Mysticism" in *The Catholic Reformation* (Milwaukee: Bruce, 1949).

[8] Albert Outler, *John Wesley* (New York: Oxford, 1964), 7.

[9] Wilson, "Influence of Mysticism," 65.

[10] J. H. Rigg, *Living Wesley* 2d ed. (London: 1891), 90.

one act of self-denial is more grateful to our Master than the performance of many lesser duties. . . ." In this the first of his mystical experiments (the years at Oxford between 1725–1727), early rising, endless resolutions, self-examination, fasting, ejaculatory prayers, and many other mystical means of purging the soul became common practice. It is no surprise that Wesley at this time began to study carefully the Catholic mystics. Some would argue that Sally Kirkham (his religious friend) was his spiritual director at this time. V. H. H. Green informs us that Wesley's Diary shows him at Stanton for Christmas 1726 where he talked with Sally about Episcopal Order and mortification. On Christmas Day they discussed Vane's reasons for becoming a Roman Catholic.[11] Unfortunately, the Diary is missing from February 1727 to May 1729, or no doubt there would be a great deal more data. But it is significant that Fénelon appears close to where the Diary ends and de Renty appears soon after the Diary begins again.

Wesley knew at least some of Fénelon's works by the winter of 1726/27. By February 1727 we find him transcribing Fénelon's *Discourse on Simplicity* for Varanese. Wesley read a great deal of Fénelon, and a surprising number of his books can still be found in John's personal library. Wesley was especially fond of Fénelon's concept of simplicity and refers to it on numerous occasions.[12] Simplicity for Wesley, as with Fénelon, came to mean "that grace which frees the soul from all unnecessary reflections upon itself."[13] One's love toward God must be *simple* and *pure*. Fénelon's phrase, "the love of God and man filling the heart and governing the life," came to represent for Wesley, "true religion."[14]

It should also be mentioned that soon after this Wesley first encountered William Law's *Christian Perfection* (1726). Law (1686–1761) completes the celebrated triumvirate (with Taylor and à Kempis) which had such a powerful impact on the early stages of Wesley's doctrine of perfection. The question which concerns us here, however, is to what extent Law introduced Wesley to mysticism. Again the question of whether or not mysticism enters into Law's *Christian Perfection* and the better known *A Serious Call to a Devout and Holy Life* (1728) has been debated at length, but most would agree that these treatises (especially the latter) represent a transitory stage in Law between a

---

[11] V. Green, *Young Wesley,* 206f.

[12] Cf. *Letters,* 5:193; 6:8, 128, 281.

[13] Ibid., 6:128.

[14] *Works,* 7:162, sermon *On Former Times.*

highly ethical period and a highly mystical period beginning in 1732. Bishop Cannon sees no apparent mystical element in the stern but practical view of religion presented in these works.[15] Although Dunn Wilson (rather unconvincingly) argues for a degree of mysticism in *Serious Call,* the fact remains that William Law did *not* introduce Wesley to mysticism. Long before Law began to figure prominently in his life Wesley had come under the mystical spell from other sources. Admittedly, Law would accelerate John's interest in mysticism later on but through a type of mysticism which Wesley soon rejected altogether and which was considerably different from the mysticism of those most influential on his spiritual growth.

Mysticism, indeed, had already made its mark on Wesley. Not only did the mystical pursuit of holiness appeal to his innate sense of morality, but the love of contemplation also appealed to his natural inclination for solitude. Soon after meeting with Fénelon John wrote to his mother, "I am so little at present in love with even company, the most elegant entertainment next to books, that unless they have a peculiar turn of thought I am much better pleased without them. I think 'tis the settled temper of my soul that I should prefer, at least for some time, such a retirement as would seclude me from all the world to the station I am now in."[16] John then spoke of the possibility of taking a position in a school at Skipton, a remote little village in Yorkshire. He stated that what he liked most was its "frightful description" and described it thus: "The town lies in a little vale, so pent up between two hills that it is scarce accessible on any side; so that you can expect little company from without, and within there is none at all."[17] Wesley was no doubt disappointed when the position passed to someone else.

John Todd's *John Wesley and the Catholic Church* cites Wesley's familiarity with the mystics and their ways as proof of his own acceptance of mysticism. After an attempt to make Wesley as Catholic as possible by implying that he was in agreement with Catholicism except for his views on "the nature and identification of the visible Church," and an attempt to make Catholicism as Protestant as possible by insisting that Catholics have always believed in the doctrines of the Reformation, especially the doctrine of grace, he argues that Wesley had

---

[15] Cannon, *Theology,* 58ff, cf. B. Green, Baker, Jeffery, etc., as to the "pre-mystical" nature of these works.

[16] *Letters,* 1:42.

[17] Ibid., 1:42f.

a great deal in common with Catholic mysticism.[18] Todd states that Wesley's emphasis on the new birth and personal experience was close to the *conversio* of the medieval mystics. Similarly, Wesley's spiritual discipline was reminiscent of the Jesuits. Then Todd identifies Wesley with the mysticism of John of the Cross using the *Ascent of Mount Carmel* and the *Dark Night of the Soul* as a measuring rod for judging Wesley's spiritual advancement. According to Todd, Wesley entered the "first active night of the senses" in 1725. Eventually styling Wesley as a "full-fledged" mystic, Todd argues that this first stage was only the start of a mystical process which would lead Wesley to a depth of spiritual awareness and conviction at Aldersgate (i.e., union with God) which would give him the power to ride and preach all over the British Isles for the next fifty years. Although Todd's theory has an obvious appeal, it is misleading. This will become apparent as Wesley's spiritual development continues to unfold.[19]

The fact still remains that Wesley drew dangerously close to the mystic way. This is especially clear in his sermons; they are particularly revealing as to the degree of mystical influence at this time.

For anyone who enters the study of John Wesley convinced that Wesley was more or less an evangelical Christian from 1725 on, it is an enormous shock to see the vast difference in Wesley's sermons before and after Aldersgate. Prior to 1738 they are infused with mysticism. Furthermore, these sermons tend to make one take Wesley more at his word, especially as he describes mysticism as the rock upon which he nearly made shipwreck.[20] The lack of justifying faith in Wesley, pre-1738, has caused some to reevaluate their appreciation of the full significance of Aldersgate. Nowhere can the impact of mysticism, and consequently of Aldersgate, be demonstrated more clearly than in

---

[18] Todd, *Catholic Church,* 21n, defends the Catholic doctrine of grace with P. Bouyer's *Du Protestantisme a L'Eglise* (Paris: Editions du Cerf, 1959), Bouyer cites the Council of Trent as proof that Catholics have always taught that "God does all" and that humankind "is always in need of divine power."

[19] Although Wesley's experience reveals some similarity to that of John of the Cross, Todd, on the whole, demonstrates (quite unintentionally) just why Wesley was *not* a mystic after this fashion. John of the Cross, like the medieval mystics and William Law (but like Wesley only for a time), was influenced by the Neoplatonists and mixed religion with a high degree of philosophy. Furthermore, even if the theory is right, the timetable is wrong. It will be demonstrated that Aldersgate was no mystical experience in the classical sense of the word.

[20] *Letters,* 1:207ff.

Wesley's sermons.[21] An even closer analysis would no doubt reveal much more, but both time and space force us to push on to the next period of Wesley's life.

Wroot: 1727–1729

It has been said that for Wesley at this time faith was either a question of pure reason or blind obedience. Up to now reason had maintained the upper hand in his search for God but this was soon to change during his second mystical experiment at Wroot. As Wesley sank deeper into mysticism, it was inevitable that he should do battle with reason. In the sermon *The Case of Reason Impartially Considered,* written long after Aldersgate, Wesley demonstrates the complete inability of reason to produce faith.[22] He writes, "Many years ago I found the truth of this by sad experience."[23] He had asked himself, "How can I be sure . . . what if I am no different than a leaf?" Piette states that these haunting doubts plunged Wesley into mysticism in search of *assurance.*[24] Furthermore, Wesley in that same sermon provides a key to the period now under observation. Reason would not give satisfactory evidence for the existence of God, and, just as he had done years before, he exhorts those determined to live by reason alone to "retire for a while from the busy world, and make the experiment yourself."[25] For Wesley, however, it had not only been an experiment with reason, but yet another experiment in mysticism.

Wesley spent most of his time from August 1727 to November 1729 in the "watery wastes" of Wroot, first as his father's curate (Wroot had become Samuel's second living) and then also as priest after his ordination as priest in September 1728. Wroot, four and a half miles west of Epworth, may not have been so isolated as Skipton, but that it was suited for another mystical experiment is abundantly clear.

---

[21] Cf. the pre-1738 sermons with sermons like *Salvation by Faith, Scriptural Christianity, Justification by Faith, Righteousness of Faith,* etc., where faith is fully a disposition of the heart involving assurance, the gift of the Holy Spirit, not the mystical "dark night." Christian faith here is a full reliance on the blood of Christ. There is no self-saving delusion here. My Ph.D. dissertation, "The Influence of the Roman Catholic Mystics on John Wesley" (Univ. of Bristol [Eng.], 1970), presents a somewhat detailed analysis of several of these earlier (pre-1738) sermons.

[22] *Works,* 6:350ff., especially 355f.

[23] Ibid., 356.

[24] Piette, *Evolution of Protestantism,* 268. My book *John Wesley, His Life and Theology* (Grand Rapids: Zondervan, 1978), discusses at length Wesley's inordinate fear of dying and his subsequent need for assurance as the siren that drew him into the mystic way.

[25] *Works,* 6:356.

Commonly known as Wroot-out-of-England, it had less than three hundred inhabitants, whom Mehetabel (Hetty) Wesley unsympathetically described as "asses dull on dunghills born."[26] Vulliamy adds that Samuel Wesley "had raised his parishioners from a level of ignorance and brutality to a level of depressing dullness, but no higher."[27] This was a contrast indeed from the more amiable life at Oxford where John had been elected Fellow of Lincoln College in March 1726.

Piette claims that when John's ailing father asked his assistance at Wroot, he jumped at the opportunity to be free from "the annoyance of university life."[28] Although John had already spent several months at Wroot (April to September 1726), this would be his first, and to some extent his last, real attempt at parish work. Curnock states that John was in some degree still marked by worldliness and describes him working in the garden, gathering flowers, shooting, swimming, and drinking tea.[29] This is, however, only part of the picture. Wesley had also decided that this would be the best means of cutting himself off from others in an attempt to approach nearer to God. Wesley performed his pastoral duties with punctiliousness, but most of his effort during these two years would be spent in sorting out his own spiritual life. Piette describes John in his country environment as "more occupied in reading mystical writers than in caring for the flock."[30] Perhaps there is more than a little truth to that.

While Wesley was at Wroot he most likely encountered Law's second treatise, *A Serious Call*, which "brightened the fire of spiritual ambition."[31] It is even more certain, however, that it was during this time that Wesley began to study carefully *The Holy Life of Monsieur de Renty*. Mon. de Renty appears soon after the Diary is resumed in the autumn of 1729 and then again in many of the successive years throughout Wesley's life. Since more will be said about this mystic later on, his influence here will not be discussed except to say that he made a lasting impression on Wesley. Mon. de Renty continues to figure prominently in Wesley's spiritual growth as Wesley was predominately

[26] Tyerman, *John Wesley*, 1:58.

[27] Vulliamy, *John Wesley*, 26f. The various biographies of Wesley abound with interesting stories concerning the people of the "Isle of Axholme," especially their struggle against the church and state which caused so much animosity against Samuel and his family.

[28] Piette, *Evolution of Protestantism*, 270.

[29] *Journal*, 1:21f.

[30] Piette, *Evolution of Protestantism*, 274.

[31] Vulliamy, *John Wesley*, 30.

concerned with the progress of his own soul throughout. While at Wroot he was susceptible to the devotional and theological slant of this French marquis. Piette reiterates that Wesley while at Wroot became "morbidly individualistic" and that his "sole happiness was to pass the time in company with mystical authors."[32] Apart from Taylor and à Kempis (who according to Piette no longer satisfied his mystical appetite), Wesley also read a great deal of the Cambridge Platonist, John Norris, who had come under the influence of Nicolas Malebranche.[33] George Herbert, Anthony Horneck, and Heylyn were also favorites at this time, all three of them having flirted with mysticism in one form or another.

It is certain that a great deal of Wesley's devotional life with regard to mysticism centered around his mother at this time. They exchanged devotional tracts and read to each other from the mystical authors on several occasions.[34] It has also been suggested that it was during this particular experimental period that Wesley perfected the practice of ejaculatory prayers. The use of devout ejaculations was common among eighteenth-century English mystics. In fact, the mystics frequently abandoned all forms of prayer except for these periodic ejaculations. Since their entire lives were spent in the attitude of prayer, they saw no real need for formal prayer. John wrote at the foot of his Diary for December 9, 1735, "No hourly prayer like ejaculations."[35] Curnock adds, however, that "the first Oxford Diary proves that Wesley adopted the habit long before the formation of the Holy Club. In all his examination work, whether for ordination or degree or fellowship, he used it freely, sometimes profusely."[36] Although the practice dwindled during the earliest years after his return to Oxford in 1729 as the Holy Club became more and more highly organized, it revived in greater force than ever after 1732.[37] In January 1734, Wesley began to mark the regularity of these prayers with the letter "e" at the beginning of every hour followed by a corresponding number (5, 6, or 7) indicating the length of the prayer. The fact that Wesley almost two years later wrote that he esteemed ejaculatory prayer more than any other type of prayer suggests the extent to which they were used and that he was

---

[32] Piette, *Evolution of Protestantism*, 420.

[33] Wesley included Malebranche's *Search for Truth* in a course for study in *Letters*, vol. 4, June 1764, p. 249. Cf. 3:163; 5:110; 7:228.

[34] V. Green, *Young Wesley*, 231.

[35] Wesley was reading *Life of Lopez* at this time.

[36] *Journal*, 1:127.

[37] Ibid.

reluctant to give them up. Although Wesley fails to record these prayers after his return from Georgia, his *Scheme of Self-Examination* for Methodists included these mystical prayers along with a strong exhortation to love God and simplicity.[38]

Toward the end of 1729 several things happened to bring this mystical experiment to a close. Henry Moore's *Life of Wesley* says, "About this time [early, probably, in 1729, when Wesley was still at Wroot], a serious man said to him, 'Sir, you wish to serve God and go to heaven? Remember that you cannot serve Him alone. You must therefore find companions or make them; the Bible knows nothing of solitary religion.'"[39] This incident, together with Wesley's call back to Oxford (junior fellows were now expected to fulfill their office in residence) by the principal of Lincoln College, Dr. Morley, ended his ministry at Wroot and initiated another period in Wesley's life.

The Holy Club: 1729–1735

The activities of the Holy Club provide still another setting for a third mystical experiment and are especially significant in the study of Wesley's partial acceptance of mysticism as he reaches the height of his romance with mysticism while still under its influence. While John was at Wroot, his brother Charles had established himself at Christ Church. Earlier, Charles had been diligent in his studies, and John informs us that Charles "led a regular, harmless life." But whenever he pressed him about religion, Charles would reply, "What, would you have me to be a saint all at once?"[40] Then, while John was still at Wroot, Charles experienced what he termed his "reformation" as his religious life began to take on definite shape. In January 1729 he wrote to John, "I verily think I shall never quarrel with you again till I do with my religion, and that I may never do *That* I am not ashamed to desire your prayers."[41] Charles goes on to write that he does not know how or when he first awoke out of his lethargy but that it was shortly after John had left Oxford. At any rate, by 1729 Charles had become increasingly concerned with the state of religion at the university. Apart from general apathy, Arianism and deism had crept in, attracting enough attention to

---

[38] *Works*, 11:521.

[39] Henry Moore, *Life of Wesley*, 2 vols. (London: Kershaw, 1824–1825), 1:162, cited in *Journal*, 1:469. Curnock argues convincingly that this "serious man" was Rev. Hoole, rector of Haxey, Samuel Wesley's friend and nearest neighbor.

[40] Green, *Young Wesley*, 145.

[41] Ibid., 147.

alarm university officials. It is against this background that in May 1729 Charles "persuaded two or three young students," so he wrote later, "to accompany me, and to observe the method of study prescribed by the statutes of the university."[42] This gained him the "harmless name of *methodist*." Then in November, John, taking the advice of his "serious friend" (Dr. Hoole) against solitary religion, quickly joined these young men who had united together for the purpose of mutual religious instruction. Furthermore, John soon emerged as the leader of the little society, or as it was commonly called, the Holy Club.

At first the Holy Club concentrated only on the study of the Greek New Testament, but by 1730, largely due to the efforts of William Morgan, one of the charter members of the Holy Club, it had also assumed responsibility for various works of charity.[43] Inspired by Morgan and again following the advice of his friend Dr. Hoole, Wesley began visiting the prisons, assisting the poor and sick, and doing what other good he could do. Gambold, in his account of Wesley at Oxford, says that Wesley even paid for a schoolmaster to teach the children of the poor.[44]

At the same time, Wesley was redoubling his efforts to purge away all "superfluities." He exhorted his friends to rise early and not to be content with just solemn devotions: Christians should "at all times and at all places make fervent returns to the mind of God."[45] It is not surprising that he should write to his mother that he had been accused of being "too strict in religion," of carrying things too far, and of spending strength on unnecessary burdens.[46] John's older brother, Samuel, after a visit to Oxford, wrote the following poem against John's excessive labor:

> Does John beyond his strength presume to go?
> To his frail carcass literally a foe?

---

[42] Ibid., 148.

[43] Wesley wrote Dr. Hoole on May 18, 1731, for advice concerning the activities of the Holy Club and received this reply: "I dare not say you would be too officious, should you of your own mere motion seek out the persons that want your instructions and charitable contributions." *Journal*, 1:99.

[44] *Journal*, 1:467, taken from *Methodist Magazine* (1798).

[45] *Letters*, 1:53ff.

[46] Remember that John criticized à Kempis six years earlier for being too strict. *Letters*, 1:85ff., 92ff., 112ff. The members of the Holy Club were called "supererogation men," among other names.

> Lavish of health, as if in haste to die,
> And shorten time to insure eternity?[47]

Susanna also felt it necessary to caution John against glorying in temptation. She wrote that John should pray to avoid temptation rather than to conquer it. This had been her primary objection to John of Castaniza, although she generally looked over his faults because of his virtue. Wesley's own devotional reading no doubt influenced his thinking along these lines. In 1730 Wesley read Taylor, à Kempis, Law, de Renty, Norris, and Heylyn. In 1731 Norris reappears and Scougal, the Scottish mystic, appears for the first time. In the same letter from Susanna she wrote "that *The Life of God in the Soul of Man* (Scougal's) is an excellent book."

One would think that the contrast of activity (although still compatible with certain types of mysticism) among the members of the Holy Club would lead Wesley away from the detached mysticism of his recent experiment at Wroot. Such was not the case, however, at least not for long.

In the sequence of his religious review written in 1738, he states that a "contemplative man" then convinced him more than ever "that outward works are nothing" and instructed him "how to pursue inward holiness, or a union of the soul with God."[48] If Wesley's interest in the interior life of the contemplatives had begun to wane, this contemplative man, most certainly William Law, reignited his interest.[49] Although Law did not introduce Wesley to mysticism, it was undoubtedly Law who was most responsible for accelerating his interest at this time. Since the days of *Christian Perfection* and *Serious Call*, Law had adopted "a new German theosophy in which elements of medieval mysticisms were harmonized with habits of modern thought."[50] Law is said to have put Wesley on a kind of internal penance. Brazier Green informs us of the "intensity of Wesley's zeal for the closely cultivated devotional life."[51] In fact, "so deep was his passion [for the interior life] during this period,

---

[47] George Stevenson, *Memorials of the Wesley Family* (London: Partridge and Co., 1876), 245.

[48] For some reason Curnock wants to identify this contemplative man with Dr. Hoole, but this is surely in error since he produced an opposite effect. *Journal*, 1:468f.

[49] *Letters*, 4:105. Law writes, "I was once a kind of oracle to Mr. Wesley." Charles refers to Law as "our John the Baptist" (Moore, *Life*, 1:107).

[50] Vulliamy, *John Wesley*, 30.

[51] B. Green, *John Wesley and William Law*, 58.

that he seriously contemplated retirement from the leadership of the Holy Club."[52]

Although the rigid asceticism continued (we know that his health was precarious, and his rigorous self-discipline imposed a severe strain on his constitution), Wesley was once again inclined to seek solitude and to abandon his social service.[53] Like Wroot, Oxford became yet another mystical experiment involving a withdrawal from the world, but at Oxford Wesley would sink even deeper into the esoteric world of mysticism. As in Wroot, the internal approach to God again got the upper hand, this time, however, not over and against reason but against any form of outward works-righteousness. Wesley writes that Law "spoke so incautiously against trusting in outward works, that he discouraged me from doing them at all."[54] About the same time he wrote his father, "By holiness I mean not fasting or bodily austerity [as his father seemed to suppose] or any other external means of improvement, but the *inward temper,* to which all these things are subservient, a renewal of the soul in the image of God."[55]

John made his first trip to visit Law in Putney in July 1732.[56] As a result of this and subsequent visits, he was persuaded to read *Theologia Germanica* and other mystical works,[57] and while he failed to understand all that Mr. Law was saying, he was nonetheless a willing student.[58] Law had combined his ethical idealism with a high degree of mystical detachment. Wilson observes that *Theologia Germanica* (which Wesley studied carefully for several years) had the same regard for "intention" as did Taylor and à Kempis.[59] Even more important, however, are the "two eyes" of the mystical treatise, the right one of which looks into eternity and has many of the characteristics of Eckhart's "spark" or Tauler's "image."[60]

But Law also recommended other mystical works, and Schmidt argues that Law directed Wesley once again to the Romanic mystics

---

[52] Ibid.

[53] Piette, *Evolution of Protestantism,* 420.

[54] *Journal,* 1:469.

[55] *Letters,* 1:168 (italics mine).

[56] The last personal conversation with Law occurred between August 28 and September 8, 1735. John was also with Law on November 28, 1733.

[57] *Sermons,* 1:264. Jeffery, *Quest,* 209, attributes the *Germanica* to Behmen.

[58] Diary entry, November 28, 1733: "with Mr. Law, not understood all he said."

[59] Wilson, "Influence of Mysticism," 143.

[60] Inge, *Mysticism,* 180ff.

whom he had known in his childhood.[61] Orcibal is more specific, stating that Law introduced Wesley to Tauler and Molinos and impressed upon him their ideal of pure love and total resignation.[62] After the eminent Putney physician and mystic, Dr. Cheyne, had fired Law's enthusiasm for mysticism with Behmen, Law became well acquainted with a wide range of mysticism. He knew the desert fathers, especially Macarius, and apart from Tauler, he was also greatly attracted to the other fourteenth-century mystics, Eckhart, Suso, and Ruysbroek. Wilson also singles out Malebranche as being influential on Law.[63] Likewise, Wesley's Diary from 1732 and 1733 reveals his own interest in the mystical authors. Rodriguez (*On Humility*), Francis of Sales (*Introduction to the Devout Life*), de Renty, Fénelon (*Maxims of the Saints* and *Pastoral Letter Concerning the Love of God*), Castaniza, Ephraem Syrus (*On Repentance*), Malebranche, A. H. Francke, Norris, Horneck, Heylyn, Taylor, à Kempis, Law, and even the *Bull Unigenitus* all find their way into Wesley's theological and devotional reading.[64] Obviously, Law's enthusiasm for the mystics was passed on to the Wesleys as they accepted Law's counsel on the methods of devotion and put them into practice.[65]

Law, however, was not the only one to introduce John to these mystical writers. For example, Dr. Cheyne was probably the first to introduce Wesley to Count Marsay. Similarly, John Byrom, a friend of Law's who contributed a great deal to the revival of mystical studies in eighteenth-century England, could have suggested some of these treatises. Furthermore, one should not forget the influence of the Holy Club, which was an important source for Wesley's knowledge of the various mystical authors. John Clayton wrote to Wesley in August 1732 that "it meant a great deal to him that he was beginning to understand what was meant by the union of souls, so much talked of by Malebranche and Antoinette Bourignon."[66] There is every reason to believe that this was Wesley's first encounter with Madame Bourignon, and indeed Clayton was probably responsible for introducing John to several of the mystical treatises. But here again Clayton was not the only member of the Holy Club, apart from John and Charles, who had an interest in mysticism.

---

[61] Schmidt, *Theological Biography*, 112.

[62] Orcibal, "Theological Originality," 89.

[63] Wilson, "Influence of Mysticism," 65.

[64] Some of these were apparently met for the first time. Ephraem Syrus (c. 306–373) will figure prominently in Wesley's attitude toward mysticism.

[65] Henry Bett, *The Spirit of Methodism* (London: Epworth, 1937), 63ff.

[66] Tyerman, *John Wesley*, 1:83–84; cf. Schmidt, *Theological Biography*, 103.

There is a great deal of evidence to suggest that the entire company developed an interest in the ascetical aloofness of mysticism. In a letter to Miss Bishop in November 1774, Wesley warned her against mystic solitude but admitted that "most of our little flock at Oxford were tried with this, my brother and I in particular." Undoubtedly, the majority of the members were impregnated with a certain degree of mysticism, especially the two Wesleys, John Clayton, John Gambold, Westley Hall, and George Whitefield. It affected different members in different ways, however. Gambold, described as "a religious seeker, living a sequestered, secluded and introspective life," made no secret of the fact that he had read widely among the mystics.[67] Westley Hall wandered into Quietism (he and Gambold were both drawn to the Moravians); but, unfortunately, he eventually became neurotic and was denounced by the Wesleys as a "smooth-tongued hypocrite" when he became unfaithful in his marriage to Martha Wesley, John's sister. Even George Whitefield, one of the most distinguished members of the Holy Club, dabbled in mysticism. His reading in Scougal's *Life of God in the Soul of Man* is said to have led to his conversion.

1735: A Climactic Year. This year is of particular importance as it marks the watershed of Wesley's mystical experience. It is also an eventful year, a year in which John's father died at Epworth and the year John and Charles set out for Georgia. It is the year when Wesley attempted to commit himself wholeheartedly to the mystic way. Richard Heitzenrater in his two-volume work *The Elusive Mr. Wesley,* writes, "By the beginning of 1735, a growing concern for the 'liberty' of the gospel (partly derived from the mystic writers) led him to begin testing his scheme of living. . . ."[68] For example, Wesley records in his Diary the practice of meditation. Unfortunately, he does not supply satisfactory detail as to the content or method. Knox exclaims that "one would give a good deal to have these meditations more fully described."[69] Wesley also demonstrates that although he was "never in the mystic way" and could find no comfort in his attempts to understand fully their particular point of view, he nonetheless came dangerously close to mysticism. Wesley undoubtedly wandered farthest from the Aldersgate concept of justification by faith at this time. All of the previous influences in his life combined here to create a system of religion based on wholehearted

[67] V. Green, *Young Wesley,* 262.

[68] Richard P. Heitzenrater, *The Elusive Mr. Wesley,* 2 vols. (Abingdon, 1984), 1:73.

[69] Knox, *Enthusiasm,* 434.

devotion to God through inward obedience. Wesley wanted to be truly religious, but most of all, he wanted an assurance of heaven. Paradoxically, even while he was so obsessed with the suppression of self-love through the mystical tools of the contemplative life (internal works-righteousness), Bishop Cannon states that a high degree of "self-love was at the very center of his life."[70]

There is a subtle but important turn here. Although Law discouraged Wesley from outward works, Law's *"mental prayer* and the like exercises" were as much one's own works as visiting the sick or clothing the naked.[71] Wesley writes that Law's effectual means of purifying the soul, the uniting it with God, were as much "my own righteousness as any I had before pursued under another name."[72] He continues, "In this refined way of trusting to my own works and my own righteousness (so zealously inculcated by the mystic writers), *I dragged on heavily, finding no comfort or help therein till the time of my leaving England."*[73] Although the standard of mysticism has a tremendous appeal to the heart hungry for righteousness, it frequently breaks down under the trial of practical application. The mystical experiments at Oxford, Wroot, and with the Holy Club provided no real test for mysticism, but Wesley was about to undertake a fourth mystical experiment, and this time he would begin to detect the inadequacy of the scale of values persistently advocated by the mystics. The idealism of the mystics would soon begin to fall to the ground under a trial by fire.

GEORGIA: A TRIAL BY FIRE

We have seen that Wesley, although committed to mysticism intellectually, lacked some of the basic mystical characteristics. Indeed, one is forced to ask at times whether he ever really understood the mystics. For example, Wesley had studied Fénelon enthusiastically, but his love for God was far from disinterested. Furthermore, Wesley was anything but indifferent to salvation and the one thing that he wanted most, the mystics could not provide—assurance. Yet Wesley's understanding of the goal of religion was essentially mystical. His negative view of the world, his misconception of faith, and his determination to

---

[70]Cannon, *Theology,* 61ff.

[71]*Journal,* 1:469.

[72]Ibid.

[73]Ibid., 469f. (italics mine).

achieve a conscious relationship with God, were all mystical ideas. Wesley, at this point, seems to have inherited many of the mystics' mistakes and few of their virtues. His experience in Georgia, however, began to put things more in perspective.

February to October 1736: The Test

On February 6, 1736, Wesley first set foot on American soil. It would not take long for him to realize that Georgia was no desert, but he took advantage of the situation as best he could.[74] On February 7 he began a long friendship with August Spangenberg. Spangenberg, previously a lecturer at Jena where he had led Peter Böhler to Christianity, had conducted the first company of Moravians to Georgia. Curnock states (and I think correctly) that although traditionally Böhler's influence on Wesley has been emphasized, it is an open question as to whether or not Wesley actually owed more to Spangenberg, both directly and indirectly.[75] Wesley and Spangenberg immediately found a great deal in common (John was just one year older), and they frequently discussed mystical divinity. The German was a great admirer of à Kempis and, in fact, acknowledged himself to be a mystic, but it is doubtful that anyone knows exactly what this meant.[76] Schmidt writes that "Spangenberg's mysticism accorded well with his previous experience with the separatist pietists in Jena and Halle."[77] We know that Francke popularized Molinos in Germany. The Moravians (although not mystics in the ordinary sense of the word) managed to combine a degree of mystical Quietism with a strong doctrine of assurance. Spangenberg pressed Wesley as to his assurance of salvation almost immediately.[78] Already impressed by the Moravian display of inner peace on board ship during a storm on the Atlantic, Wesley was primed for the encounter with them. *At first,* however, he was more inclined to their Quietism than to their assurance of faith. This would be reversed in two years' time, but for the present one must agree with Dr.

---

[74] Wesley's plans to convert the Indians fell through, and he was almost immediately caught up in the pastoral duties of the community at Savannah.

[75] Although Spangenberg's Quietism really came to the surface at Fetter Lane, Wesley's affection for him continued. After conversing with Spangenberg in April 1741, Wesley marvels at how he can refrain from joining the Moravians; his "heart burns" within him. Wesley conversed with Spangenberg frequently in Georgia and after his return to England. Spangenberg had a significant influence on Wesley before and after Aldersgate.

[76] *Journal,* 1:169.

[77] Schmidt, *Theological Biography,* 156.

[78] *Journal* 1:151.

Bett that the Moravians were yet another contributing factor in Wesley's partial acceptance of mysticism.

Spangenberg no doubt introduced Wesley to some mystical treatises. On February 27 Wesley and Spangenberg spent the afternoon discussing mysticism. That evening, after a period of meditation, they discussed the mystics and the conversation turned to Wesley's mystical friend, John Gambold. The next morning Spangenberg and Wesley again discussed mysticism. That afternoon Wesley began Madame Bourignon's *Light of the World,* and then a battery of mystics began to appear in Wesley's Diary. On February 23 Wesley read Scougal to a Mrs. Hawkins. In March Wesley read *The Life of Tauler* and in April and May Madame Bourignon (*Treatise on Solid Virtue*), Fleury, de Renty, and à Kempis all figured prominently. On March 14 Wesley meditated in his garden, à Kempis in hand. On his first trip to Frederica, à Kempis and Bourignon's *Light of the World* went with him. And on Easter Day Wesley refreshed his spirit with Fleury. All of these Roman Catholic mystics were encountered or reencountered in fairly rapid succession during Wesley's first few months in Georgia.[79]

During the summer of 1736, Law, Scougal, and Macarius occupied much of Wesley's time. Macarius emphasized a highly individualistic Christian ideal. Like many of the mystics, he taught one to expect the fulfillment "of being born from on high" and that this should lead to a measure of Christian perfection. Especially significant at this point, however, is the fact that he also added a strong doctrine of *progress* in the Christian life. In September Macarius was reinforced along these same lines by Ephraem Syrus, who, like Macarius, extended the rigid, static concept of perfection (*disciplined* love) to include a more dynamic progressive concept of perfection (*aspiring* love). Outler believes that Macarius and Ephraem probably first interested Wesley in perfection. They were certainly known long before Georgia. Ephraem appears in the Oxford Diary for 1732 and Wesley surely knew Macarius by this time, if not through William Law (who was strongly influenced by Macarius), then through someone else. At any rate, Macarius and Ephraem were the mystics to whom Wesley now pinned his faith.

Their particular brand of mysticism gave him a brief glimmer of hope. Still convinced intellectually of the truth of mysticism, he plunged once again into the midst of his mystical advisors. In preparing for the pulpit, John studied Ephraem on the nineteenth of September. On the

---

[79] Schmidt, *Theological Biography,* 214n, notes Piette's neglect of the Catholic mystics encountered in Georgia.

twenty-third of September he wrote about the mystics in his Journal. On the twenty-fourth, after morning prayers and coffee, he spent six hours with the mystics. On the twenty-fifth the mystics absorbed most of the morning. On the twenty-seventh his day's study again began with the mystics. Then Ephraem reappeared on the sixteenth, seventeenth, nineteenth, and twentieth of October and on the first, second, third, and twenty-second of November. This last frantic interest in the mystical authors, however, had a surprising effect on Wesley. For this reason it is necessary to bring additional factors into the discussion, perhaps the most crucial factors of all relative to Wesley's attitude toward mysticism.

October to December 1736: Seeds of Disillusionment

Wesley's encounter with the concept of the Christian life as going on to perfection in continuous process (introduced by Macarius and Ephraem Syrus) renewed his determination to explore the depths of mysticism, but it did not produce the desired results. Wesley now understood the necessity of continuing to build upon a foundation, but the foundation itself had not yet been established.

Wesley's utter frustration as a missionary and pastor reached a climax at Frederica, a little settlement south of Savannah. Curnock wrote that "the weakness . . . lay in this—that he did not as yet fully understand the mystery of 'the law of the Spirit of life in Christ Jesus.' "[80] Wesley admitted that in Georgia he had no understanding of faith. He wrote, "Being ignorant of the righteousness of Christ, which, by a living faith in Him, bringeth salvation 'to everyone that believeth,' I sought to establish my own righteousness; and so laboured in the fire all of my days."[81] His own works-righteousness (both external and internal) was revealing its lack of power to transform. Frederica was teaching John a painful lesson. The mystic "form of godliness" revealed its impotency most clearly at Frederica. If one reads the fourth and fifth Frederica Journals and the corresponding Diaries it is difficult to overlook Wesley's almost fatalistic expectation that his parishioners would backslide. On the sixteenth of October, for example, the Diary informs us that he reached Frederica at half past three in the afternoon. He then noted that he "met Mark Hird, 'in trouble, alas! in trouble. Oh, my Frederica!' "[82] Again, on a later visit to Frederica, Wesley revealed

---

[80]*Journal*, 1:282–83n.

[81]Ibid., 470.

[82]Ibid., 282.

his frustration. He wrote, "Most of those we met with were, as we expected, cold and heartless. I could not find one who had retained his first love."[83] Many of Wesley's attitudes began to change as a result of his realization that his mystic theology (such as it was) had been ineffectual at Frederica. The Journal in general and the Diary in particular begin to tell the story of "the complete collapse of the elaborate structure of outward (and inward) righteousness—of a religion built up according to rule and law, but without life or root in itself."[84]

Between the end of September and the twenty-third of November, Wesley began to pinpoint at least a part of his problem, realizing more and more that the mystical system which he sought to follow just did not work out in practice. First of all, he was psychologically incapable of total commitment to its theology. In his January 1738 statement against mysticism, he wrote, "*I could never fully come into this, nor contentedly omit what God enjoined;* yet, I know not how, I fluctuated between obedience and disobedience."[85] Secondly, even its more practical side was untenable. Wesley wrote to William Law just prior to Aldersgate that the ethical ideal of *Christian Perfection* and *Serious Call* (these treatises were not truly mystical, but they had a great deal in common with the initial stages of mysticism as demonstrated by the letter as a whole) was "too high for man."[86] Wesley had learned that by "the works of the law [mystical or otherwise] shall no flesh be justified."[87] The task which confronted him now was the acceptance of an evangelical alternative.

On November 22 Wesley again labored over Ephraem Syrus, but by this time a change had taken place in his experience. Consequently, Ephraem, his constant companion for nearly three months, disappeared for over a decade (until March 4, 1747). Wesley's reason for discarding Ephraem (and several of the other mystics as well) can be seen in an important letter written the next morning to his brother Samuel in which he describes his troubled state of mind.

---

[83] Ibid., 310.

[84] Ibid., 282n.

[85] Ibid., 420. It is uncertain that Wesley suspected weaknesses in the mystic scheme from his earliest encounter. His high church background, if it influenced him toward the mystics, also made him uncomfortable in denying or neglecting the ordinances of God. If Wesley could ever be correctly termed "mystic," he was a reluctant one at best.

[86] *Letters*, 1:239.

[87] Ibid.

The Letter to Samuel, November 23, 1736. H. B. Workman states that "Wesley was more influenced by mysticism than he was aware." But the fact is (at this stage at least) that no one was more keenly aware of his mystical susceptibility than John Wesley.[88] He wrote to his brother, "I think the rock on which I had the nearest made shipwreck of the faith was the writings of the mystics: under which term I comprehend all, and only those, who slight any of the means of grace."[89] In this same letter (thought by many to represent Wesley's "final break" with mysticism), he drew up a short scheme of their doctrines and asked for Samuel's opinion. Having pinpointed mysticism as the source of his failure, he now needed someone who would agree with his conclusion. It is not surprising that he wrote to Samuel who was already highly suspicious of mysticism—as evidenced by his poem citing the "whims of Molinos."[90] In fact, an earlier letter from Samuel could have assisted this initial break. At any rate, John, no doubt confident of approval, took a large part of the scheme that he had devised from the writing of Molinos as well as from Tauler and the author of *Theologia Germanica*.[91] Wesley demonstrates here that he understood mysticism (to a large extent) along the classical lines of purgation, illumination, dark or passive night, and union. Although his understanding of mysticism continued to cling to this basic skeleton throughout his life, his objections to mysticism changed or deepened as he drew nearer to Aldersgate. His earliest objection, for example, was against its "strictness"; but here his objection is against the slighting of the means of grace.[92] Perhaps the bulk of Wesley's definitive statement about mysticism in this letter can best be understood under three headings: the mystic advice to *seekers* (the imperfect seekers after the mystical experience); to *attainers* (the perfect finders); and to *teachers* (those who advise seekers that they have not yet reached their goal).[93] Wesley interprets the mystical advice to seekers in this manner: They must have love as their only end. They must choose such means as lead

---

[88] W. J. Townsend, H. B. Workman, G. Eayrs, eds., *A New History of Methodism*, Vol. 1, p. 55. This quotation is taken from a misleading article entitled "Mysticism and Methodism."

[89] *Letters*, 1:207.

[90] *Journal*, 1:104.

[91] The hymn "O God, my God, my all Thou art," (*Journal*, 1:240) which John translated on July 2, 1736, was probably written by Molinos.

[92] Wesley's break with mysticism, however, would not be completed until he recognized the mystical denial of the Atonement.

[93] Jeffery, *Quest*, 286ff.

most to love while remaining flexible toward these means. They must never become fixed or static at any one level of mystical experience. They must judge for themselves the efficacy of "conversation, meditation, forms of prayer, prudential rules, fixed return of public or private prayer, fasting, Holy Communion, and the Holy Scriptures."[94] All of these may be beneficial for a season, but, lest they become wedded to the means as the end is attained, the means must cease.

For attainers, pure love possesses all virtue in essence. Even good works are worked essentially, not accidentally. As sensible devotion in prayer is a hindrance to perfection, attainers need no public prayer since they pray without ceasing. Scripture is not needed by those who converse face to face with God.[95] Furthermore, Holy Communion is not needed by those who never cease to remember Christ in the most acceptable manner; finally, fasting is not needed by those who by temperance keep a continual fast.

Seekers become finders or attainers when they have divested themselves utterly of free will, self-love, and self-activity and entered into a passive state of pure love. In these "deified" men and women, the superior will have extinguished the inferior. They "enjoy such a contemplation as is not only above faith, but above sight, such as is entirely free from images, thoughts, and discourses, and never interrupted by sins of infirmity or voluntary distractions."[96] Attainers absolutely renounce their reason and understanding, preferring obscure or general knowledge over the particular.[97] For them, Christ died for the world, but they rarely applied redemption to themselves since this might suggest the desire for a reward which is both mercenary and inconsistent with perfect love. For attainers, the "means" have ceased. Hope is swallowed up in love. Union with God replaces the inferior faith (the dark night where one must proceed on blind trust).[98] This conscious union is the gift of God, and in order to gain it one must be content to live without it. Only pure, disinterested love leads to union.

---

[94] *Letters,* 1:209.

[95] Both Madame Bourignon and Madame Guyon received their "impressions" straight from God (or so they believed).

[96] *Letters,* 1:209.

[97] Cf. Jeanne Marie Guyon, *Life of Lady Guion* (Bristol, Eng.: S. Farley, 1772), 43.

[98] For the mystic, faith involved *passive resignation;* for Wesley, faith (via the Moravians) would involve assurance. For the mystic, darkness was a sign that faith was at work, "to believe further than one can see." Faith was an inferior stage, but Wesley came to associate it with union, as an end involving the indwelling witness of the Holy Spirit. Romans 8:16 would be his favorite sermon text for the next fifty years.

A part of Wesley's scheme also applies to the mystical teachers. They should not press seekers to pray, to read the Scripture, to fast, to communicate, or even to practice self-denial. They should speak little of eternity. Above all, they should not argue. They should let the seekers themselves apply any lesson. They may advise as to religious books, but they must stop there. They must not interfere with the seekers as their own wills must guide them. The seekers are so guided by the Spirit as not to need the teachers' direction. It is worth noting that William Law adopted this method of teaching, and Wesley strongly attacked it in a letter just prior to Aldersgate. Yet Wesley himself was slow to discard many of his mystical habits. Once, traveling in a coach after his return to England, he had an opportunity to speak "a well chosen word" but adds that "following the advice of the mystics, I left them to themselves."[99]

Now that the contents of this letter have been established, it should be mentioned that many scholars have attempted its analysis. Most are baffled, calling it one of the most obscure points in Wesley's life. Perhaps a part of the key, however, can be found in Wesley's sermon *On Self-Denial*. Here he states that most of the devotional writers of the church were mystics, but that mysticism spoke "of self-denial in so dark, so perplexed, so intricate a manner" as if they designed to conceal it from the vulgar rather than to explain it to the ordinary reader.[100] Since Wesley's ministry in Georgia (as in England) was largely to common people, he needed a message palatable to common people.

Furthermore, several scholars have interpreted this letter as if it were totally unexpected. Although there was obviously a fairly rapid change of heart, it should be mentioned that the crisis which brought about this change had been building up for some time. Almost the moment Wesley landed in Georgia he found it difficult "to serve God without distraction" in the midst of his secular business.[101] On February 11, 1736, Wesley wrote in his Diary, "Did nothing. Got no good."[102] It is interesting to speculate what the effect would have been on Wesley if Georgia had been the desert that he had anticipated. He still could not have given himself completely to mysticism, but it is safe to assume that if he had been able to venture into the wilderness to minister among "savages athirst for the Gospel," an Aldersgate experience would have been postponed and perhaps even missed altogether.

---

[99]*Journal*, 1:441.
[100]*Sermons*, 2:283.
[101]*Journal*, 1:150.
[102]Ibid., 155.

By November 1736 the tension had mounted. To make matters worse, the more he failed the harder he tried to salvage something out of the Georgia experience by an even stricter obedience to the mystic discipline. If a fanatic can be defined as "one who, having lost his vision, redoubles his effort," then Wesley was a fanatic. He observed all the external and internal rules of religion that his strength would allow. He observed and strictly enforced the rubrics of the church, the feasts, the fasts, and other similar exercises. He was also highly critical of any breach of discipline among his flock. The inevitable resentment and bitterness which he evoked prompted him to cry out, "O discipline! Where art thou to be found? Not in England, nor (as yet) in America."[103] As long as John remained among his parishioners he could hold them together tolerably well. The moment he left, however, things rapidly disintegrated. His problems seemed to increase daily, forcing him into an agonizing period of self-examination. His mystical frenzy intensified (especially during the months of September, October, and November) almost to the degree of panic but he could find no satisfaction. Schmidt attempts to interpret John's thoughts at this time. He writes that Wesley must have thought that

> . . . if it was no longer necessary to be an example to one's fellowmen or to attend to their needs, if it was enough to feel compassion without doing anything practical, if speaking about salvation was forbidden, if nothing other than a great silence remained, in which the mystic was plunged solitarily into union with God, then he was unable to detect in such a faith the presence of the Spirit of God.[104]

The general thrust of Wesley's scheme tells us clearly that he perceived two things to be central: the high value given to love and the depreciation of definite means toward salvation. It is interesting to note that although Wesley criticized the mystics for denying the means of grace (at least in theory), he, at the same time, contrasted mysticism with antinomianism.[105] Perhaps the key to this apparent paradox can be found in Wesley's use of the terms *instituted* and *prudential* to classify the means of grace.[106] Many of the mystics (but by no means all) tended to neglect and even discourage the instituted means (prayer, Communion, fasting, etc.); but they frequently encouraged the prudential means

---

[103]Ibid., 271.

[104]Schmidt, *Theological Biography,* 253.

[105]*Journal,* 4:201f.

[106]*Works,* 8:322ff.

(e.g., the art of holy living, watching, self-denial, taking up the cross, and exercising the presence of God). The mystic denial of the instituted means remained a stumbling block for Wesley throughout his life, but the ultimate break was far from complete. The major battle was yet to be fought. Wesley would find that his greatest problem lay in a much more basic error of which the denial of the means of grace was only a symptom, a tip of the iceberg.

Ambivalence and Confusion: 1737

Wesley's failure to understand fully the real nature of his problem simply meant that his second year in Georgia would be no more successful than his first. Furthermore, since his failure was attributed largely to the mystical denial of means (although there is no evidence to suggest that Wesley himself denied such means apart from the statement "the rock on which I had the nearest made shipwreck"), he tended to exaggerate this lesser problem. In fact, after Aldersgate and out of the heat of personal struggle when this same objection is raised again in the sermon *The Means of Grace,* Wesley reveals a far more sober judgment. He states that, although far from uniform, the mystics were "burning and shining lights standing in the gap against ungodliness."[107] They "intended only to show that outward religion was worth nothing without a religion of the heart but in so doing they appeared to despise the means of grace."[108] Lawson's *Notes* adds that the mystics taught that the "highest form of religion is the immediate union with God in soaring contemplation and ecstatic rapture, quite apart from outward forms of prayer and worship."[109] Although Wesley deeply appreciated the mystical counterbalance to externalism, he detested their neglect of the means of grace which caught the full force of his frustration.

It is important to reiterate that the real problem with many of the mystics who were most influential on Wesley at this time lies at the heart of Christianity. Until Wesley realized that much of mysticism in fact held a different view of religion, denying the very atonement of Christ, he would continue to struggle on, being tossed about with the various winds of doctrine. For this reason, Wesley's Diary reveals little sign of the mystic break other than the sudden disappearance of Ephraem Syrus. John Todd suggests that Wesley (rather than breaking away) is

---

[107] *Sermons,* 1:240; cf. 240fn.
[108] Ibid.
[109] Lawson, *Notes,* 104f.

just getting down to mystical business. According to him this letter to Samuel simply confirms the "dark night."[110] He argues that one does not have to have a conscious love of mysticism to proceed along the mystic way of spiritual development. Again Todd grossly overstates and oversimplifies. But it is, nonetheless, interesting to note that Wesley returned almost immediately to à Kempis and Francke. The mystics had undoubtedly dropped in Wesley's estimation, but they continued to hover on the fringe of his experience for another nineteen months.

Wesley, therefore, went to Georgia expecting to find a spiritual climate conducive to yet another mystical experiment (his fourth). His disappointment, however, rather than leading him to alter his methods, caused him to redouble his efforts in an almost frantic attempt to achieve a constant awareness of God. Out of his subsequent frustration he unleashed an attack on his mystic masters, thinking them to be the source of his failure as a pastor and missionary. Although his general diagnosis was correct, he still failed to understand the true nature of his lack of power. The disease went far deeper than he imagined. He still had no faith, no peace, and no assurance. Dunn Wilson insists that before Wesley left for America he had already begun to choose a better way, the way of faith. Wilson sees the mystical internal works-righteousness as an improvement over mere external works-righteousness. In reality, however, mysticism in many respects was as much a detour as a sign post to Aldersgate. With regard to a sound doctrine of justification by faith (in the Reformation sense), he was probably as close to Aldersgate in 1725 as at the end of 1737. Wesley's journey home proves this conclusively. Wesley had learned precious little from his trial by fire. He left America with ambivalent feelings about the mystics but, most of all, utterly confused.

---

[110] J. Todd, *Catholic Church*, 57ff.

4

mysticism unmasked:
a reluctant rejection

Something had to give and quickly. Wesley felt betrayed. He had asked for a loaf and received a stone, the rock upon which he had nearly made shipwreck.

THE JOURNEY HOME

Wesley, almost before losing sight of land, registers "unaccountable apprehensions of I know not what danger (the wind being small and the sea smooth)."[1] More than anything, Wesley desired a faith which would prosper under the prospect of death; and, again, his first reaction was to turn to the mystics.

Monsieur de Renty

Unfortunately, the Diary is missing from September 1, 1737, to March 31, 1738, although the fact that the mystic Fleury appears at the point where the Diary leaves off and the mystic de Renty appears soon after it begins is indicative of his continuing interest in the mystics. Wesley's Journal for January 6, 1738, tells us that he completed the "abridgment of Mr. de Renty's life." Wesley strongly criticizes the historian's (Jean Baptiste de Saint-Jure) presentation of de Renty's *Life* since he casts the "shade of superstition and folly over one of the brightest patterns of heavenly wisdom."[2] Wesley admired de Renty

---

[1] *Journal*, 1:414.
[2] Ibid., 414f.

more than any other Roman Catholic mystic, properly so-called, and de Renty would soon become a household word among the people called Methodist. In light of this it would be important to discuss briefly the attraction of de Renty at this point in Wesley's pilgrimage.

Wesley expresses few (if any) open criticisms of de Renty's life, and de Renty's area of influence runs wider and deeper than that of any other mystic. In fact, Wesley frequently defended him. We have already mentioned his complaint against the biography (by his Jesuit confessor, Jean Baptiste de Saint-Jure);[3] and he reiterates this complaint to Bishop Lavington, claiming that de Renty has been "misunderstood."[4] Yet only a casual glance at Wesley's own extract of the biography placed alongside the original reveals that Wesley liked and disliked a great deal about de Renty.

Gaston Jean Baptiste de Renty, known only by his biography entitled *The Holy Life of Monsieur de Renty, a Late Nobleman of France and Sometime Counsellor to King Lewis the Thirteenth*,[5] was born in 1611. One should not be surprised to learn that at an early age de Renty was first awakened by reading à Kempis' *Imitation of Christ*.[6] Wesley's extract says that no sooner had de Renty read it "than he felt new thoughts and affections, and resolved seriously to pursue 'the one thing needful' [one of Wesley's favorite phrases not in the original], the working out of his salvation and ever after he so esteemed that book, that he always carried it about him, and made use of it on all occasions."[7] Wesley then omits from the original many of the events and letters from de Renty's early life, moving on quickly to the time of his marriage at the age of twenty-two. When he was twenty-seven, God touched his heart more closely, "and this time he marked as the beginning of his entire change, and perfect consecration to God's service."[8] It is interesting that the original

---

[3] Ibid.

[4] *Letters*, 3:328f., 1751.

[5] This book by Saint-Jure originally appeared in French under the title *Le Chrétien Réel ou la vie du Marquis de Renty, servant de modéle à la vie vraiement Chrétienne, et d'apologie effective aux maximes et voies spirituelles de la vraie theologie mystique, vainement combattue par les esprits du siécle*. The edition that Wesley abridged was almost certainly the 1657/58 edition translated by E. S. Gent (London: printed for John Crook) and which reappeared in 1684. Henceforth this edition will be referred to as the *original*.

[6] Wesley's *Farther Appeal to Men of Reason and Religion*, vol. 2, *Works*, 8:190f., cites à Kempis and de Renty in support for "rules," self-denial, and love. De Renty's charity is also mentioned.

[7] Wesley, *Extract from the Life of M. de Renty* (pub. independently, 1741), 2; cf. *Original*, 4f. This extract also appears in the first edition of Wesley's *Works* (Pine, 1771).

[8] Ibid., 2; cf. *Original*, 17.

refers to this as a "call to a high Perfection," but Wesley omits any reference to perfection at this point. He merely records de Renty's need for a guide. On the advice of his guide (the Reverend Father de Candrien, unnamed by Wesley), a person of deep learning, of great piety, "and of high capacity for matters interior" (the last phrase was omitted by Wesley), de Renty "withdrew altogether from court, he renounced all visits of pure compliment, and all unnecessary employments to give himself up to those which might glorify God, and help his neighbour."[9]

The publisher's note to the reader points out that de Renty "was not a retired or cloistered person, but one who practised the rules of perfection in a secular and married condition, with the ordinary worldly impediments . . . as living in the world, and yet dying to it."[10] De Renty, like Loyola, practiced a mysticism of service and Wesley goes to great lengths to record his depth of piety and works of charity (much is quoted verbatim) but he omits the *excessive* mortification and *any* reference to the highly philosophical mystical path and to material leaning toward Rome.

Wesley's extract reduces 347 pages of the original to only 67. The extract deals almost exclusively with aspects of his personality (according to Schmidt this is where his true greatness lay), his supreme love for God, and his works of charity. This means that the abridgment upholds a strong Christian ethic while playing down so much mystical theology. The original devotes considerable space to de Renty's "retired life," and "his great skill in interior matters of the soul," especially to the two central features in de Renty's life, his "mystical prayer" and "the state of his mystical death and annihilation,"[11] none of which appears in the extract or figures greatly in Wesley's life and thought.

Wesley, focusing on the practical outworkings of a vital mystical religion, sifted away most of the dross and would eventually give to his societies a record of Christianity lived to its ultimate conclusion. Now, however, de Renty's exemplary holiness, his remarkable self-control, and his diligence in the service of God and people would illustrate for Wesley "the ideal Christian life."[12] Perhaps this comment on de Renty's

---

[9] Ibid. Wesley frequently condenses entire chapters into mere sentences.

[10] *Original,* iv–v.

[11] De Renty's "ladder of prayer" involved four stages: reasoning and discourse (meditation); will and affection; active or acquisite contemplation; and passive or infused contemplation. *Original,* 285.

[12] Cf. *Letters,* 8:171.

"corporal death" is a proper place to end our discussion: *"Sir, I have one word to say to you before I dye. The perfection of Christian life, is to be united* un *to God,* in the [*by*] *faith* of the church: [. *Let us*] we ought *not* to *entangle ourselves in novelties; let us adore his conduct over us, and continue faithful to him unto the end;*[. *L*] *let us adhere to that one God, crucified for our salvation;*[. *L*]*let us unite all our actions*[,] *hoping that if we continue faithful to him*[,] *by his grace, we shall be partakers of the glory of his Father.*[13] Note that by 1741 (the time this extract was published) Wesley fully understood the issue of personal faith. "The faith of the church," for example, is altered to read "by faith," leaving room for the personal dynamics at work. On the journey home, however (just three years earlier), this was still a mystery to Wesley.

It is apparent that Wesley now, as in Oxford and Georgia, was suffering from a lack of faith complicated by almost constant confusion of mind and spirit. He could find no real peace, yet he was obeying every commandment (not only according to the letter but the spirit as well). He knew that there had to be a reason for his lack of faith. He had the option of accepting the mystic explanation that God was withholding the Spirit intentionally in order to ensure an ultimate union dependent upon pure love; or of admitting that everything he had done thus far was for nothing. This, then, was the dilemma. Should he be content with his misery and hold on to the hope that he was on the brink of divine union where light would flood his soul and give him the coveted awareness of God (de Renty's "experimental verity")? Or should he go back and start afresh? Wesley tells us on January 24, 1738, that a "wise man [no doubt William Law] advised me some time since, 'Be still, and go on.'"[14] Following this advice on January 6 and 7, Wesley seriously contemplated once again sinking wholly into mysticism. On January 8, 9, and the days following, however, the second major crisis (the first being those events prompting the November 1736 letter to Samuel) was reached in Wesley's partial break with mysticism.

St. Cyprian

The days that followed the completion of his abridgment of de Renty were troubled ones and crucial to Wesley's spiritual development. On the eighth of January he wrote that by "the most infallible of proofs,

---

[13] *Original,* 329f.; *Extract,* 66. Words italicized denote the text of the extract. Words in regular face denote words Wesley deleted. Words in brackets denote those added by Wesley.

[14] Ibid., 418.

inward feeling, I am convinced, of unbelief, pride, gross irrecollection, levity, and luxuriancy of Spirit."[15] Then in his Journal for the ninth of January and following Wesley wrote:

> I reflected much on that vain desire, which had pursued me for so many years, of being in solitude in order to be a Christian. I have now, thought I, solitude enough. But am I therefore the nearer being a Christian? Not if Jesus Christ be the model of Christianity. I doubt, indeed, I am much nearer that mystery of Satan which some writers affect to call by that name. So near that I have probably sunk wholly into it, had not the great mercy of God just now thrown me upon reading St. Cyprian's works. "O my soul, come not thou into their secret!"[16]

This passage has been quoted in full because of its importance. Our task is two-fold: first to identify the expression "mystery of Satan"; and secondly, to discuss the influence of St. Cyprian.

For anyone who has studied Wesley and mysticism, it is more than obvious that by the phrase "mystery of Satan" Wesley means mysticism. The whole context of comments and events makes the identification certain. In Wesley's mind, for example, solitude was always associated with mysticism. The books he read, the letters he wrote, the diaries he kept, the sermons he preached, and the life he led all pointed to mysticism. Yet some (especially those with a particular bias like Ronald Knox who attempts to identify the phrase with Catholicism)[17] are still not convinced and for this reason I add a few more facts to reinforce the argument for mysticism. Wesley, for example, in other places in his works uses similar phrases when referring to mysticism: it is called the "fairest of Satan's devices,"[18] the "specious snare of the devil,"[19] and the "mystery of iniquity."[20] Behmen is labeled "demonospher" as his mysticism was considered to be Satanic in origin. Wesley, while still on the journey home, writes that mysticism is "set on fire of hell."[21] Furthermore, the words of St. Cyprian in this context make more sense contrasted with mysticism (they certainly are not anti-Catholic). Surely

---

[15] *Journal*, 1:415.

[16] Ibid., 416.

[17] Knox, *Enthusiasm*, 435.

[18] *Sermons*, 1:378n.

[19] *Journal*, 6:10.

[20] Wesley, *Notes Upon the New Testament*, 2 Thess. 2:7.

[21] *Journal*, 1:420.

it is safe to say categorically that the "mystery of Satan" was a reference to mysticism.

The question now is how the works of St. Cyprian kept Wesley from "sinking wholly" into mysticism. Curnock writes that "Cyprian had no sympathy with the dreamy and speculative genius of the East. His stern assertion of ecclesiastical order and sacerdotal domination, his rigid asceticism and his dauntless heroism in the time of pestilence (the "Diocletianic persecution") appealed to Wesley at this juncture."[22] Curnock then added that "a study of Cyprian would probably reveal one of the many sources of Wesley's scheme of life and discipline."[23] In fact, one need go no further than Wesley's own extract entitled *The Acts of the Christian Martyrs* to pinpoint Cyprian's stand against mysticism.[24] Remember that Wesley at this time was deliberating as to whether his misfortune was divinely imposed (as taught by the mystics) or lay within himself. St. Cyprian said, "We must confess that this calamity, riseth chiefly of our own wickedness, while we walk not in the way of the Lord."[25] Here lies the answer and one need go no further than *The Christian Library* to find it. After Aldersgate it could be demonstrated time and again that for Wesley "darkness" had its roots in *sin* not in God.[26]

An even closer examination of St. Cyprian's works is still more revealing. Cyprian, for example, wrote a treatise, *On Works and Alms,* which is diametrically opposed to much of what Wesley understood mysticism to mean. Cyprian quotes from Proverbs 16:6, "By almsgiving and faith sins are purged" and Ecclesiasticus 3:30, "As water extinguisheth fire, so almsgiving quencheth sin"; and he himself wrote that "by almsgiving and works righteousness the flame of sin is subdued."[27] Cyprian throughout this treatise uses Scripture to exhort men to works of mercy, prayer, and fasting (e.g., Matt. 25:31–46; Gal. 6:9–10).[28]

---

[22] Ibid., 416n.

[23] Ibid.

[24] This extract is included in *The Christian Library,* 2:272ff.

[25] Ibid.

[26] Cf. Wesley on Madame Guyon and the sermon *The Wilderness State* (*Works,* 6:80, "[God] never *deserts* us, as some speak; it is we only that *desert* him.") In the *Journal* (3:318) for September 2, 1747, Wesley states that *in orco* or darkness seems far deeper than it really is. "If we look into a dark pit it seems deep; but the darkness only makes it seem so. Bring the light, and we shall see it is very shallow." Cf. *Sermons,* 2:253, where Wesley speaks out against the Romish "dark night."

[27] *The Writings of Cyprian* in the *Ante-Nicene Christian Library* 10 vols. (Edinburgh: T. and T. Clark, 1868), 1:1–20.

[28] Ibid.

Furthermore, Wesley maintained his admiration for St. Cyprian, defending him in a letter to Dr. Conyers Middleton, on January 4, 1749, and later in the Journal referring to the famous bishop of Carthage as a "governor of the Church."

THE GAP WIDENS

The events which followed Wesley's encounter with St. Cyprian reiterate (although not without exception) even more strongly what has been said thus far. On the thirteenth of January a violent storm broke over the sea. At first John was afraid but was strengthened after crying unto God. As soon as the storm ceased, he once again found relief from his heaviness through a renewed resolution to preach and apply "the word of God to every single soul in the ship."[29] Then he added:

> I am sensible one who thinks the being *in orco,* as they phrase it, an indispensable preparative for being a Christian, would say, I had better have continued in that state; and that this unseasonable relief was a curse, not a blessing. Nay, but who art thou, O man, who, in favour of a wretched hypothesis, thus blasphemest the good gift of God?[30]

Here we see Wesley take yet another stab at mysticism. When he was out of danger and found comfort in his various spiritual exercises, he lashed out at the mystics because they (Law, Guyon, de Renty, etc.) discouraged these sensible comforts as they (or so the mystics thought) could easily become motive for religion and prevent further growth in perfection. Wesley was frequently blind to his own inconsistencies, however. Any gift of God must be well received (in spite of the mystic *in orco*), but the moment death looked him in the face and his comforts vanished, he invariably turned once again to the mystics where even fear and doubt were the instruments of God.

On January 24, in a review of his thoughts at that time, Wesley admitted that he had "a fair summer religion." He could talk well and even believed himself while no danger was near, but when danger threatened his spirit was troubled and all of the old doubts came flooding in upon him. He then added, "Perhaps this is best, to look upon it as my Cross; when it comes, to let it humble me, and quicken all my good resolutions, especially that of praying without ceasing; and at

---

[29] *Journal,* 1:417.
[30] Ibid.

other times, to take no thought about it, but quietly to go on 'in the work of the Lord.'"[31] These are strange words considering the fact that he had called another aspect·of the same idea a "wretched hypothesis" just a few days earlier. The battle with mysticism had not been won.

We may summarize events on the ship so far as follows: When Wesley was troubled, his first instinct was to turn to mysticism (de Renty) where his spiritual dryness could be attributed to *in orco* (the mystical "dark night") instead of to himself. St. Cyprian made him realize that the real source of his fear and doubt lay in his own wickedness and in his own lack of faith. In the quiet after a storm, Wesley lashed out at what nearly consumed him, realizing that *in orco* stifled spiritual growth, making one content to remain still. Old habits are not easily broken, however. At the time of writing his review (January 24, 1738), he paused once again to consider the advice of his mystical mentors. Wesley, now beginning to realize his inconsistency, was baffled. He was still a desperate man "grasping at the edge of a precipice."[32] At this point we return to the Journal review which continues from a "private paper" quoted by Moore.[33]

John admits to being "tossed by various winds of doctrine." At first he was warned against too much stress on outward works. At the other extreme, however, the Lutherans and Calvinists "magnified faith to such an amazing size that it quite hid all the rest of the commandments." Wesley "did not then see that this was the natural effect of their overgrown fear of Popery."[34] As he became acquainted with the mystic writers, their "noble descriptions of union with God and internal religion made everything else appear mean, flat, and insipid . . . even good works appear so too; yea, and faith itself."[35] At this point Wesley more or less repeats an abbreviated form of the mystical scheme presented to Samuel earlier. He cites their exaltation of love at the expense of the means of grace. John states, "I had no heart, no vigour, no zeal in obeying; continually doubting whether I was right or wrong, and never out of perplexities and entanglements."[36] Again we are reminded that Wesley (because of all that had gone before) was unhappy in his mysticism. This review then concludes with the statement that the

---

[31] Ibid., 418.

[32] Wilson, "Influence of Mysticism," 89ff.

[33] Moore, *Life*, 1:342.

[34] *Journal*, 1:419.

[35] Ibid., 420.

[36] Ibid.

mystics are the most dangerous enemies of Christianity (all others being but triflers). "They stab it in the vitals; and its most serious professors are most likely to fall by them. May I praise Him who hath snatched me out of this fire."[37]

Many who do not interpret John's statement to Samuel in November 1736 as the ultimate break with mysticism find it here. Dunn Wilson writes that by the time Wesley landed in England he was a man freed from mysticism's fatal snare. This conclusion, however, is still premature. Apparently, Wilson (like Wesley) does not fully understand what the fatal snare of mysticism really is. A careful comparison of the statement in November 1736 with this statement of January 1738 reveals that Wesley's objection to mysticism is still concerned almost wholly with the denial of the means of grace. Wesley's description of mysticism here states that "love is all; all the commands beside are only means of love: you choose those which you feel are means to you, and use them as long as they are so." A quick glance at the statement in 1736 reveals that all of Wesley's objections here were taken almost verbatim from one paragraph in that letter.[38] Nothing new as to the nature of Wesley's complaint against mysticism appears here. As long as he had not the witness of the Spirit he would be vulnerable to mysticism. Even after Aldersgate his brief moments of despair almost inevitably lead him to cast a longing look back to the way of the mystic.

Schmidt writes that Wesley, upon examining his spiritual state on the voyage home, found that the "greatest form of self-deception was a reliance upon solitude as the way to God."[39] Schmidt argues further that Wesley's reiteration of a categorical "No! to the mystics" was a result of the fact that the mystics, under the cloak of love, "avoid every concrete, practical act of obedience and leave a person fluctuating in a state of uncertainty between a sense of obligation and freedom."[40] Although Wesley now sees that many of the mystics do not hold the religion of Christ, in fact, that mysticism is potentially a dangerous enemy to Christianity, their promise of final union with God and of being inwardly bound to him still holds an appeal for Wesley during the days from January to May 1738. The language against the mystics in

---

[37] Ibid.

[38] Wilson ("Influence of Mysticism," 93f.) notes the similarity of the two statements but fails to recognize the significance. The objections registered by Wesley in May 1738 reveal the nature of the ultimate (but still partial) break with mysticism. Cf. chapter 5.

[39] Schmidt, *Theological Biography*, 252ff.

[40] Ibid.

early 1738 is stronger than that of 1736 because the threat was greater. But Wesley still failed to understand the greatest mystical weakness that, when fully understood, would break the back of their strong appeal. Since November 1736, Wesley had learned almost nothing more about the nature of his mystical error or of his lack of justifying faith in Christ. St. Cyprian's two-fold influence pointed out the fallacy of *in orco* (that darkness originates in sin, not in God) and no doubt helped Wesley to reassess the value of works. But he was still without the witness of the Spirit; until this was his, mysticism remained a serious threat indeed. Until John's fits of darkness left him reasonably free to grow in the faith, mysticism hung just on the fringe waiting to move in at the slightest sign of weakness.

Before moving on to the next section, I should mention that Wesley's last mystical experiment (now drawing to a close) was not a complete failure. As we examine the abiding mystical influences, it will become more and more apparent that the journey to Georgia had, at the same time, a positive contribution which to a large extent can be attributed to mysticism. Curnock writes:

> The crowning achievement was the slow moulding of the Methodist system. The circuit, the society, the itinerant ministry, the class meeting, the band meeting, the love feast; leaders and lay assistants; extempore preaching and prayer; and even the building of a meeting-house,—all this, and much else in the form and spirit of early Methodism, came to John Wesley in Georgia, and was transplanted by him to English and Irish cities and villages—a tree of life the leaves of which were to be for the healing of the nations."[41]

The seeds of Methodism were then sown in the soil (however shallow) of mysticism but transplanted in time into the deep fertile soil of an evangelical faith in Jesus Christ.

THE MORAVIAN SYNTHESIS

The Journal and Diary for the period extending up to Aldersgate demonstrate that Wesley's ultimate break with mysticism had not yet occurred. It is interesting to note, for example, that Wesley writes in his Journal for February 18 that on a trip to Stanton Harcourt he found his old friend John Gambold "recovered from his *mystic* delusion, and convinced that St. Paul was a better writer than either Tauler or Jacob

---

Behmen."[42] Ironically, however, Wesley himself had not yet recovered. The next day the Moravian missionary Peter Böhler (more about him shortly) exhorted John to purge away "that philosophy of yours." Wesley writes that he "understood him not," but the meaning can be seen more readily in the account found in Böhler's own diary for February 18, 1738, and following. Böhler writes, "The art which we have to learn to believe in the Saviour is much too easy for the Englishmen, so that they are not able to adjust themselves to it, though if it were a little more ingenious they would accommodate themselves to it. The best people in England, especially the scholars, talk only of 'imitating Jesus.' "[43] Wesley was still not free from the philosophy of à Kempis and the mystics. Wesley's harsh words against mysticism thus far prove only that the tide had turned, but the final battle (as we shall soon see) had not been fought.

Böhler was not the only one to recognize the lingering appeal of mysticism. On February 27, Wesley writes that he had several opportunities for serious discussion with his fellow travelers on a coach trip to Salisbury, "but endeavouring to mend the wisdom of God by the worldly wisdom of prefacing serious with light conversation, and afterwards following that advice of the *mystics,* 'leave them to themselves,' all I had said was written on the sand."[44] On March 2, no doubt determined not to make the same mistake again, he renewed his former resolution "to use absolute openness and unreserve with all I should converse with."[45] Then, just when it seemed almost certain that he had severed all of the mystical ties, the Diary begins again and de Renty reappears almost immediately.[46] Wesley writes for April 6, "Began M. de Renty's life." Haliburton appears on the ninth of April and on the eleventh Wesley read de Renty to Miss Molly (who was ill) and to those in attendance on her. On the thirteenth Wesley read de Renty once again; Haliburton follows on the fifteenth; and on the seventeenth he began *Life of A. M. Schurmann.* Anna Maria Van Schurmann (1607– 1678) was a Dutch mystic, a blue-stocking and Quaker, and was frequently called "the most learned woman in Europe" or "the modern

---

[42] Ibid., 440.

[43] Peter Böhler's *Diary,* London, February 18, 1738 to the end of May. A manuscript in the archives of the United Brethren at Hernhutt, quoted in Schmidt, *Theological Biography,* 82n.

[44] *Journal,* 1:440f.

[45] Ibid.

[46] The London and Bristol Diary fragments (Colman collection) began April 1, 1738.

Sappho."[47] In the Journal for February 14, 1774, Wesley writes that perhaps the world had never seen a woman with a stronger understanding. "She was likewise deeply devoted to God. So was Antoinette Bourignon, nearly her equal in sense, though not in learning; and equally devoted to God."[48] On April 20, John went with James Hutton to Mr. Stonehouse's at Islington where they dined and talked of the mystics.

In spite of the fact that Wesley was not yet completely free from the appeal of mysticism (which tended to inhibit any further experience of saving grace), between the end of January and the end of May he virtually lost interest in most aspects of mystical theology. The reason for the broken spell, which had held him captive for nearly thirteen years, is the topic of interest to us now. Jeffery discusses four stages in Wesley's rejection of mysticism, and the fourth stage is listed as the influence of the Moravians, especially Spangenberg and Böhler.[49]

After 1735, the height of Wesley's mystical experiment, the Moravians are associated with many of the critical phases in his spiritual development. The impression of their sense of peace during the Atlantic storms, Spangenberg's questions concerning Wesley's inner witness (Vulliamy describes this encounter as a "momentous experience"), and finally the introduction to Peter Böhler are all important to Wesley's evangelical conversion and have a direct bearing on his ultimate break with mysticism as well. The Moravians were to serve as a kind of decompression chamber for Wesley in that they had a strong Reformed doctrine of justification by faith tied to a rich mystical heritage. According to Alexander Knox, the Moravians "weaned" Wesley from mysticism.[50] The Moravian synthesis of mystical piety and Reformed theology appealed to Wesley's greatest weakness and fulfilled his greatest need. Both Spangenberg and Böhler combined a strong sense of mystical piety with the internal witness of the Holy Spirit appropriated through faith in Jesus Christ. Their experience in both of these areas impressed Wesley, and the resulting synthesis was most appealing to him, especially now.

Earlier, in Georgia, Wesley had ears only for the mystical Quietism of the Moravians. They dotted all the "i's" in Lutheran theology and consequently taught that there would be no salvation by any action or

---

[47] *Journal*, 6:10n (#5).
[48] Ibid., 10.
[49] Jeffery, *Quest*, 285.
[50] Southey, *Wesley*, 2:322.

work.[51] They recommended a completely passive attitude very close to the mystical writers whom he had been reading at the time (Madame Bourignon, for example). Deeply involved in yet another mystical experiment, Wesley had found it relatively easy to seize upon Spangenberg's Quietism and then substitute his own internal works righteousness for the Moravian faith in Christ. By February 1738, however, Wesley was ready to listen to the other side of the Moravian synthesis, but it would take someone who understood Wesley's mystical mind to lead him from it. In Georgia he had continued in his mystical exercises in hopes of raising himself to a "coveted pitch of Christian rectitude."[52] The bankruptcy of his mystical self-discipline during that season of trial, "humbled him almost to despondency, and predisposed him for listening to the lessons of Peter Böhler."[53]

Before we turn to the influence of Böhler, however, we should examine briefly the history of the Moravians, which reveals the origin of the synthesis and discloses a little of the mystical continuity of our study at the same time. Toward the latter part of the seventeenth century, Philipp Spener rallied the devotional circles within Lutheranism in order to recall personal piety (thus he is known as the founder of Pietism). Spener, partially through the influence of Jean de Labadie (the Labadists, like the Quietists, emphasized "immediate inspiration," and they rarely celebrated the Eucharist) and, according to Ronald Knox, partially through the influence of the Roman Catholic devotional authors like Gregory Lopez, gave a mystical turn to his evangelical fervor.[54] The personal interior religion of Spener and his "collegia pietatis" (devotional meetings which met twice weekly in his house) greatly impressed A. H. Francke who extended the influence of the Pietists at Halle, where in 1696 he founded his "Paedagogium" and his orphanage. In turn, Francke (whose mystical bias we have already mentioned) passed this synthesis of mysticism and Reformed theology on to Nikolas Zinzendorf, the founder of the "Herrnhuter Brudergemeine," who was educated at the orphanage in Halle.

Ronald Knox writes that the Moravians owed their existence, as a system of thought, to Spener and the pietists.[55] Yet the Moravians had no creed as such. Their particular brand of spirituality simply empha-

---

[51] Knox, *Enthusiasm,* 410.
[52] Southey, *Wesley,* 2:300f.
[53] Ibid.
[54] Knox, *Enthusiasm,* 398ff.
[55] Ibid.

sized a high degree of spiritual discipline. In many ways Moravianism (like Jansenism and even Methodism) involved a reaction against the deistic thought which offered Christianity without Christ. The Moravians, therefore, while appealing to Wesley's inbred fear of external works, also struck a blow at the root of his mystical philosophy of internal works-righteousness.

Peter Böhler on Justification by Faith

Wesley first met Peter Böhler on the February 7, 1738, "a day much to be remembered." Böhler, like Spangenberg, immediately sensed John's need. Although the mystical common denominator in both Böhler and Wesley recognized in religion much the same end, the means were vastly different. Böhler, like Wesley and the mystics, emphasized holiness, but as the *fruit* of faith, not the *cause*. He stressed the means of justification more than the end result of sanctification. Yet Wesley was drawn to Böhler because he could build upon a "new" foundation—justification by faith, and still retain holiness and perfection as the end of religion. H. B. Workman makes a basic mistake here by insisting that Methodism and mysticism *build upon the same foundation* of "conscious spiritual experience."[56] The fact is that although they share a common goal in religion, they build upon entirely *different* foundations. The lesson that Workman apparently fails to understand is the very lesson that Wesley was learning from the Moravians at this time. The mystical ideas of "conscious spiritual experience," constant communion with God, a heart filled with love, holiness, and perfection—all of these were reasonably compatible with the Moravian (and later the Methodist) concept of the end of religion. But the mystical means of internal works-righteousness (although both shunned external works) were entirely incompatible. The divine spark of the mystic eliminated the need for "satisfaction." For the mystics (as we have defined them), there was no atonement (at-one-ment) to be realized in Jesus Christ, but rather a union to be achieved by contemplating the "God within us."[57] Whereas Methodism was Christocentric, mysticism was basically theocentric[58] (in spite of a few exceptions). Although Wesley continued to share a common end with

---

[56] Workman, *History*, 1:55.

[57] This is spelled out more clearly in the discussion of Wesley's correspondence to William Law in May 1738. See below.

[58] It should be mentioned that although Wesley's approach to religion was Christocentric between 1738 and 1764, there is a slight shift after this time.

mysticism (compare, for example, the Journal entry for January 7, 1760), he was now beginning to see that the mystics traveled a route different (in effect putting sanctification before justification) from that of faith in Jesus Christ.

On March 5, 1738, Peter Böhler advised Wesley, "Preach faith *till* you have it; and then, *because* you have it, you *will* preach faith."[59] Wesley was now "clearly convinced of unbelief, of the want of that faith whereby alone we are saved." Brazier Green marks the period from March the fifth to the seventh as Wesley's "intellectual conversion."[60] Wesley was now determined to preach what his mind knew to be true until his heart revealed it as well. Wesley, in a sense, believed in the doctrine of justification by faith, without being justified.

Even more significant for our study, if this can be correctly termed Wesley's intellectual *conversion*, it was his intellectual *break* with mysticism as well. Wesley's sermons at the time certainly suggest this.[61] According to his Journal, he began now to preach justification by faith alone. He was still *emotionally* involved with mysticism (remember that he was still reading the mystics during the month of April), but *intellectually* he had chosen a different path by which to travel. Surely he understood now (or at least by the end of April), as his correspondence with William Law in May, 1738, will demonstrate, that the mystics denied not only the means of grace but the very basis upon which our acceptance with God is grounded—faith in the "blood of Christ."

Wesley's thought continued to develop along these same lines. His brief renewal of interest in the mystics in April could mean almost anything. He continued to use the mystics (especially de Renty) in the course of his spiritual instruction for those under his care. Yet, he was undoubtedly considering most of the aspects of mysticism critically and in the light of his new doctrine of faith. On April 20 he discussed the mystics, but two days later he wrote that he "had now no objection to what [Peter Böhler] said of the nature of faith; namely, that it is 'a sure trust and confidence which a man hath in God, that through the merits of Christ his sins are forgiven and he reconciled to the favour of

---

[59] *Journal*, 1:442.

[60] B. Green, *John Wesley and William Law*, 61ff.; cf. J. E. Rattenbury, *The Conversion of the Wesleys* (London: Epworth, 1938), 70f. The religious, or Catholic, or moral conversion in 1725 was followed by this intellectual conversion and the "heart" conversion at Aldersgate.

[61] By May 7, 1738, he was being refused permission to preach in many churches because of his "new" doctrine.

God.' "62 Mysticism virtually denied both faith and external works. Schmidt argues that Böhler (with his emphasis on faith in an objective atonement) pointed out the error in a doctrine of salvation achieved largely through works or a "high Christian ethic" (even though interpreted according to the "spirit of the law" and appropriated through *inner* righteousness).63 Böhler unmasked the subtle refinement of mysticism as the highest and most dangerous form of legalism.64

By the time Böhler left for Carolina (May 4, 1738), Wesley was intellectually prepared for Aldersgate.65 Whereas previously he had understood faith only in the mystical sense of a blind trust in God (an inferior state eventually to be "swallowed up in love"), he now understood faith in the evangelical Reformed sense, or perhaps it is more accurate to say in the sense of the sixteenth-century Anglican Reformers.66 Consequently, his statement in the Journal (January 1738) that "he had from the very beginning valued faith" carries little weight since it was written at a time when he did not really understand faith. John insists in a letter to Charles dated July 31, 1747, that before this time (1738) he had heard nothing about either justification by faith or a sense of pardon.

At this point it should be mentioned that Wesley was prone to overreact at times. When he exaggerated or overreacted to the doctrine of justification by faith, most would agree that it was in the area of assurance.

The Doctrine of Assurance

It has been suggested, just in passing, that Wesley struggled in mysticism for as long as he did because he was seeking there an experience of assurance which did not exist, at least in the initial stages. For the mystic (in spite of the deluge of phrases concerning an immediate communion with God) there was *no* assurance and *no* sensible comfort from God for those who could not master the dark

---

62 *Journal,* 1:454, the definition of faith is quoted from the Homily "Of Salvation," which deals with the subject of justification by faith.

63 Schmidt, *Theological Biography,* 83ff.

64 Ibid.

65 After the end of April 1738, an unexplained break in the Diary occurs. The next entry, on the same page, is Wednesday, May 23, 1739.

66 Although various books (Cannon, Cell, Deschner, Williams, Schmidt, etc.) portray Wesley as heir to the Continental Reformers (Outler adds, "a notion which would have shocked Wesley"), Wesley's concept of faith at this time is taken largely from the sixteenth-century Anglican Reformers. Neither Luther nor Calvin appear in *Christian Library.*

night of the soul. Since Wesley was incapable of reaching even this inferior stage of mysticism, assurance was perhaps the one thing that he wanted most. One can imagine the impact of a Moravian synthesis on Wesley that offered (within the context of a quasimysticism) the promise of assurance, involving not the dark night of the soul but faith in Christ.

For the next decade (in the letter to Charles on July 31, 1747, he seems to alter this opinion), "faith" for John Wesley was nearly synonymous with assurance. Later, assurance would become the "common privilege" of Christians; but for now at least, it was an indispensable quality of faith.[67] One does not have to agree with Wesley here to understand how the doctrine evolved. Most of the mystics, but only *after* years of struggle, enjoyed a fellowship with God which Wesley interpreted as assurance. Being constantly plagued by fear and doubt, Wesley needed a "sure trust" in God. Some are content to live with their doubts, but he, convicted first by the illusion of mysticism and then by the example of the Moravians, wanted to *feel* that he was accepted by God.[68] Wesley's father had praised the "inner witness" on his deathbed. It is difficult to say how much emphasis to put on any one event, but the Moravian doctrine of assurance must have sounded familiar. The mystics exhorted one to practice a *blind* trust in God; the Moravians promised a *sure* trust in God. Admittedly, some of the differences here involved only a question of words. The mystic, for example, called the *process* of acceptance with God, faith; whereas the Moravian called the *awareness* of acceptance with God, faith. Nonetheless, for Wesley the issues seemed very great indeed. The important thing to remember is that the mystical concept of faith (although using the same word) is not faith in the evangelical sense, but a process of "mystical matters" directed toward union with God.

This mystical union involved holiness and perfection (with a degree of assurance) while the Moravian faith involved assurance (with a degree of holiness and perfection). Ronald Knox, in fact, sees this period between November 1736 and May 1738 as a watershed between Quietism (with its emphasis on perfection) and Jansenism (with its

---

[67]It is interesting to note here that Wesley later in life (after 1767) seems to reach a compromise between the mystic and Moravian concepts of faith.

[68]*Journal,* 1:415, cf. 471. Aldersgate will interpret "inward feeling" as the "most infallible proof"; "I well saw no one could, in the nature of things, have such a sense of forgiveness, and not feel it."

emphasis on assurance).[69] By the first of May, however, Wesley had left this fence in favor of the promise of assurance, which was perhaps the one thing most responsible for Wesley's leaving the mystics for the Moravians. Pope's *Compendium of Christian Theology* states that the mystic teaching is opposed to the doctrine of assurance, or at best is indifferent to assurance.[70] Although the Moravians nurtured the Quietistic approach to grace (both were against making worship formal and both minimized external works-righteousness), the major difference between the Moravian and the Quietist (apart from the question of the Atonement) lay in the area of assurance. The Moravian enjoyed a peace of mind through the conviction that one stood in the favor of God while the Quietist mystic preferred to remain ignorant of acceptance with God altogether.[71] The mystic wished to love God regardless of the prospect of assurance. Faith which led to "pure love" coveted no sense of divine protection. The mystics (William Law in particular) exhorted Wesley to accept his heaviness as the discipline of God.[72] Ronald Knox writes that Wesley hated Law's "darkness."[73] His formula of trust without assurance made a melancholy thing of religion. Spangenberg and Böhler, on the other hand, reinterpreted this mystical *in orco*, exhorting Wesley not to be content, but "to *believe* in *your* Jesus Christ."[74] It is significant that Wesley now turns to the very personal application of Böhler's doctrine and away from the broad generalities of Law's.

Yet, having said this in an effort to contrast (as well as to compare) the Moravians and the mystics on assurance, some would emphasize the comparison far more than the contrast. H. B. Workman, for example, in his statement that the Methodist doctrine of assurance is not far from the mystical inner light misses this point altogether.[75] Confounding the problem, Eric Baker, in support of Workman, claims that assurance is essentially a mystical doctrine.[76] In actual fact, little could be further from the truth. It is true that Methodism and mysticism both contained an intuitive experience, but they were vastly different. Methodist assurance (an inner witness associated with the indwelling of the Holy

---

[69] Knox, *Enthusiasm*, 435.

[70] Ibid., 410ff.

[71] W. B. Pope, *A Compendium of Christian Theology*, 3 vols. (New York: Phillips and Hunt, n.d.), 3:123f., quoted in A. S. Yates *Doctrine of Assurance*.

[72] Cf. Law on the dark night of the soul, Law's *Works*, (London, 9 vols.), 4:135f.

[73] Knox, *Enthusiasm*, 480ff.

[74] A letter from Böhler to Wesley (May 8, 1738), quoted in the *Journal*, 1:461.

[75] Workman, *History*, 1:55.

[76] Baker, *Evangelical Revival*, 108ff.

Spirit), based to a large extent on Romans 8:16, was a far cry from the mystical inner light or inner guide—being little more than intuitive knowledge—that led inevitably into a wilderness state in which assurance was abhorred. The path to union plotted by the inner light led through darkness while assurance brought comfort. Wesley (understandably) detested the doctrine of the inner light and registered his criticism against it on several occasions.[77] He strongly condemns the "impressions" of Madame Guyon as "enthusiasm." Similarly, his sermon *On the Wilderness State* ridicules the *naked* faith of the mystic which was spawned by the inner light.[78]

Knox argues that Wesley was no slave to the inner light.[79] He was too logical. Wesley would have been the last one (so Knox continues) to obey "unaccountable impulses" or make quick "instinctive decisions."[80] Knox adds that although Wesley sympathized with enthusiasm, even in its most violent forms, he was never carried away by it. He "obeyed no inner light."[81] Unlike the mystics and Quakers (George Fox is the obvious example), Wesley made no claim for "instinctive certainty."[82] The inner light compelled the mystic to trust God further than one could see. For a season, the resulting dark night provided a reasonable explanation for Wesley's own heaviness of fear and doubt. But rather than being content to wait patiently for union with God, he was miserable in it. He could not in good conscience deny the means of grace and he detested his heaviness. Madame Guyon, on the other hand, followed the instructions of her inner light (or her "intuitions") to the letter. She endured her darkness with resignation and without a thought for assurance or spiritual comfort, feeling that the absence of assurance forced her to rely on pure faith.

Lastly, the mystical inner light originated more within the nature of human understanding than within the nature of God. Every mystic had *his* inner light, whereas the Methodists had *the* witness of the Holy Spirit. Outler, therefore, traces the doctrine of assurance correctly to the Moravian Pietists but not to the mystics.[83] Wesley, in the final analysis,

---

[77] Cf. *Journal*, 8 vols. (2:226—June 22, 1739); *Universal Magazine*, December 1760.
[78] *Sermons*, 2:246, 248, 255, 261, 278; cf. *Works*, 6:84.
[79] Knox, *Enthusiasm*, 450.
[80] Ibid.
[81] Ibid.
[82] Ibid.
[83] Outler, *John Wesley*, 210. It should be mentioned that this attempt to dissociate assurance and inner light should not imply that the mystics, or quasimystics, did not later

although *drawn* to the Moravians through their mysticism, was eventually *driven* to the Moravians because their synthesis emphasized the one thing that he wanted most and that mysticism alone could not promise: assurance.

Before moving on to the next chapter and the crisis days from May 14 to May 24, we should ask whether Wesley himself was aware of the significance of the Moravian synthesis for his partial break with mysticism. In answer to this question, evidence seems to suggest that he did not fully understand the nature or the significance of this synthesis. There is a good possibility that just as Wesley's preoccupation with mysticism in early 1736 blinded him to the theological strengths in Moravianism (faith and assurance), so his preoccupation with faith and assurance in 1738 blinded him to the theological weaknesses in Moravianism (mystic Quietism). Yet the effectiveness of the Moravian influence resulted from its synthesis. The mystical flavor in Moravianism made their doctrine of faith palatable. After practicing the art of self-denial and mental refinement, justification by faith must have seemed intolerable. John Gambold (in a letter to Charles Wesley recorded in the Journal) describes the doctrine of faith as it must have appeared to *religious* persons whose wealth lay in the quality of their own righteousness ("acquired by much painful exercise").[84] It "is a downright robber. It takes away all this wealth, and only tells us it is deposited for us with somebody else, upon whose bounty we must live like mere beggars."[85] Furthermore, "they who have long distinguished themselves from the herd of vicious wretches, or have gone beyond *moral* men,—for them to be told that they are either not so well, or but the same needy, impotent, insignificant vessels of mercy with the others, this is more shocking to reason than transubstantiation."[86]

Consciously or unconsciously, the Moravian appeal for Wesley was as strong as it was because they couched a "new" doctrine within a familiar setting. If, however, the Moravian affinity for mysticism in 1738 was an asset for Wesley (which it undoubtedly was as it served to wean him from his mystical "depths"), it later revealed itself as a liability. Perhaps Wesley did not fully appreciate the nature of the Moravian

---

influence Wesley's doctrine of assurance; cf. B. Green, *John Wesley and William Law*, 28 on Malebranche and Norris.

[84] *Journal*, 1:462f.

[85] Ibid.

[86] Ibid. Cf. *Journal*, 2:256n (#1). Dialogue with the Bishop of Bristol (August 1739) on "Justification by Faith."

synthesis until the events of Fetter Lane.[87] Once free from the subtlety of the mystical trap, he was able to react against what he had earlier failed to understand. In a letter to the Moravian brethren, dated August 8, 1740, he writes that "they mix religion with man's wisdom and accommodate it to the mystic theory." Again on April 2, 1741, he criticizes their scheme as "mystical and not scriptural." These and other similar accusations will be touched on later. Suffice it to say that for now Wesley's partial break with mysticism was near completion. The fruit of the Moravian synthesis would reveal itself even more clearly during the crisis period leading up to Aldersgate. Here it became obvious that the very nature of the Atonement was at stake.

---

[87]The controversy at Fetter Lane over Moravian "stillness" dates roughly from November 1, 1739, to July 20, 1740.

5

atonement: the missing link

Thomas Jeffery's detailed analysis of Wesley's religious quest traces his ultimate break with mysticism to the eleven-day period prior to Aldersgate.[1] Perhaps it would be more accurate to say that during this crisis period the fruits of that break are manifested more clearly.

THE CRISIS: MAY 14 TO MAY 24, 1738

We have established that the Moravian inner tranquillity and assurance (seasoned with just enough of the mystical spirit to make it palatable) appealed to John Wesley's troubled mind and melancholy spirit. Yet the Moravians also unmasked the true depths of the mystical error. The problem with mysticism went deeper than Wesley's objections registered in November 1736 and again in January 1738 had indicated. There he criticized their denial of the means of grace while the most dangerous mystical heresy (a more subtle form of Pelagianism) extended to the very nature of the Atonement itself. All of this is demonstrated clearly in Wesley's correspondence during this period.

Dunn Wilson mistakenly interprets the January 1738 statement as Wesley's ultimate break with mysticism and implies that Wesley's criticism here has little significance in that it is guided simply by the previous break. He states that after the January break "one of the *first* tasks . . . was to write Law."[2] The fact is, however, that it was over four months before he wrote to Law. Furthermore, it is doubtful that Wesley

---

[1] Jeffery, *Quest,* 291.
[2] Wilson, "Influence of Mysticism," 95.

could have written these letters any earlier. Even a cursory comparison reveals that they were not the product of the January revelation (which was simply a rehash of the earlier statement in 1736). The letters are clearly the result of knowledge imparted through the Moravian synthesis. This break is vastly different. Here the means of grace are never mentioned. This correspondence reveals the mystic denial of faith in Christ as the greatest stumbling block to Aldersgate. Knox, therefore, is suspicious (and with good reason) of those who argue that Wesley never mistrusted mysticism as such, only its contempt for good works. He states that Wesley's objection to mysticism is much more basic.[3] Jeffery writes that "naught else came so near bringing his quest to futility and himself to ruin as did mysticism."[4] Once mysticism had been conquered (and for Wesley the only alternative was assurance of faith since he was unable to enter the depths of mysticism as William Law had done) Aldersgate was the next logical step. The lack of justifying faith (preventing Aldersgate) was one side of the coin and mysticism the other. If, in fact (as Wilson supposes), Wesley had made the ultimate break in January, Aldersgate would have occurred four months earlier. The Moravians, however, turned the coin and disclosed the anti-evangelical nature of mysticism. Aldersgate came in May because mysticism had not been sufficiently conquered until that time.

Wesley's Correspondence With William Law

The fruit of Wesley's struggle against mysticism can be seen in his letters to his old friend and mentor, William Law. On May 14 and 20, Wesley wrote to him to criticize his substitution of "mystical matters" for justifying faith. Whether or not John was right or wrong in his judgment of Law (there was undoubtedly some substance to his charges), his condemnation of mysticism is still important to us. It is also good to remember that these letters were not written in a vacuum. For over eighteen months John had been seriously questioning the validity of the mystical approach. Since Frederica he had been reexamining the very foundations of his faith. He greatly admired Law's genuine piety, but still needed the warmth of a personal awareness of God.

Scholars have allowed Law's influence on Wesley to cloud their understanding of the mystical influence on Wesley largely because they

---

[3] Knox, *Enthusiasm*, 479.
[4] Jeffery, *Quest*, 281.

fail to understand Law's role in Wesley's relationship with mysticism. Law's contribution was *not* primarily mystical. Nonetheless, these letters to Law mark the climax of Wesley's rejection of mysticism. For Wesley, Law at this time personified mysticism.[5] Jeffery concludes that Wesley rejected mysticism when he rejected the mystic, William Law.[6] This is an oversimplification, but it is true that since so much of mysticism is closely related (its sheer scarcity attracts strange alliances), the part frequently casts suspicion upon the whole. Although Wesley had read widely among the mystics, Law was one of the few (and undoubtedly the most influential) whom he knew personally. While John had not actually seen him since before leaving for Georgia, they had maintained (either directly or indirectly) fairly close contact. Charles Wesley's Journal for August 31, 1737, and September 9, 1737, records conversations with Law, and Charles may have discussed his brother's "scheme" (November 1736) with Law at that time.

Peter Böhler had also visited Law just weeks earlier, probably with the intention of sorting out the Wesleys' old mentor. Wesley records a part of that interview between Böhler and Law in his letter to Law on the fourteenth of May. "'I [Böhler] began speaking to him of faith in Christ: he was silent. Then he began to speak of mystical matters. I spake to him of faith in Christ again: he was silent. Then he began to speak of mystical matters again. I [Böhler] saw his state at once.' And a very dangerous one in his [Böhler's] judgement, whom I know to have the Spirit of God."[7] Law's absorption into mysticism and Wesley's own narrow escape from a similar fate (or so he thought), linked with a conscientious attempt to be reconciled with his brother, prompted the letter. Wesley was also burning his bridges behind him. Law's advice to "renounce yourself and be not impatient" had been discarded for Böhler's advice to "*strip thyself naked* of thy own works and thy own righteousness [the mystical part of the Moravian synthesis] and *fly to Him*. For whosoever cometh unto Him, He will no wise cast out."[8]

It is also useful to note that although Wesley was most influenced by the works of Law produced during his ethical period (1726–1732), by 1736 both he and Law felt the need of some further dynamic to supplement their practical mysticism. Baker, interestingly enough, suggests that both Law and Wesley experienced conversions from law to

---

[5] Baker, *Evangelical Revival*, 103.
[6] Jeffery, *Quest*, 289.
[7] *Letters*, 1:240.
[8] Ibid., 239 (italics mine).

grace.[9] Law, via Behmen in 1737, *chose* a route deeper into mysticism; Wesley, via Böhler in 1738, incapable of the mystical alternative, *was driven* deeper into the Reformed tradition. In spite of their parting sentiments concerning the means of religion, however, their concept of perfection as the end of religion remained much the same.

Any eventual similarities should not lead one to underestimate their differences, which Tyerman claims (somewhat naively) led to "an estrangement between two great and good men which ought never have existed."[10] The differences between Wesley and the mystics (as represented by Law) at this point were perhaps even greater than Tyerman imagined. Law, placing sanctification before justification, proclaimed the *duty* of holiness, but lacked the *power*. Wesley's earlier reaction against the mystic denial of the means of grace had not even begun to fathom the subtle depths of mysticism revealed in these two letters. Here the whole of the Atonement is in question. Wesley in the first of these letters asks, "Why did I scarce ever hear you name the name of Christ? Never, so as to ground anything upon 'faith in His blood'?"

Brazier Green informs us that a "complete union of the soul with God is, for Law and for mysticism in general, the essence of religion."[11] Furthermore, "this Pearl of Eternity" (the favorite metaphor in the *Spirit of Prayer*) or this "touch of the Divine loadstone" is to be sought, not by an external quest, but "by looking within."[12] According to Law one must "search and dig in thine own field" allowing "the eye of thy spirit to enter the naked faith."[13] Green rightly concludes that this is "a concept of salvation emanating from what is *within* the nature of man" and not of an acceptance by faith in an *objective* atonement.[14] The mystical substitution of this internal subjective element for faith in the atoning work of Christ is the crucial issue in Wesley's break with mysticism. Wesley now insisted upon the objectivity of salvation as revealed in Scripture.

His open letter to William Law, January 6, 1756, reiterates many of the objections first raised in 1738. He writes concerning the later works of his old mentor, "The person I greatly reverence and love, the doctrine

---

[9] Baker, *Evangelical Revival,* 29.
[10] Tyerman, *John Wesley,* 1:188.
[11] Green, *John Wesley and William Law,* 121.
[12] Ibid., 121f.
[13] Ibid., 121, cf. notes #47 and 48.
[14] Ibid., 126.

I utterly abhor." It is "totally subversive to the very essence of Christianity."[15]

In the second letter written to Law in May 1738, Wesley again objects to the fact that Law had never advised him "to seek first a living faith in the blood of Christ."[16] Law, on the other hand (in a reply to Wesley's first letter), insisted that he had advised Wesley along these lines and suggests how he had done so. First he had recommended the treatise *Theologia Germanica* (Law commented, "If that book does not plainly lead you to Jesus Christ, I am content to know as little of Christianity as you are pleased to believe"); then he had published an answer to the *Plain Account of the Sacrament*. Law then reminded Wesley that two fundamental maxims had governed his life and work— "without me ye can do nothing," and "if any man will come after me, let him take up his cross and follow me."[17] In his retort Wesley insists that "in *Theologia Germanica* I remember something of Christ our pattern, but nothing express of *Christ our atonement*. The answer to the *Plain Account* I believe to be an excellent book, but not to affect the question. Those two maxims may imply but do not express that third—'He is our propitiation through faith in His blood.'"[18] Wesley, in his exaltation of faith in the blood of Christ, had come to the position expressed so clearly by B. B. Warfield: the question which mysticism raises is "whether we need, whether we have, a provision in the blood of Christ for our sins or whether we, each of us, possess within ourselves all that can be required for time and eternity; both of these things cannot be true, and obviously *tertium non natur*. We may be mystics, or we may be Christians. We cannot be both."[19] One does not necessarily have to agree with all of the implications of this dogmatic statement to realize that this was Wesley's attitude at present. Law's soteriology lacked any concept of a substitutionary atonement. Law's demands concerning the imitation of Christ were closer to the moral influence theory of the Atonement than to the strong sense of imputed righteousness in Reformed theology. Lindström states that "Law's concept of salvation depends upon perfection and the sincerity of our endeavors to obtain it."[20]

---

[15]*Letters*, 3:345.

[16]Ibid., 1:241.

[17]Ibid.

[18]Ibid.

[19]B. B. Warfield, *Biblical and Theological Studies* (Philadelphia: Presbyterian Publishing Co., 1952), 462.

[20]Harald Lindström, *Wesley and Sanctification* (Grand Rapids: Zondervan/Francis Asbury Press, 1980), 56ff.

Some Wesley scholars would have us believe that Wesley's theology did not change during this period.[21] The fact is, however, that before Wesley's ultimate break with mysticism his theology focused on the role of internal works and his religion was basically theocentric. God was primarily a God of love, and recapitulation characterized his view of the Atonement.[22] After the mystical break, however, his theology focused on the role of faith in Christ and his religion was basically Christocentric. God was primarily a God of justice, and satisfaction characterized his view of the Atonement. Most of these changes are clearly recorded in these letters. For the moment enough has been said about the question of the Atonement. Wesley also directs a blow at the mystical disparagement of good works. Wesley writes that there are several reasons why Law is "chargeable with my not having had this faith."[23] First of all Law did not tell him plainly that he lacked it. He never advised him to seek or pray for it. He assumed that he had it. His advice led him from it; and, finally, he "recommended books to me which had no tendency to plant this faith, but a direct one to *destroy good works*."[24] The mystic exhorted one first to tend to one's own conversion and *then* to strengthen one's neighbors. One must first be charitable, *then* one can do works of charity if one is careful to avoid all pride and vanity (remember Wesley's earlier criticism of Law for being so injudicious about works that he discouraged them altogether).[25]

Another change in Wesley's theology is associated with the mystic exaltation of love. His strongest criticism of this imbalance appears in the 1756 letter to Law. According to mysticism, God's love "postulates an ultimate unity and singleness of being and will behind all manifestation."[26] Behmen (who influenced Law) had one bias: "God is love," and consequently the phrase, the "wrath of God," was for Law a contradiction in terms.[27] This, of course, affected mystical concepts of original sin. Law's *Spirit of Prayer*, for example, denies the imputation of sin; contrarily, the volume of Wesley's *Works* in the Jackson edition entitled

---

[21] Cf. V. Green, *Young Wesley,* 287.

[22] Cf. Law's *Works,* 8:7, 74, 87 (especially p. 74), on "recapitulation."

[23] *Letters,* 1:241f.

[24] Ibid. Cf. Wesley, *Poetical Works,* 13 vols. Collected and arranged by C. Osborn (London: 1868–72), 1:xix–xx and Wilson, "Influence of Mysticism," 265.

[25] Ibid. 210. Cf. *Journal,* 1:469.

[26] Green, *John Wesley and William Law,* 102.

[27] Cf. Law's *Works,* 5:156; even hell is a creation of God's love. Cf. Law's *Spirit of Prayer* (Pt 1:27): "No wrath (anger, vindictive justice) ever was or ever will be in God" and *Letters,* 3:346.

Original Sin strongly emphasizes this doctrine within the context of God's justice and righteous indignation.

Consequently, yet another key to Wesley's rejection of mysticism can be seen in the fact that Wesley emphasized sin and repentance leading to faith in Christ while the mystic emphasized *love* and *self-discipline*. The mystical "imitation" was concerned primarily with sanctification, not justification. Wesley, on the other hand, exalted faith as the condition of pardon and justification. Salvation and faith presumed God's initiative. The only condition of faith was one's yielding to prevenient grace that led to repentance as one turned grief-stricken with sin, fleeing the wrath to come, to the love of God revealed in his crucified but risen Son.[28]

For the mystic, however, there was no need for divine reconciliation since there was no wrath between God and humankind, except humankind's.[29] Humankind, therefore must allow the example of Christ to turn one's own wrath to love. Wesley replaced the mystical reproach for the historical Incarnation and the objective Atonement with a strong doctrine of original sin.[30] Justification had to precede sanctification. This is absolutely key in understanding the theological issues at stake at this point. Wesley, in effect, was combining the best of continental Reformed theology (with its emphasis on justification) and Catholic spirituality (with its emphasis on sanctification). This places Wesley more firmly within the tradition of Latimer and Ridley (of the English Reformation) than of Luther and Calvin. One of the keys that turns this lock should now be discussed.

May 24, 1738

This is a day to be remembered by Methodists and all followers of Wesley for as long as they continue to exist. If its significance has been exaggerated in the past, perhaps the tendency is to underestimate its significance in recent times. The Journal states, *"Monday, Tuesday, and Wednesday* (May 22, 23, 24), I had 'continual sorrow and heaviness' in my 'heart,'"* something of which he described in a letter to a friend dated May 24, 1738[31] This letter clearly describes what might well have been Wesley's last real struggle with mysticism. Probably writing (in light of the previous correspondence) to John Gambold, Wesley depicts

---

[28] Ibid. Cf. Wesley, *Poetical Works,* 1:xix–xx and Wilson, "Influence of Mysticism," 265.

[29] Ibid., 117.

[30] Ibid., 119.

[31] *Letters,* 1:245.

the state of his soul. If one has studied Wesley's letters and Journal for the period between 1725 and 1738, it is easy to read between the lines. He writes, "I feel that 'I am sold under sin.'"[32] On the other hand, he hears a voice saying, "Believe, and thou shalt be saved."[33] He then adds, "Oh let no one deceive us by vain words, as if we had already attained this faith! By its fruits we shall know. Do we already feel 'peace with God' and 'joy in the Holy Ghost?'"[34] Can anyone who has carefully read the correspondence with Law deny the fact that this is still another caution against Law and the mystics? Who else had advised Wesley to be content in his present state except Law and the mystics whom he represented? Surely mysticism was riddled with "vain words" and the dark night of the soul certainly lacked the "fruits of peace and joy." Furthermore, the words which follow, "O thou Saviour of men, save us from trusting in anything but Thee," are they not also aimed at the mystical delusion of internal works-righteousness?[35] Wesley was cutting the mystic cord. Just as he once believed intellectually in the truth of mysticism, he now believed intellectually in the truth of justification by faith alone.[36] His failure to *experience* the truth of one, however, would not be repeated with the other. After all, "what is impossible with man is possible with God." Where mysticism had failed justification by faith would succeed.

Charles, who had been fighting much the same battle with mysticism, found peace on May 21, 1738 (ironically on the occasion of a sermon by Dr. Heylyn whose mystical interests have already been mentioned). On the evening of May 24, John too received the experience of conversion as an inner assurance of faith. At long last he was free forever from any serious threat from mysticism. Previously his spasmodic fits of darkness and doubt had always carried him back into mysticism. Now, however, he could boldly proclaim, "Now, I was always conqueror."[37]

THE ROLE OF ALDERSGATE

Signs of Aldersgate appear as early as 1725 (Wesley received a foretaste of "sensible comfort" from à Kempis), and Wesley was

---

[32] Ibid., 1:244f.

[33] Ibid.

[34] Ibid.

[35] Ibid.

[36] There is a slight shift in Wesley's concept of justification by faith after 1767, but for now Wesley's mind is set.

[37] *Journal*, 1:477.

convinced intellectually of his need for faith as early as March 1738. Yet no one dare deal with a particular influence on John Wesley without discussing the role of the experience of May 24, 1738. This is not to exaggerate the experience. It is simply to recognize that Aldersgate touched Wesley at virtually every level of life. If, therefore, one realizes the degree of influence of the mystics thus far, one can also understand the importance of Aldersgate in breaking their spell. In fact, an understanding of Wesley's mystical wanderings should cause some to reevaluate Aldersgate. It was not just a watershed between law and grace or between an outward form of religion and a religion of the heart, but also between mysticism (an inward form of religion) and assurance of faith.

The Immediate Effect

It does little good to rehash the old problem of whether John was a Christian prior to this time.[38] That is an issue which John had difficulty in settling himself and is not really to the point, which is that regardless of the exact moment of justification, Aldersgate is still significant for the study of mysticism. The Christian experience is never an isolated experience. Events both precede and follow every level of Christian development. Aldersgate is the sum total of Wesley's agonizing search for the "life of God in the soul of man." Wesley believed that struggle alone never justified the Christian, but he also believed that one was rarely justified without it. What some have experienced in minutes Wesley experienced over thirteen years. Eric Baker explains the 1725 awakening (more narrowly defined as the conviction of sin) in light of the total experience.[39] An "ethical" conversion (emphasized in Roman Catholicism) must precede an "evangelical" conversion (if only by a few seconds). Law must precede grace. It is a fatal antithesis to set one

---

[38] In recent years the tendency has been to emphasize the 1725 experience as Wesley's Christian conversion. Theodore Jennings' article "John Wesley *Against* Aldersgate" (*Quarterly Review*, 8, no. 3 (Fall 1988): 3–22) argues that too much emphasis upon Aldersgate is fraudulent. Unfortunately, he overstates his case. Nevertheless, Leger, Piette, and Outler, insist that Wesley was a Christian in 1725. Piette, in an attempt to take Wesley out of the Reformed tradition, claims that Aldersgate led not into the experience of faith without works, but into the experience of works "inspired by love." Böhler's faith was "nothing else but the love of God, felt and lived intensely" (Piette, *Evolution of Protestantism*, 306f.). B. Green, *John Wesley and William Law*, 19, contrasts the opposing view held by men like Tyerman, Cannon, and Jeffery who emphasize Aldersgate and who portray Wesley pre-1738, not as a saint, but as a "self-centered bigot."

[39] Cf. *Journal*, 1:465ff; B. Green, *John Wesley and William Law*, 19.

experience against the other. In fact, it could be argued that the nature of Wesley's 1725 experience made Aldersgate inevitable once he was freed from the excessive weight of mysticism. The 1725 awakening created in John a desire for holiness which would find fulfillment only through faith in Christ. Perhaps in order to purify his motives, to intensify his desire, or even to increase his ultimate joy, God tarried; but ultimately Aldersgate was God's answer to Wesley's prayer first registered in 1725.

However, one should add at this point that although Wesley was never really far from the kingdom of God for the duration of his spiritual quest, to refer to the accelerated religious fervor of 1725 as *the* conversion is to detach it arbitrarily from his experience as a whole. To disregard the full significance of the fact that Wesley continued to fight his own personal battle until Aldersgate when he was virtually beaten into submission is to substitute one exaggeration (1725) for another (1738). John, in 1725, had yet to learn by experience that internal and external righteousness are the effect, not the cause of saving faith. Wesley's venture into mysticism blinded him from recognizing the need for faith in Christ and delayed his experience of the heart until 1738.[40] Although he realized his need for power and correctly identified its source in the Holy Spirit, in his romance with mysticism he failed to understand that the Atonement and the subsequent power of the Holy Spirit were appropriated through a personal faith in Christ. Most of the classical works on Wesley (written or edited by men like Curnock, Telford, Sugden, Tyerman, Jackson, and Simon) emphasize the fact "that until his heart was 'strangely warmed' in Aldersgate Street, he neither knew, as a normal experience, the meaning of saving faith nor had he the power to fulfill his Lord's mission."[41] Aldersgate linked his understanding of the Atonement and the work of the Holy Spirit to God through justification by faith. Thus, whether or not the Aldersgate experience was a "saving experience" is irrelevant to this study. Aldersgate still marks a significant change in Wesley's attitude toward mysticism.

In his analysis of Aldersgate, Harold Lindström notes the emphasis on *human* response and obedience to God in the letter to John Gambold (May 24, 1738). Thomas à Kempis, Law, and the mystics in general all leaned to Arminianism. Lindström then adds perceptively that this Arminianism appealed to Wesley as he was too impatient and too much

---

[40]*Letters,* 2:65.
[41]*Journal,* 1:33.

of an activist to wait around for God to act in God's own time.[42] Perhaps a manifestation of this can be seen in his inability to marry.[43] Jeffery suggests that Wesley had an overactive sense of reason.[44] A lesser man would have failed in his attempt at self-saving acceptance much sooner and would have recognized the need for faith much more easily. In the final analysis, perhaps the words of Curnock sum up Aldersgate as well as any: "On Wednesday, May 24, 1738, he found the peace for which, during thirteen weary years, he had striven, toiled, suffered, and prayed."[45] Ultimately his greatness as well as his effectiveness had a great deal to do with his shrewd determination. Wesley's secret lay in the fact that he sought God just as wholeheartedly by grace through faith as he had previously done by law.

Most Wesley scholars recognize the influence of the mystics on Wesley before Aldersgate, but an overemphasis on William Law has tended to submerge the ultimate influence of mysticism as a whole (especially the Roman Catholics abridged by Wesley). It is important, therefore, to realize that these mystics were a contributing factor for many of the tools which Wesley would fashion for the Evangelical Revival.

Since Aldersgate influenced every aspect of Wesley's life, the study of any ultimate influence of mysticism in the Wesleyan tradition must first examine the factors contributing to Aldersgate and then begin again to rebuild. Obviously Wesley had already established patterns and characteristics which would remain with him for the rest of his life. All the same, there was virtually nothing in Wesley left untouched by Aldersgate. Although Wesley was still Wesley, for all practical purposes (especially as far as this study is concerned), he was a different man. His works (particularly his sermons) demonstrate this beyond doubt. Consequently with Wesley, as with anyone who wipes the slate clean, the historian must begin the task anew.

Wesley wrote to his brother Samuel, "*nihil est quod hactenus feci.*"[46] Perhaps this phrase demonstrates Wesley's use of hyperbole, but the fact remains that Aldersgate marks a point of redeparture when dealing with an ultimate influence on John Wesley. The need for complete spiritual

---

[42] Lindström, *Wesley and Sanctification,* 128ff.

[43] See Heitzenrater, *Elusive Wesley,* 1:174ff. on "The Would-Be Husband."

[44] Jeffery, *Quest,* 70.

[45] *Journal,* 1:32.

[46] "What I have hitherto done is nothing"; *Letters,* 1:263. *Imitation,* Bk. 1, chap. 19, sec. 1.

reconstruction expressed in this Latin phrase (it was also stated in January 1738 when Wesley was struggling with his heaviness on board ship) reveals the magnitude of the Aldersgate experience. It is significant that Wesley from this point on uses two systems of chronology: one *anno domini* and the other *anno meae conversionis*.[47] By May 24, Wesley had overcome his objections to "faith alone" (cf. the letter from John Gambold to Charles recorded in the Journal of May 14, 1738). Faith had triumphed, exchanging its wealth of imputed righteousness for the poverty of self-righteousness.

Thus far when referring to Wesley's ultimate break with mysticism we have also used (or implied) the term *reluctant*. Wesley's break was not only reluctant but partial because the mystics (especially the Roman Catholics abridged by Wesley) continued to influence him for the rest of his life. In fact, if the mystical influence before Aldersgate was (for the most part) negative, the mystical influence after Aldersgate was positive. Aldersgate equipped Wesley with the necessary tools for separating the good from the bad. If, therefore, the break with mysticism was in any way complete (as so many seem to think), its completeness was only momentary. Although the mystics at this time must have seemed a part of an unwanted and distant dream, Wesley soon began again to see the value of their examplary lives for convicting sinners and for challenging Christians to go on to perfection. This is not, however, justification for saying (as do Todd and Wilson) that Aldersgate was a mystical experience.

John Todd, following through with the scheme of St. John of the Cross, interprets this experience in light of the mystical union with God. He refers to Wesley's doctrine of faith alone as a mystical scheme where God and the mystic meet in the "cloud of the unknowing."[48] We have already demonstrated, however, the vast difference between the mystical faith (with its appeal to darkness) and the faith of Aldersgate (with its assurance).

Even less convincing in many ways is the thesis by Dunn Wilson, where Aldersgate is interpreted as a mystical "illumination of the mountain top."[49] Wilson argues that Wesley, in rejecting a perverted

---

[47] Cf. *Letters*, 1:262; 4:298; 5:358, etc.

[48] Todd, *Catholic Church*, 127.

[49] Wilson, "Influence of Mysticism," 105. Only a few mystics (commonly so-called) are used by Wilson for the sake of comparison (e.g., Teresa and John of the Cross, neither of whom Wesley is likely to have read). Cf. also Yates, *The Doctrine of Assurance* (London: Epworth, 1952), 204ff.

Hellenistic mysticism (in January 1738), accepted New Testament mysticism (at Aldersgate). Unfortunately Wilson's thesis is of little help to us here as he completely redefines mysticism along the lines of ordinary Christian experience. In fact, it is difficult to understand exactly what he means by the term *mystic*. He apparently takes at least a part of his lead from Gordon Wakefield who at one point describes Methodism as a *prophetic mysticism:* "It is the mysticism of the Old Testament prophets—an immediacy of communion with God, realized in the sheer, ardent rapture of response to His mighty acts of grace."[50] While all of this is certainly true (and relevant to Methodist devotion), for our purposes here it tells us little of the role of the mystics most influential in Wesley's life in that it describes little of their common experience. If the "mysticism" that Wilson describes for Aldersgate has little to do with the mystics whom Wesley knew and read, then it is irrelevant to the study of the influence of these mystics on Wesley. Wilson's section on "the mystical experience of Aldersgate" deals more with the influence of Christianity as revealed in St. Paul than with mysticism commonly so-called. Moses, Jeremiah, and St. Paul are far removed from the mysticism of Lopez, de Renty, and Madame Guyon. It would be pointless for *this* study to speak of mysticism as perhaps it *ought to be*. In order to learn about the influence of the mystics studied by Wesley, it is necessary to speak of mysticism as it *is*. Either Aldersgate was a meaningless, watered-down mystical experience, or it was no mystical experience at all.

It is the firm conclusion of this study that Wesley had left the mystic path (remember that he never really progressed spiritually beyond the first stages) as we have come to understand it. Dimond's *The Psychology of the Methodist Revival* states that "Wesley's character stopped short of mystical ecstasy and neither the mystic death nor union can be said to describe any experience in Wesley's life."[51] Whether or not Wesley accepted some vague type of prophetic Christian mysticism is irrelevant to our present study. Of course it could be said that Aldersgate was mystical in that it brought Wesley insight into God's mystery, but so does every other Christian experience involving the witness of God's Spirit.

Consequently our task from this point on is not to describe the

---

[50]G. Wakefield, *The Spiritual Life in the Methodist Tradition 1791–1945* (London: Epworth, 1966), 35.

[51]S. Dimond, *The Psychology of the Methodist Revival* (London: Oxford University Press, 1926), 77.

ultimate influence of mysticism as it *should have been* according to the New Testament, but as it actually *was*. Wesley had temporarily severed his ties with mysticism, but for the next fifty-three years we find him continually sifting the gold from the dross.

The Long-Term Effect: The Gold From the Dross

Before launching out into the study of the ultimate influence of mysticism following Aldersgate, we need to establish a few basic guidelines. At this point, the obvious question to ask concerns any permanent mystical influence that remained to affect the Evangelical Revival. Henry Bett quickly labels as an inept statement Leslie Stephen's comment that "Wesley thought mysticism to be simple folly."[52] Wesley himself provides a key. On September 8, 1773, he writes of the mystics that they had "an amazing genius . . . we have all the gold that is in them without the dross. . . ."[53] In the Preface to the extract of *The Life of Madame Guyon* (1776), Wesley writes, "Yet with all this dross how much pure gold is mixed. So did God wink at involuntary ignorance! What a depth of religion did she enjoy."[54] Aldersgate supplied Wesley with a formula for extracting the gold from the dross. The task now is to anticipate that formula in the form of a hypothesis in order to extract from Wesley's future relationship with the mystics their ultimate influence.

Urlin's *Churchman's Life of Wesley* states that "in the *better sense of the word* he never rejected mystic influences. They continued to cling around his deeper devotional language."[55] Briefly, the gold of mysticism lay in its practical and pietistic outworkings over and against its highly philosophical and theological theory, but this needs to be explained in greater detail.

A Hypothesis Stated

Wesley at Aldersgate did not so much exchange a bad mysticism for a good mysticism as learn to extract the good from the mystics that he had already known. It is wrong to imply that Wesley substituted St. Paul (or so-called New Testament mysticism) for an earlier brand of mysticism. Rather, the experience known to St. Paul enabled Wesley to

---

[52] Bett, *Spirit of Methodism*, 59.
[53] *Letters*, 6:39.
[54] *Works*, 14:275ff.
[55] Urlin, *Churchman's Life of Wesley* (London: S.P.C.K., 1880), 58.

appreciate that which would be of value to Methodism from his previous (as well as future) encounter with mysticism. Although Wesley found a different application for the mystic truths, he continued to read many of the same mystics and more. In essence the hypothesis is this: *Of the five mystical stages (1. awakening, 2. purgation, 3. illumination, 4. the dark night of the soul, and 5. union with God), Wesley continued to practice and encourage the "tools" known to the first three stages.*[56] *He also admired and commended the many other practical outworkings of these stages manifested in the lives of the mystics whose utter devotion to God was a continual inspiration to him. Similarly he continued to uphold the mystical concept of perfection (the mystical fifth stage) as the end of religion. Yet Wesley detested the vain irrational philosophy that sought to link the noble beginnings of religion (stages one to three) to the ultimate end of religion (stage five) by the dark night of the soul (the mystical fourth stage involving a lifeless theory of "in orco"), and it was precisely at this point that he substituted the Aldersgate experience of justification by faith in Christ.* The remainder of this study examines many of the various ramifications of this hypothesis as they appear in Wesley's theological and ethical schemes. But, first, a brief review of the gold and the dross from the data collected thus far.

The Gold of Mysticism. Alexander Knox states that Wesley's concept of spirituality contained the "very spirit of Macarius and Chrysostom, of Smith and Cudworth, of de Sales and Fénelon, simplified, systematized, rationalized, and evangelized."[57] Wesley was no longer drawn to mysticism as such; but he continued to admire the individual mystics. Their personal piety and pattern of Christian holiness would soon be woven into Methodism. The mystics (like Wesley) are best known by what they did, not by what philosophers may suspect that they thought.[58] In fact, that which appealed to Wesley most about the mystics was that which was most incompatible with mysticism as a whole. The importance of our hypothesis (and the sharpness of the break) is underscored once this fact is fully understood. From this point on the mystics that were deeply involved in highly speculative theology

---

[56] E.g., humility, poverty of spirit, and the other instruments of purgation were vital to Methodism. Humility was the first step to faith and the new birth, "a participation in the divine nature." Cf. *Sermons,* 1:321.

[57] J. A. Faulkner, "Wesley the Mystic," *London Quarterly Review,* 153 (April 1930): 145–60.

[58] *Journal,* 2:275.

(like Tauler, Behmen, and Law) had less of an appeal for Wesley. Wesley admired the mystical marks of piety, the communion with God, and most of all the external works of charity, but he utterly rejected much of the mystical theology (especially that of the fourth stage). John, therefore, will be seen condemning the mystics on one day and praising them the next (thus Tyerman insists that Wesley was in *no* sense a mystic).

Just six weeks after Aldersgate (July 7, 1738) John writes to his brother Samuel applying Law's chapter (from *Serious Call*) on "Universal Love and Intercession" as if it were the Word of God. Again on October 30, 1738, he makes an even stronger application of the same chapter. One might well ask how Wesley could both praise and condemn the mystics. A part of the answer lies in this paradox: although the mystics discouraged works theoretically (for they dare not speak of them), they were encouraged and even compelled by their experiences to practice them. Dunn Wilson reminds us that St. Teresa, for example, founded a convent, Suso began religious houses, and Guyon (to mention only one of the mystics abridged by Wesley) maintained intense activity with a ministry of teaching and healing.

Consequently one major difficulty in understanding Wesley and mysticism can be removed if one realizes that even though much of mystical theology (in essence a self-achieved union of the soul with God) seemingly obviated any need for rite, discipline, or rule. The mystical life (or ethic) always manifested these very things as an effect of such union. In almost the same moment, therefore, Wesley could strongly criticize the mystical disparagement of works of charity and then publish a mystical biography (especially from the Roman Catholics) illustrating such works. Wesley, from the mystics encountered both before and after Aldersgate, retained an active "mysticism," that is a vital piety that practiced the presence of God in daily activity and led to wholehearted devotion to God in love.

This is not, however, to forget for a moment the wide differences between Wesley and mysticism. Mystic theology still cut at the root of Wesley's new-found understanding of faith in Christ. Yet the mystical lives demonstrated the "ethical condition of fellowship with God," and Wesley was still enough of a moralist to recognize the absolute necessity of this for practical piety. It is interesting to note that Findlay's *Fellowship in Life Eternal* makes a study of 1 John in relation to this ethical condition. Findlay writes that St. John's first epistle affirms "the disciplinary element in the Christian experience; he never allows us, for many paragraphs, to get away from the plain ethical condition of fellowship with God: 'He that keeps His commandments dwells in God and God in him.' "[59]

Likewise, for the mystic, union between God and humankind is impossible apart from obedience. Mysticism, however, then moves from the ethical to the whimsical, from external means to internal means. The moral and ethical obedience, so strong in the preliminary discipline of mysticism, was seized upon by Wesley and linked with God through an evangelical faith in Christ before it had an opportunity to wander off into the dark night of the soul. Therefore, Wesley's understanding of justification by faith retained the supremacy of the moral principle. Alexander Knox writes that "in his attitude to justification by faith it is again the ethical aspect that meant most to Wesley."[60] Similarly Lindström strongly emphasizes Wesley's *practical mysticism* and writes that Law and the mystics influenced Wesley toward "ethical activism."[61] Keying on the expression *practical mysticism,* Lindström goes on to state (and correctly) that "the purport of the breach with the mystics can be summed up in the statement that he changed his mind about the way of salvation. But as to the goal of salvation, he remained in agreement with Law and practical mysticism. . . . He continued to regard sanctification as the true aim and essence of religion."[62] Ultimately mysticism provided a necessary supplement for Aldersgate. Wesley embraced the Reformers (English and Continental) on justification. On one occasion he wrote that he was "but a hair's breadth from Calvin on justification."[63] On another occasion, however, he wrote that although Luther was good on justification he knew nothing of sanctification (as understood by Wesley).[64] This, therefore, would be one of the areas of greatest influence from among the Roman Catholic mystics. Wesley again wrote that Sales and Castaniza, for example, confused justification but fully comprehended sanctification.[65] He also boasted that the Methodists knew both.[66] Bett seems to be justified in his statement that apart from Law's and Byrom's interest in Behmen there was little knowledge of mysticism during Wesley's century. Bett continues, "It might be seriously argued that Wesley stood almost alone in his age for

---

[59] Findlay, *Fellowship in Life Eternal,* 290; quoted in Yates, *Assurance,* 124ff.

[60] Southey, *Wesley,* 2:339ff.

[61] Lindström, *Wesley and Sanctification,* 14–16.

[62] Ibid.

[63] *Letters,* 4:298; cf. sermon *On God's Vineyard, Works,* 7:202ff.

[64] Outler, *John Wesley,* 97ff.

[65] Ibid.

[66] Ibid.

his knowledge of some of the great mystics, and for his appreciation of what was best in them."[67] If, however, Wesley understood what was best in them, he also (following Aldersgate) understood what was worst in them.

The Dross of Mysticism. Although Wesley never really discarded the mystics and continued (somewhat paradoxically) to view them as exemplary Christians, he still rejected the subtle refinement of mysticism, which he felt led away from the grace of God so necessary to Christian conversion. Perhaps Wesley's greatest criticism of mysticism was that it was *inventive, irrational,* and *unscriptural.* This was especially true of the medieval mystics, and there was sufficient overlap of these weaknesses among the post-Reformation (and for that matter the pre-medieval) Catholic mystics to make Wesley temporarily uncomfortable even in their company.

The mystics as a whole were inventive in that they expounded a new gospel. They were irrational (although John Fletcher insists that mysticism does not necessarily decry reason and that Wesley could retain a rational and Scriptural mysticism)[68] in that their doctrine frequently led to illogical conclusions. Their overactive fear of external works, for example, tended to discourage even the means of grace (although there were many exceptions). Wesley, in his first sermon on the *The Witness of the Spirit,* states that the Spirit perfects reason against mystical notions.[69] Workman also notes that although Methodism and mysticism vindicate the spiritual rights of the uneducated against the pretensions of mere learning (both hold religion superior to reason),[70] the mystics sometimes degenerated into a contempt for learning; thus, the quotation from Tauler: "Children, ye shall not seek after great science."[71] The mystics were unscriptural in that they taught, as essential doctrine, that which the Scriptures failed to teach. Wesley complains, for example, that the mystical scheme asserts the efficacy of physical evil (fire, floods, etc.) to cure moral evil, and the necessity of suffering to purify lapsed beings. He could find a basis for neither in the Scriptures,

---

[67] Bett, *Methodism,* 62.

[68] Cf. *Works,* 8:11–12; and Fletcher's "Evangelical Mysticism" in his *Works,* 2:17.

[69] *Sermons,* 1:199ff.

[70] Cf. the Methodist hymn "Where reason fails with all her powers, there faith prevails, and love adores."

[71] Workman, *History,* 79ff.

although he had taught the identical doctrine himself prior to Aldersgate.[72]

Wesley also reacted against the mystics (especially the highly contemplative) as solitary and individualistic. According to Bishop Cannon, "Wesley (in 1736) conceived of mysticism as a retreat from the world and as an attempt to purify the soul by isolating it."[73] After Aldersgate, however, solitary religion was counted as dross and remained one of Wesley's most consistent objections to mysticism.[74] Orcibal insists that Wesley merely confused mysticism here with the love of solitude and that Byrom, a man of "deep and strong understanding" and Wesley's "guide of youth," tried to set him straight by recommending mystics who combined action with contemplation.[75] There may be some truth in this, and Byrom may have been an important link with the Roman Catholics abridged by Wesley. But the fact remains that although Wesley may have exaggerated his case against mystical solitude, mystics like Lopez, Molinos, Guyon, and Bourignon used dangerous enough language along these lines to cause Wesley considerable concern.

Perhaps Wesley's most basic objection to mysticism was registered against its Pelagianism. Here we find that the controversy between Wesley and the mystics was not just a miserable squabble, but that the principles involved were vital to the fundamentals of the Christian religion. Prior to Aldersgate Wesley's primary concern was with imitating the suffering Christ. Like the mystics, he stressed the Incarnation as the central fact in Christianity, not the Cross. Again, like the mystics, Wesley emphasized humankind's reconciliation to God, not God's reconciliation to humankind. After Aldersgate, however, he emphasized the triumphant Christ and the Cross as an atonement for sin that assured one's victory over the power of Satan. The basic differences here can be clearly observed in a comparison between Wesley's sermons before and after Aldersgate.[76] Compare *The Almost Christian, The Lord our Righteousness,* or even the expositions on the *Sermon on the Mount,* with any of the earlier sermons. The first of Wesley's sermons in the series on the Sermon on the Mount argues that Christianity begins

---

[72]Cf. Sermons *Trouble and Rest,* and *Public Diversions,* with *Works,* 14:214 and Faulkner, "Wesley the Mystic," *LQR,* no. 153.

[73]Cannon, *Theology,* 61ff.

[74]Cf. "Preface" to *Hymns* (1739).

[75]Orcibal, "Theological Originality," 91ff.

[76]Pre-1738 sermons can be found in *Works,* vol. 7 and "New" *Works,* vols. 3 and 4 (Outler edition).

where other religions leave off.[77] Most religions maintain a degree of morality, most emphasize the poverty of spirit, conviction of sin and renouncing ourselves; but, the "first point in the religion of Christ is the not having our own righteousness."[78] This, of course, cuts across the heart of any Pelagian tendencies in mysticism. The self-saving illusion of the mystical divine spark has no place in Wesley's post-1738 theology. Human sin makes it necessary to assimilate the Atonement through faith in Christ. Lindström, citing this same sermon, remarks that Wesley "split with the mystics as a result of a deepened conception of the gravity and depth of sin."[79] The mystics simply failed to understand the degree to which sin corrupts human nature.

This brief section has sought to establish a few guidelines upon which to begin our study of the ultimate influence of mysticism on John Wesley. It will obviously be expanded as the study progresses. Our hypothesis will serve to identify parts of mysticism with many of the great sources of strength for Methodism. Brazier Green, for example, states that Methodism, because of its mystical ties, has not surrendered its spirituality even when intellectual, social, and modern scientific materialism have threatened its search for inner experience.[80] Green surmises that direct communion with God is necessary to animate those who know only the traditional means of grace.[81] On the other hand, our hypothesis will also identify parts of mysticism with the negative characteristics of extreme Quietism, Quakerism, Rantism, and cheap, half-digested spiritualism, all of which Wesley had grown to despise. Wesley's communion with God was not a dreamy reverie in which the soul, devoid of personality, swoons away into the unseen.[82] For this reason the dross of mysticism needs further exposure, and the gold of mysticism needs further exposition. There are features in both which call for more extended explanation and comment in order "to clear out the mind's corners."[83] Few influences carry so much weight in both directions, not only in Wesley's time but (as we shall soon see), in our own time as well.

Now that Wesley had successfully worked through most of the problem areas of mysticism—"its wide departures from good begin-

[77] *Sermons,* 1:314ff.
[78] Ibid.
[79] Lindström, *Wesley and Sanctification,* 60ff.
[80] B. Green, *John Wesley and William Law,* 312–13.
[81] Ibid.
[82] Ibid.
[83] Jeffery, *Quest,* 312–13.

nings; its flagrant contradictions; its pervading passivity of God as agent; its manipulation of God by man's efforts; and the almost total immanence of God, the root of all its errors"—he was (at long last) ready to extract its most healthful fruit, fruit that would strengthen himself and Methodism devotionally, theologically, and spiritually for many years to come.[84] The remaining task, therefore, is the identification of that fruit as Wesley continues to react and counter-react to the works and lives of his favorite mystical writers.

THE ABRIDGMENTS: JUSTIFICATION BY FAITH REPLACES THE MYSTIC FAITH OF THE "DARK NIGHT"

Relative to justification by faith, two examples from the mystic Extracts will illustrate our point dramatically. Between 1738 and 1749 Wesley was openly cool toward the mystics. Then between 1749 and 1757 he published *The Christian Library* (a fifty-volume collection of abridged works on "Practical Divinity"). Eight out of the ten mystical extracts published by Wesley appear in that collection (Macarius, Fénelon, Pascal, Brother Lawrence, D'Avila, Lopez, Bourignon and Molinos).[85] Since Macarius and Fénelon are especially important for the abiding influences discussed in chapter 6 (the quasimystic Pascal, Brother Lawrence, D'Avila and Lopez to a lesser extent), here we will focus on two of the more controversial to illustrate the importance of justification by faith as the replacement for the mystic "dark night"— Bourignon and Molinos.

Antoinette Bourignon

Wesley knew Madame Bourignon's works as early as 1736. On February 28, 1736, he writes in his Diary that he began *Light of the World*.[86] Again on April 2, 1736, the Diary reads:

6 at home: garden, began *Solid Virtue*
7 *Solid Virtue*
8 bread, conversed 1/2, *Solid Virtue*

---

[84] Ibid.

[85] De Renty (1741) and Guyon (1776) were published independently.

[86] Remember that during this period he had been discussing mystical divinity with Spangenberg. On April 4, 1736, he is again reading *Light of the World*, and this apparently went with him on his first Frederica journey.

Since Wesley abridged *Solid Virtue,* this will be our main tool in exploring Madame Bourignon's influence.

The original treatise was "written in twenty-four letters to a young man, who sought after the perfection of his soul," and was entitled *An Admirable Treatise of Solid Virtue,* "which the men of this generation know not, seeing they take the appearance of virtue, for true virtue, taught by Jesus Christ, in these words, *learn of me, for I am meek and lowly, and humble of heart*; as well as in the other salutary doctrines, which he hath given for true *Christians.*"[87] The first ten letters were designed to implant *virtue,* teaching (according to the title page) "that it consists in the *knowledge* of ourselves, and the mortification of our five natural senses." The remaining letters were designed "to evert and root out what may hinder its increase." As a part of the editing process, Wesley reduced 251 pages to 154, and, according to Ronald Knox, deleted every paragraph, sentence, and clause containing distinctive doctrines.[88] Although this is an exaggeration, one must agree with Knox that this extract is one of the most important keys to Wesley's method of abridgment.

Wesley includes the original "preface of the publisher" (under his title "To the English Reader"), adding a brief introductory paragraph and a statement in defense of Madame Bourignon's treatise. Anticipating some who would say that there is nothing of Jesus Christ and nothing of faith because it deals with virtue, Wesley writes, "What God has joined, men ought not to put asunder, or to make a contrariety between them. True faith, and faith in *Jesus Christ,* is certainly the divine principle of solid virtue. We are bidden to add to our faith the other divine virtues; and are told that faith worketh by love, and that the end of the commandment is charity, and that is the essence of virtue."[89] Wesley encourages the readers to read "without an evil eye" that they might see that they are still directed to Christ and that he alone merits our pardon and favor; that nothing is pleasing without his grace, and that his Holy Spirit sheds divine virtue into our hearts.[90] Finally, one is instructed to put these directions (Madame Bourignon's) into practice as one finds them conformable to the gospel of Christ.[91]

---

[87] The edition of the original that Wesley probably abridged (although he could possibly have used a later one since letters xx–xxv of the extract were taken from another edition or another source) was the 1698 edition by Henry Wetstein; cf. *Library,* 36:177ff.

[88] Knox, *Enthusiasm,* 352ff.

[89] Wesley, *Library,* 36:178f.

[90] Ibid.

[91] Ibid.

This is not to say, however, that Wesley was uncritical of Madame Bourignon's works. In one of his own letters he writes that she was "a person dead to the world and much devoted to God; yet I take her to have been very many degrees beneath Mr. de Renty and Gregory Lopez."[92] He then adds, "The new expressions of Madame Bourignon naturally tended to give you a new set of ideas . . . set your imagination at work, and make you fancy wonderful things; but they were only shadows."[93] Yet Wesley was ambivalent. One has to reconcile, for example, his answer to Hartley's *Defense of the Mystics* in the Journal for February 5, 1764, with his appreciation of Bourignon's battle against antinomianism.[94] Wesley objects to Hartley (who was a great admirer of Madame Bourignon) that the mystics have no conception of church communion; they slight works of piety, the ordinances of God, even works of mercy, and yet they all hold justification by works.[95] One can easily document each of these objections with references from *Solid Virtue*.[96] Wesley admired her enough to abridge her treatise as one much "devoted to God," but he was constantly cleaning up after her. He reinterprets her mystical exercises (including the "dark night") on almost every page. As observed in his own preface, while affirming her ethic he insists on faith (in the evangelical sense) as the source of power both to love and obey. This same pen-quicker-than-the-eye is even more apparent in the abridgment of Molinos.

Michael de Molinos

If *The Christian Library* holds any real surprises, then this is certainly one of the biggest. It is difficult to understand how or why Wesley, considering the battles he would have with Quietism (which would be a lingering menace among some of the societies), included Molinos' *Spiritual Guide* (an archetype of Quietism) in volume thirty-six of the *Library*. The full title of the original is *The Spiritual Guide, Which Dis-Intangles the Soul; and Brings it by the Inward Way, to the Getting of Perfect Contemplation and the Rich Treasure of Internal Peace.*[97] Wesley

---

[92] *Letters*, 7:66, June 10, 1781 (Miss Loxdale).

[93] Ibid., 67.

[94] *Journal*, 5:46. Madame Bourignon fought the antinomians on the level of *internal* works and then weakened her position on the level of *external* works.

[95] Ibid.

[96] Cf. Bourignon, *Solid Virtue*, Letter 15, for example. There she refers to works as "devices of Satan."

[97] No place of publication is given; printed 1699, translated from Italian. Wesley's extract is almost verbatim but for the frequent but significant omissions.

reduces the original 180 pages to 44. If Ronald Knox's statement about Wesley's abridgment of Madame Bourignon concerning the complete removal of essential doctrine was an exaggeration in that instance, it would certainly be true in this. One could read descriptions of the original *Spiritual Guide* and Wesley's extract and never suspect that they were describing the same book. To examine the emphasis of the original in comparison with the extract is to realize that Wesley has cut out the heart of what Molinos was really attempting to say.

Molinos' path to perfection is alien to Wesley. Although Molinos gives lip service to the necessity of God's grace, his basic approach assumes that one can achieve perfection (union with God) by one's own efforts. Wesley, therefore, seeks to correct this inconsistency. He omits Molinos' claim that perfection can be reached in two to six months.[98] If God's grace is really responsible, then why not *instantaneously?*[99] Again Wesley is seeking to sort out the problem of internal works-righteousness. The passage below compares the original with the extract and illustrates the mood. Words not in italics were omitted by Wesley, and he added the words in the brackets.

> *God will do all this in thy soul by means of the cross* and dryness, *if thou freely givest thy consent to it by resignation,* and walking through those darksome and desert ways. *All thou hast to do, is to do nothing by thy own choice* alone. The subjection of thy liberty, is that which thou oughtest to do, *quietly resigning thyself up in everything, whereby the Lord shall think fit internally* [*or*] and *externally to mortifie thee.*[100]

It is interesting how Wesley strengthens the concept of grace here by eliminating the internal works ("and dryness") while retaining the idea of free will. Similarly, he omits any concrete reference to the principle of the "dark night of the soul." Another comparison reads: "*It is no small gift of God . . . to walk by holy faith only,* through the dark and desert paths of perfection, to which, notwithstanding, it can never attain, but by this painful, though secure means. Wherefore *endeavour to be constant. . . .*"[101]

Along these same lines Wesley omits Molinos' emphasis on the efficacy of an "obscure faith" where the Christian suffers "blindfold,"

---

[98]*Original,* p. 14 (*Library,* 36:253).

[99]*Library,* 280. Here Molinos seems to be saying: perfected "in a moment."

[100]*Original,* 27 (*Library,* 36:257); cf. *Original,* 93 where Wesley's omissions make the same point. Remember, the words not in italics were omitted from the original.

[101]*Original,* 18 (*Library,* 36:254).

seemingly abandoned by God and desolate.[102] Wesley admits that God *uses* dryness, but he denies that God *induces* dryness.[103] Compare the following example: *"Possibly thou wilt find within thyself* a passive *dryness, darkness,* anguish, contradictions, continual resistance, inward desertions, horrible desolations, *continual and strong suggestions, and vehement temptations of the enemy."*[104] Wesley simply extracts the more practical thoughts from their mystical context. He takes the "dark night of the soul," for example, denies its necessity as a means to perfection, and uses the principle of the efficacy of suffering and temptation to encourage his Methodists to persevere. Furthermore, he omits the various tools of the mystical path (*via negativa*: the concept of faith as blind and obscure, and the utter disdain for sensible comforts and assurance) and then retains the fragments of practical advice and encouragement as yet another aid for the Evangelical Revival.[105] One might well wonder why Wesley went to the trouble to sift the gold from this Spanish Quietist when so many other authors wrote practically without the mysticism. The answer is of course that Molinos, as well as the other mystics, had a unique contribution to make apart from their mysticism (although obviously related to it).

For example, Wesley was most impressed by the characteristics which are associated with the nature of (rather than the approach to) perfection. Although he was unimpressed by Molinos' emphasis on the highest form of contemplation or mystical silence, the effects of perfection as the "one thing" in religion impressed him deeply. Pure or perfect love, for example, figures prominently in Molinos' scheme. As with Fénelon (and to a lesser degree Brother Lawrence and others), this love involved disinterested resignation. Molinos names "perfect disinterestedness" as one of the "perfections of spiritual beauty."[106]

Wesley was also deeply impressed with what Molinos had to say concerning humility (he included almost all of one chapter and most of another from the original on the subject, a rare occurrence), turning adversity into means of grace and internal peace (perhaps simply using other words for Brother Lawrence's "practice of the presence of God"). Yet despite all the gold, our point here relates more to the dross. When

---

[102]Wesley omits these ideas from *Original,* 24ff., 38, 95ff., 99.

[103]*Original,* 20 (*Library,* 36:255).

[104]*Original,* 93f. (*Library,* 36:276).

[105]*Original,* 13, "blindfold without reasoning"; cf. p. 21, Molinos argues that "sentiments" (Wesley substitutes "joy" for "sentiments" but omits the context) are "manifest cheats."

[106]Ibid., 292f.; cf. pp. 268, 270, 289, 291.

push came to shove, Molinos, like Bourignon, taught that faith as the mystic dark night was the route to perfection (an internal works-righteousness). Once this was sorted out and Wesley's understanding of the Atonement was firmly in place, he would return to the gold as impetus for the Evangelical Revival. With these two illustrations in mind, it is important now to say that the one who perhaps helped him most in reevaluating the mystics was John Fletcher.

JOHN FLETCHER'S EVANGELICAL MYSTICISM

John Fletcher, Swiss by birth and education, emigrated to England in 1752. Although Wesley knew Fletcher almost from the time of his arrival, it was during the early 1760s (Fletcher went to Madeley in 1760) that their real friendship developed. His influence on Wesley was paramount, and that he contributed greatly to Wesley's readjustment is more than conjecture. Furthermore, it is almost certain that he reintroduced Wesley to a higher appreciation of mysticism. The "Shropshire Saint," or the "Methodist Mystic" as he was sometimes called, impressed Wesley enough that he chose Fletcher to be his successor. But Fletcher predeceased him. Piette, with good reason, refers to Fletcher as the "mystical writer of the movement."[107] Wesley writes that "the reading of those poisonous writers the Mystics confounded the intellects of both my brother and Mr. Fletcher and made them afraid of (what ought to have been their glory) the letting their light shine before men."[108] Wesley nonetheless records with apparent admiration (if not envy) the facts of Fletcher's life, which read like the story of a born mystic and which undoubtedly served to associate Fletcher with mysticism.[109]

Wesley's *Life of Fletcher* portrays a man constantly pleading with God to take greater possession. Once while prostrate in prayer he received a vision of Christ bleeding on the cross.[110] Wesley emphasizes his continual, yet cheerful and valiant, self-denial. He sat up two whole nights a week in order to enter more deeply into communion with God through reading, meditation, and prayer. Wesley frequently underscores this communion with God, stating that he would not even move from

---

[107] Piette, *Evolution of Protestantism,* 391.

[108] *Letters,* 8:93f.; cf. 8:88–91. The mystics persuaded Mrs. Scudamore "to put her light under a bushel."

[109] *Works,* 11:273–365, Fletcher's *Life.*

[110] Ibid.

his chair without first looking to God. Like Wesley in Georgia, Fletcher was a vegetarian, sometimes eating only bread, water, and milk. Wesley also states that he rarely saw anything before him but the Bible and the *Christian Pattern.*[111] Wesley then concludes Fletcher's *Life* with this interesting and revealing comment:

> I would only observe, that for many years I despaired of finding any inhabitant of Great Britain, that could stand in any degree of comparison with Gregory Lopez, or Monsieur de Renty. But let any impartial person judge if Mr. Fletcher was at all inferior to them. Did he not experience as deep communion with God, and as high a measure of inward holiness, as was experienced by either one or the other of those burning and shining lights?[112]

Orcibal attributes Wesley's "reintroduction to mysticism" in part to the influence of John Fletcher on the one hand and to the threat of Calvinism on the other.[113] Wesley and Fletcher (as evidenced by his *Checks to Antinomianism*) were forced to do battle with a deterministic antinomian trend in contemporary religious movements that threatened to confuse his society members relative to their ethical distinctions and their religious enjoyments.[114] It has already been established that Wesley saw in mysticism and its emphasis on personal holiness an effective weapon against antinomianism. On August 18, 1775, he comments on the progress of predestinarianism in a letter to Fletcher: "Does not [Dean Tucker of Gloucester] show beyond all contradiction that it was hatched by Augustine in spite of Pelagius (who very probably held no other heresy than you and I do now)?" Without attempting to push this point too far, it is interesting to speculate whether Wesley, who earlier criticized the mystics for Pelagianism, now under the influence of Fletcher was prepared to drop this objection in light of a

---

[111] *Works,* 11:286ff. Several mystical books can be found in Fletcher's personal library. Besides Taylor and à Kempis, one can find works like the following published by P. Poiret: *Recueil de Divers Traitez de Theologie Mystique qui entrent dans la célèbre dispute du Quietisme qui s'agite presentement en France* (A Cologne, chez Jean de la Pierre, 1699). It contains a preface on *La Vie de M. Guyon; Le Moyen Court et Tres-facile de faire oraison* (Guyon); *L'Explication du Cantique des Cantiques* (Guyon); *L'Eloge, Les Maximes Spirituelles,* et quelques *Lettres du Fr. Laurent de la Resurrection; Les Moeurs et Entretiens du même Fr. Laurent,* et so pratique de *L'Exercice de la presence de Dieu.*

[112] *Ibid.,* 364.

[113] Orcibal "Theological Originality of John Wesley and Continental Spirituality," 95ff.; cf. *Journal,* 5:59; during the crucial month of April 1764, Wesley exclaims, "Oh that our brethren were as zealous to make *Christians* as they are to make *Calvinists.*

[114] Workman, *History* (1909), 1, 54f.

current controversy. In spite of their continued emphasis on faith, Wesley and Fletcher both seem to join forces with the mystics and Pelagius against the demoralizing effects of antinomianism.[115]

Wesley, between 1738 and 1764, objected to what he thought to be an unevangelical, inactive, philosophical mysticism that was intent on contemplating abstruse metaphysical questions; a mysticism which thought more of speculation than Scripture, more of the inner light and the vision of God than doing God's will here and now.[116] Similarly, after Aldersgate he no doubt exaggerated its dangers owing to the intensity of that experience. Furthermore, Wesley's growing appreciation for the authority of Scripture, validated by the experiences of countless Methodists, continued to act as the spring of his reaction against mysticism in general.[117] Between 1764 and 1767, however, there is considerable evidence to suggest that Fletcher confronted Wesley with a view of mysticism which was not only Scriptural but thoroughly evangelical. In Fletcher's *Works,* one finds a tract entitled "On Evangelical Mysticism."[118] Contrary to Wesley's earlier "Earnest Appeal" (1744), Fletcher denies that the mystics decry the use of reason.[119] According to Fletcher there is a "rational mysticism found in many excellent works, both ancient and modern," which "is a thin veil, covering the naked truth, to improve her beauty, to quicken the attention of sincere seekers, to augment the pleasure of discovery, and to conceal her charms from the prying eyes of her enemies."[120]

Fletcher writes that a "judicious mysticism enables us to speak the greatest truths with impunity, and to deliver them in the most energetic and striking manner."[121] He illustrates this with the example of Nathan the prophet, who, "by concealing a terrible rebuke under a well-chosen apologue, brought King David to pass a just sentence upon the seducer of Uriah's wife"; and Fénelon, who, "under the character of mentor . . . presumed to give lessons of wisdom and moderation to Louis XIV,

---

[115]Cf. *Works,* 7:312ff. and Fletcher's *Checks, Letters,* 5:274f. Wesley and Fletcher defend the *Minutes* (1770) against the Countess of Huntingdon's attack. Cf. *Letters,* 4:158. Somewhat recklessly, Pelagius is called "both a wise and holy man."

[116]Faulkner, "Wesley the Mystic," *London Quarterly Review,* 153:148.

[117]Ibid., 149. Cf. *Letters,* 4:234ff. Although one wonders at times exactly what Wesley meant by "man of one book," few would question his reverence for the testimony of Scripture.

[118]*Works* (London: 1860 edition), 9:382–91. This tract is addressed basically to those prejudiced against mysticism.

[119]Ibid. Cf. Wesley's *Works,* 8:12

[120]Ibid., 382.

[121]Ibid., 383.

which would not have been received but through the prudent mysticism of the authors."[122]

Fletcher goes on to contrast "extravagant" and "true" mysticism, admitting first of all that extravagant mysticism "turns all into allegories, vain subtleties, and curious refinements unworthy of holy Scripture."[123] He then objects that "to avoid these excesses many imagine that they must run to the other extreme," and in so doing, as enemies to true mysticism, they injure religion. "They enervate the Gospel of Jesus Christ, as the Pharisees did the law of Moses; leaving only a dead carcass without a soul."[124] Fletcher finally exhorts his reader (as he no doubt exhorted Wesley) to avoid both extremes. One should profit from the errors of the mystic who turns all into spirit, and one should profit from the errors of the philosopher who turns all into "bodies and natural philosophy," and then "preserve the way of truth equally distant."[125] Judging from Wesley's attitude toward mystics in the following chapter, we have every reason to conclude that he learned his lesson well.

Wesley was now secure enough in his understanding of justification by faith and the Atonement to allow the influence of certain mystics to flow more freely. Read carefully this quotation from his sermon *Salvation by Faith* as he defines the Atonement in the evangelical sense and appropriated by a personal faith in Jesus Christ, not as our model but as our substitute for sin and death.

> This then is the salvation which is through faith, even in the present world: A salvation from sin, and the consequences of sin, both often expressed in the word *justification*; which, taken in the largest sense, implies a deliverance from guilt and punishment, by the atonement of Christ actually applied to the soul of the sinner now believing on him, and a deliverance from the power of sin, through Christ *formed in his heart*. So that he who is thus justified, or saved by faith, is indeed *born again*. He is *born again of the Spirit* unto a new life, which "is hid with Christ in God." And as a new-born babe he gladly receives the "*sincere milk of the word, and grows thereby;*" going on in the might of the

---

[122]Ibid. Cf. p. 385. Fletcher states that "a wise mysticism gives body and weight to moral precepts" (a bundle of arrows broken one at the time). Cf. Wesley's *Works*, 10:438 where Fletcher refers to Solomon as the "chief mystic."

[123]Ibid., 388.

[124]Ibid., 385ff.

[125]Ibid., 388ff. Fletcher argues that one should never confine everything in the Bible to literal truth. This was Nicodemus' problem in John 3. Since the carnal mind cannot discern the things of the Spirit, truth must be explained in terms of circumlocution (pp. 385ff.).

Lord his God, from faith to faith, from grace to grace, until, at length, he come unto "a perfect man, unto the measure of the stature of the fulness of Christ."[126]

Here is the classic evangelical approach to salvation with room enough for the mystic "gold" to underscore a balance between faith and works (Wesley's peculiar genius) that would only strengthen as the years advanced.

---

[126]*Works,* 5:11–12.

6

abiding mystical influences in the wesleyan tradition: a mysticism of service

In my book *John Wesley: His Life and Theology*, I gave a considerable amount of space to Wesley's theological readjustment between the years 1762–67. Without retelling that story, it is significant here to state that after 1767 Wesley would preach justification by faith as confirmed by works. Although justification by faith is still the primary doctrine in all of his sermons, Wesley now realized that faith has its *inevitable* fruit— the loving of one's neighbor as oneself.[1] By the same token, if faith had its inevitable fruit, then evidence of the inevitable fruit was a sign of faith. Where the mystics were concerned, if a mystical life manifested fruit that only faith could produce, even if the understanding of faith was incomplete, then faith, saving faith, was still evident.[2] All of this would serve to create a wider appreciation for mystical influences. Each of these influences would surface, however, with a pragmatic turn.

Few would deny that John Wesley was at once a wonderfully complex man and yet a powerfully practical theologian. He never did theology in a vacuum. His theological treatises appeared only in answer to potentially dangerous controversies or in response to particularly pressing needs. The abiding influences of the mystics always speak to a specific need as related to the spiritual development of the people called Methodist. In most instances these same needs persist today.

---

[1]Tuttle, *John Wesley*, 311–20; 335–45.
[2]Wesley, *Works*, 6:160.

THE NEED TO PERSEVERE

Perhaps the best way to illustrate what has just been stated is to describe a need and then discuss Wesley's prescription for meeting that need. From the early days in Georgia through the years of revival, one of the most perplexing problems for Wesley was persistent, nagging (if not haunting) backsliding. Already mentioned in other contexts, Wesley developed a sophisticated doctrine of perseverance necessarily linked (as we shall soon see) to a doctrine of perfection. Our focus here will be on the need to persevere as preface to the even more important teaching on perfection as the only solution.

It has been our assumption that from his earliest days in Georgia Wesley's emphasis on spiritual discipline leading to perfection was geared to his doctrine of perseverance. Wesley not only stressed perseverance to ensure perfection, he stressed "going on to perfection" to ensure perseverance. Again and again, perseverance is the one great issue. Wesley insists that "if we do not grow spiritually, we die spiritually."[3] Perfection is frequently seen in light of perseverance. He states that it is better to *retain* perfection than to *attain* perfection.[4] Wesley predicts that "hardly three in five of those that are either justified or sanctified keep the gift of God a year to an end."[5] On January 26, 1772, he writes that two recovered is better than three new.[6] Perfection served a practical end indeed. Not that his hatred of backsliding was greater than his love for holiness. He simply believed that going on to perfection and then increasing degrees of perfection was the only way to persevere. On November 22, 1772, he writes, " 'Go on to perfection'; otherwise they cannot keep what they have."[7] Much of Wesley's practical theology (including his doctrine of perfection) seems to turn on the belief that those saved could lose their salvation and in fact, "it is a miracle if they do not."[8]

The relevance of this for mysticism can be detected on several occasions. First of all, Wesley's scheme of spiritual exercises aimed at perseverance follows the example of the mystical writers, at least in

---

[3] Cf. *Letters*, 8:184.

[4] Ibid., 8:188.

[5] Ibid., 5:273; cf. 6:241f.; 8:188; cf. also *Works*, 11:441f. Wesley insists that perfection is always improvable.

[6] Wesley's emphasis on perseverance dominates his letters during the 1770s.

[7] *Letters*, 7:109; cf. 7:229f.

[8] *Journal*, 6:33.

part.[9] His *Plain Account of Christian Perfection,* for example, states that the best aids to growing in grace are affronts and losses and that "we should receive them with thankfulness, as preferable to all others."[10] Similarly, "the readiest way to escape from our sufferings is, to be willing they should endure as long as God pleases."[11] God afflicts those God loves and the love of God is revealed by granting them the grace to bear such affliction. Furthermore, true resignation is presented as the key to perseverance. Wesley exhorts us to abandon all, strip ourselves, and follow naked the naked Christ: "True humility is a kind of self-annihilation; and this is the centre of all virtues . . . suffering evils in meekness and silence, is the sum of a Christian life."[12] Wesley's sermon *On Self-Denial* reiterates these points. There he insists that perseverance requires self-denial, while backsliding is ceasing to deny oneself.

Although Wesley might well have derived many of the characteristics of his doctrine of perseverance from several sources, it seems certain that many of his general impressions were taken from the mystics.[13] Take Macarius, for example. Macarius taught that after receiving the Holy Spirit one needed to improve the gift imparted in order to persevere.[14] Macarius speaks of the degrees or stages of perfection.[15] He writes that "sometimes the love flames out and kindles with greater strength; but at other times more slow and gentle."[16] Eventually, however, the humble soul is received into "the mystical fellowship in the fullness of grace."[17] This filling of the Holy Spirit implies an entire redemption from sin, but perfection is gradual: "There are heights which the soul does not reach all at once; but through many labours and conflicts, with variety of trials and temptations, it receives spiritual growth and improvement."[18] Although Wesley on occasion spoke of

---

[9] An interesting comparison could be drawn with Ignatius Loyola. Cf., for example, *Meditation on Two Standards* (*Spiritual Exercises,* 100ff.) where Loyola emphasizes the advantage of affliction (in reality more of a psychological warfare) for perseverance and perfection (G. Wakefield, *Puritan Devotion,* 132).

[10] *Works,* 11:425ff.

[11] Ibid.

[12] Ibid. Cf. Wesley's reference to self-annihilation here with his disparagement of the same below. Wesley's hand-corrected hymnbooks, frequently changed "salvation from self" to "salvation from desire," etc.

[13] Wakefield's *Puritan Devotion* (pp. 131ff.) develops the Puritan influences.

[14] Ibid., Homily 11:122f.

[15] *Extract,* Homily 5:102ff.

[16] Ibid., 102.

[17] Ibid., 106.

[18] Ibid., 107.

"instantaneous sanctification" (that is, one grows gradually to the *moment* of full delivery), he certainly appreciated Macarius' emphasis on continual growth. Macarius taught that no matter how high the state of perfection, one could always grow in grace.[19] It is foolishness to boast that one has no sin (even if sinless) since one must grow to persevere.

Macarius' caution against backsliding (remember Wesley was also reading Macarius before the crisis at Frederica) also greatly appealed to Wesley. Although he strongly emphasized the grace of God, this grace was clearly not irresistible. Macarius answers the question as to whether one can fall from grace in this manner (Wesley's extract is almost verbatim): "If he grows careless, he certainly falls. For his enemies are never idle, or backward in the war. How ought you then never to desist from seeking after God? For the damage which you sustain by your neglect is exceeding great, tho' you may seem to be even established in the mystery of grace."[20] What better treatise could Wesley use to remedy the problem of backsliding in the societies? Even the "perfect" were not exempt from the snare of Satan, who is perfectly void of mercy. Macarius describes the experiences of some who "had no sin," yet "the corruption that lurk'd within, was stirr'd up anew, and they were well nigh burnt up."[21] Is it any surprise, then (in light of the needs of the Methodist societies in particular), that Wesley should abridge these homilies and quote from Macarius in his sermons?[22] Macarius, like Wesley, felt that Christians should never underestimate the danger of sin. For this reason, Macarius continued to be a pattern for Wesley's own doctrine of perfection and continued to illustrate the meaning of perfection for Methodists.

In the sermon *On Self-Denial*, it is the mystics who are singled out for their emphasis on self-denial. On May 30, 1772, Wesley writes, "Oh, it is a blessed thing to suffer in a good cause." He illustrates with the example of Xavier, the apostle of the Indies, who, forsaken of all men, was left dying in a cottage. Wesley writes, "Here was a martyrdom, I had almost said, more glorious than that of St. Paul or St. Peter!"[23] Through suffering, God "will confirm your soul against too great sensibility." Wesley then adds, "Whatever you read in the *Life* of Mr. de

---

[19] Ibid., 112ff.

[20] Ibid., 109.

[21] Ibid., 114 (Homily 9).

[22] *Sermons*, 2:447 (*Scripture Way of Salvation*); and *Notes Upon the New Testament*, 2 Cor. 5:2.

[23] *Letters*, 5:320.

Renty and Gregory Lopez . . . is for you. Christ is ready! All is ready!
Take it for simple faith!"[24]

Since we have associated Wesley's emphasis on suffering and self-
denial relative to perfection and perseverance with the mystics, we must
now point out at least one grand exception. Whereas the mystics include
darkness among the afflictions of God, Wesley once again strongly
affirms that in spite of all affliction one need never leave or lose the light
of God. He writes on March 25, 1772, that he fears that Betsy Johnson
"has met with some of those that are called 'mystic writers' who abound
among the Roman Catholics. These are perpetually talking of 'self-
emptiness, . . . , self-annihilation,' and the like."[25] In *Plain Account*, he
insists that God afflicts but that he never brings darkness.[26] We may
suffer but darkness is never the will of God, who is always willing to
give more light. Since darkness results from the failure to return to the
source of our strength, to persevere we must continually return to
Christ. Then, however, with a remarkable turn of logic, Wesley (on
another occasion) takes a proof text from the mystics themselves to
substantiate his case against mystical darkness. On August 3, 1771, he
quotes from both de Renty and Lopez. He writes that Lopez is an
illustration of "faith's abiding impression" where there is no unbelief, no
darkness—"all is midday *now*."[27] He goes on to exhort his correspon-
dent "to glorify God like Mr. de Renty or Haliburton, in death as well
as in life."[28] Thus, once again we find Wesley almost irresistibly drawn
to the mystic gold as he seeks to refine it from so much dross in order to
use its example for the edification of those under his care. Wesley uses
the mystical extracts during this period more than any other, specifically
to exhort Methodists to persevere, to move away from backsliding and
toward Christian perfection.

CHRISTIAN PERFECTION, A PURE AND DISINTERESTED LOVE: THE SOLUTION

As Wesley's views developed over the years, the area of Christian
perfection is where the mystics make their most continuous and lasting

---

[24] Ibid., 320f.

[25] Ibid., 313.

[26] *Works*, 11:414–20.

[27] *Letters*, 5:271 (italics mine). Wesley omits that for the mystic this "abiding light" can
be reached only through "darkness"; cf. p. 283 where Lopez's "uninterrupted communion" is again cited.

[28] Ibid., 271.

impression. Since Wesley and the mystics were concerned with perfection as the end of religion, this is the area where Wesley's mystical heritage carried him far beyond Aldersgate. The degree of continuity relative to perfection before and after Aldersgate, as well as the variations, can (at least in part) be traced to the influence of these mystics.

Although the years between 1756 and 1763 mark the heaviest emphasis on perfection, Wesley insists that he maintains a basic continuity of thought from a period long before Aldersgate. Since the pre-1738 period was the time when he was most involved with mysticism it is only natural to look among the mystics for the roots of Wesley's perfection as well as for the influence on his more mature doctrine. Wesley's views on perfection represent his most consistent line of thought reaching back to his religious awakening in 1725; for that reason this is the doctrine least affected by Aldersgate. Wesley rarely (if ever) refers to that experience when explaining the origin and development of this Christian ideal.

On March 5, 1767, he writes to the editor of *Lloyd's Evening Post* in defense of his doctrine of Christian perfection recently attacked by Dr. Dodd. He states that "five and six-and-thirty years ago I much admired the character of a perfect Christian drawn by Clemens Alexandrinus."[29] Wesley goes on to say that taking the example of this noted mystical Father he developed a scheme of his own in *The Character of a Methodist*.[30] Lindström writes that under the influence of "practical mysticism" Wesley first became preoccupied with Christian perfection: "He never abandoned the general position with regard to Christian perfection which first derives from his introduction to practical mysticism in 1725 and was then first expressed. . . ."[31] By "practical mysticism" Lindström refers to the quasimysticism of Taylor, à Kempis, and Law whose concept of perfection as an "ethical goal" for all men continued to influence Wesley throughout his life. Since our hypothesis states that Wesley's partial break with mysticism concerned for the most part only the philosophical and theological means of religion, this ethical end in its pietistic, practical, and ascetical form remained the area of greatest pre-1738 influence on Wesley. Furthermore, although men like B. Green, Baker, and Wilson emphasize Law (and perhaps Scougal), the

29 *Letters,* 5:43.

30 It would be interesting to compare Clemen's seventh book of the *Stromateis,* read by Wesley in 1731–1732, with Wesley's *The Character of a Methodist, Works,* 8:339–47.

31 Lindström, *Wesley and Sanctification,* 126ff., 157.

Roman Catholic mystics have, in certain respects, an even closer parallel to the Wesleyan doctrine. Lindström cites the examples of François de Sales and Juan de Castaniza whose Christian perfection (as in practical mysticism) "was conceived as an inherent *ethical* change in man and the Christian life was represented as a progressive development towards it."[32] Even more important, however, is the example of the mystics abridged by Wesley. Most of the basic characteristics of Wesley's doctrine find parallel consideration among these mystics whom he was reading while his ideas on perfection were first being formulated. The following statement by Wesley concerning the implications of Christian perfection could just as easily have been written by any of the Roman Catholic mystics already discussed: Perfection is "the loving God with all the heart, so that every evil temper is destroyed; and every thought and word and work springs from and is conducted to the end by pure love of God and our neighbour."[33]

Although Wesley's *Plain Account of Christian Perfection* makes virtually no reference to the mystics as such,[34] the pre-Aldersgate development of perfection in this treatise follows the pattern established by the mystical authors. Perfect love is the end; and the imitation of Christ (rather than justification by faith) is the means.[35] Likewise, the earliest hymns and poems expressing the nature of perfection assume the mystical scheme.[36] Again, the first tract written on the subject was admittedly inspired by a mystic. Consequently, Wesley's earlier doctrine of perfection contained most of the essential elements present in the more mature doctrine (pure disinterested love attainable in this life, resignation, the continual practice of the presence of God; that is, praying without ceasing and in everything giving thanks), but couched more deeply within the tradition of his mystical heritage. The fact

---

[32] Ibid., 128; cf. 171ff. Lindström writes that Wesley shared the teleological leaning of Law and the mystics; that is, he saw salvation as a process of several means to one end. Wesley frequently viewed man as a spirit come from God and returning to God (Preface to *Standard Sermons*; *Plain Account of Christian Perfection*; and his sermon *The Circumcision of the Heart*). Lindström, p. 218, also writes that the Christian (as in mysticism) is above all a pilgrim, one's life on earth is a journey, the path of sanctification, of real spiritual change.

[33] Flew, *Perfection*, 326, from the 1758 Conference *Minutes*.

[34] De Renty is mentioned (*Works*, 11:394f.) to illustrate one who was perfect yet whose mistake in judgment occasioned a mistake in practice.

[35] *Works*, 11:366–69. Although no reference is made to Aldersgate, Wesley's treatise introduces faith at a point immediately following this experience. Prior to this point, faith is not mentioned as Wesley speaks of the Spirit returning to God through the imitation of Christ (p. 368).

[36] Cf. *Hymns and Sacred Poems* (1739); cf. Ibid., 369f.

remains, however, that although the mystical means dropped away, the unmistakable influence of the mystics can still be detected in Wesley's doctrine of Christian perfection.

Furthermore, it is significant that for Wesley, as for the mystics, perfection is not merely a moral and ethical aspiration or a set theological creed: it is a doctrine related to practice, a dynamic concept validated by actual experience. Wesley insisted that if he could be proved wrong on any particular doctrine by the overall experience of believers he would "preach it no more."[37] Undoubtedly, therefore, perfection increased in stature as it continued to reveal its value in and for Christian experience. Many of Wesley's letters at this time document the point. Wesley's personal care for souls through his correspondence discloses a wealth of practical advice strikingly similar to that of the Roman Catholic mystics.[38]

Between 1756 and 1763 Wesley's letters are full of advice related to the pursuit of perfection. He exhorts those under his care to quit trifling companions;[39] to praise God continually;[40] to reject all comfort which flows not from the spirit of adoption;[41] to maintain all simplicity, watching unto prayer and yielding not to indolence or spiritual sloth;[42] to control wandering thoughts, bringing all into the captive obedience of Christ;[43] and to hold some time daily for reading and other private exercises.[44] Furthermore, Wesley frequently exhorts Methodists to meditation. He instructs Sir James Lowther that light will be given directly from God "in meditation and private prayers."[45] He advises another to fix his eyes upon Christ.[46] He exhorts still another to "Gospel obedience and holiness of life."[47] His letter to Mrs. Ryan (November

---

[37] *Works*, 1:405. Evidently experience taught Wesley that those perfected could fall at any level. At one point (*Letters*, 3:213), Wesley seems to imply that those perfected could *not* fall, but he later insists (cf. *Works*, 11:426) that absolutely no one was invulnerable; cf. *Letters*, 5:20 (where Wesley claims that his doctrine of perfection is confirmed by five hundred witnesses).

[38] Cf. the letters abridged in *The Christian Library* from Bourignon, Fénelon, Brother Lawrence, and D'Avila.

[39] *Letters*, 3:206.

[40] Ibid., 208.

[41] Ibid., 212.

[42] Ibid., 215; cf. 218f.

[43] Ibid., 243.

[44] Ibid., 240; 4:103; cf. Conference *Minutes*, 1762.

[45] Ibid., 4:66; cf. 3:141.

[46] Ibid., 4:70.

[47] Ibid., 4:327–30; cf. 85f. On January 7, 1760, Wesley completed Fénelon's celebrated *Telemachus*. On March 4, 1760, he concludes a letter to Miss March with the words: "May

12, 1761) is especially revealing. He questions her as to her self-examination, her practice of the presence of God, and her "experimental proof of the ever-blessed Trinity." It would be difficult to deny the influence of the Roman Catholic mystics in these and other letters which breathe the spirit of de Renty, Macarius, Madame Bourignon, Fénelon, Brother Lawrence, D'Avila, and Lopez.

Equally significant is the fact that Wesley did not always feel compelled to omit the mystical phrase "union with God."[48] Green suggests that there is considerable evidence that Wesley had a deep appreciation of religion as an ultimate union with God.[49] Wilson writes that Wesley "stands in a noble mystical tradition" when he asserts that union with God is the ultimate end of the Christian experience.[50] He finds it difficult to resist the conclusion that Wesley thought of his relation to God in terms of a mystical union.[51] A word of caution is needed here, however. Although some evidence suggests that Wesley thought of perfection in terms of one's return to union with God through the restoration of a divine image—that is, an ethical or moral perfection of the human nature—it is dangerous to push this idea too far.[52] Wilson's insistence that this is evidence of Wesley's post-1738 mysticism completely disregards Wesley's rejection of the mystical means of solitude, darkness, and contemplation to mention only the most important.[53] Admittedly, Wesley does speak of a "ladder of ascent"[54] which leads to perfection and which assumes an element of prevenient grace that is similar in some ways to Law's "divine spark or seed," Scougal's "divine life," the Quaker's "inner light," and the

---

He who loves you fill you with His *pure love*' (italics mine). In the *Journal* (4:370) for March 6, 1760, with Fénelon still fresh in his mind, he defines perfection as "constant communion with God" and a heart filled with love.

[48] Most of these treatises expound a doctrine of union with God to be achieved in *this* life.

[49] B. Green, *John Wesley and William Law*, 191.

[50] Wilson, "Influence of Mysticism,"256.

[51] Ibid., 338.

[52] Although Wesley (*Works,* 11:435) writes, "For as the rivers all return into the sea, so the bodies, the souls, and the good works of the righteous, return into God, to live there in his eternal repose," he himself rarely uses the phrase "union with God." Wilson's references ("Influence of Mysticism," 227, 256) are not too convincing in this respect; cf. *Notes,* 2 Peter 1:4; Rom. 14:17; 2 Tim. 3:17; 1 John 3:2, 9; *Sermons,* 1:164, 207f., 217, 345.

[53] Cf. Wesley's reaction to Hartley's *Defense* in *Letters,* 4:234f.

[54] *Sermons,* 1:316ff. Wesley concludes from the Sermon on the Mount that "the Son of God . . . is here showing us the way to heaven . . . the Beatitudes are the successive steps in the ladder of ascent to God . . . til the 'man of God is made perfect.'"

Platonist's "reason."[55] Wesley and the mystics would agree that this element was the gift of God to everyone and that it is the necessary starting point for the work of God in the soul. *But* this is as far as one can go. Wesley's more mature doctrine of perfection from this point on parts from the mystics in that it recognizes human depravity and the futility of the mystic "way of purgation" as an ascent to God purely by means of self-purification and personal growth in inward holiness. Colin Williams states that Wesley combined his pessimism of nature with his optimism of grace and thereby attained the mystical end (the perfect *com*-union with God in love) within the framework of justification by faith.[56]

Although Wesley never emphasizes the role of Aldersgate in his descriptions of the nature of perfection, one should never underestimate the impact of that experience on his doctrine of perfection. For Wesley the actual nature of perfection remained largely the same as it was for the mystics. But the means change. This fact, of course, once again underscores our hypothesis concerning the gold and the dross; and, knowing this, one should not be too surprised to find Wesley criticizing the "mystic foxes" who continue to spoil true religion with a "new gospel" one moment, and then insist that the Spirit is grieved by not following the mystic example of self-denial and holiness of life the next.[57]

Wesley's concept of spiritual discipline and Christian perfection ring loudest during the latter part of the 1760s. In fact, Wesley's reaction to the antinomian controversy (cf. the Conference *Minutes* for 1770) might lead some to think that he now thought of perfection as achievable by guts, grit, and gumption more than by grace.[58] The mystical graces of lowliness, meekness, and resignation are emphasized continually, and wholehearted devotion to God still stands as the only real criterion for Christian faith. Perfection has but one common denominator—perfect love.

Wesley's application of the mystic gold carried over into many other areas as well during this period. Although perseverance was frequently an underlying motive, perfect love still persisted as the heart

---

[55] Wilson, "Influence of Mysticism," 218ff.

[56] C. Williams, *Theology*, 77f.

[57] Cf. *Letters*, 3:214f., May 18, 1757; 3:218f., June 18, 1757; Wesley's *Journal* (5:23) for August 28, 1763, again condemns the "poison of mysticism." But the following June (*Letters*, 4:249) he recommends Malebranche's *Search After Truth* for a course of study.

[58] *Letters*, 5:132ff. Wesley wrote a classic letter on the rules of discipline for Methodist ministers. Cf. *Letters*, 5:274 (he defends the 1770 *Minutes*).

of true Christianity. On July 13, 1771, Wesley writes that 1 Corinthians 13 presents "the height and depth of genuine perfection; and it is observable St. Paul speaks all along of the love of our neighbour, flowing indeed from the love of God. Mr. de Renty is an excellent pattern of this."[59] The pure or perfect love of the mystic is frequently cited by Wesley as the pattern for Christian perfection. As mentioned earlier, Lindström attributes the connection here to Wesley's teleological approach.[60] For Wesley, love is the essence of sanctification which he (like the mystics) accommodates (or teleologically determines) to a state of progression toward the goal of salvation. Lindström writes that "an examination of love in its relation to its divine object will make it clear that into the Reformed outlook is woven another derived from mysticism and in line with Augustine's conception of love."[61] The Reformed emphasis on the *cause* is aligned with the teleological emphasis on the *end*. Wesley sees perfect love as both the desire *to* enjoy God and the *way* back to God. Lindström concludes, "Accordingly, Wesley sees perfection in terms of the mystics' idea of purity in intention and affection. Love is a wholehearted attitude to God, a means to attain the end of perfect and final union with Him."[62]

Undoubtedly the one who influenced Wesley most with regard to "pure love" was Fénelon. The sections from Fénelon in *The Christian Library* could just as easily be called a discourse on Christian perfection. Olive Wyon quotes the modern French writer François Varillon who says, "'Like everyone who has a deep experience, Fénelon always had one thing to say—and only one.' This 'one thing' . . . was his doctrine of *Pure Love*: 'It is the love which God has for us which gives us everything; but the greatest gift that he can give us is (in the words of so many mystics) to give us the love which we ought to have for him.'"[63] Wesley equated perfection (a wholehearted devotion to God) with pure or perfect love. For Wesley, "perfect love" implied rejoicing evermore,

---

[59] *Letters*, 5:268; cf. *Letters*, 5:129. De Renty is praised for his full acquiescence in the will of God. Wesley also included the extract from de Renty's *Life* in the first edition of his *Works* published in 1771.

[60] Lindström, *Wesley and Sanctification*, 171ff.

[61] Ibid., 185; the teleological approach deals with *means* and *ends*, emphasizing the latter; the Reformed approach deals with *cause* and *effect*, emphasizing the former.

[62] Ibid., 186; cf. *Works*, 11:367.

[63] Olive Wyon, *Desire for God* (London: Fontana, 1966), 34. She provides a brief survey of perfection as presented by Fénelon, Wesley, and Evelyn Underhill. Unfortunately for our purposes, she makes almost no comparisons. In fact, her statement (p. 76) that Wesley and Fénelon meet in Wesley's changing view of full assurance (as if this were the only point of contact) is misleading.

praying without ceasing (Fénelon strongly encouraged prayer and the frequent recollection of the presence of God),[64] and in everything giving thanks.[65] In the Journal for June 27, 1769, he defined perfection as "loving God with all our heart . . . a heart and life all devoted to God . . . having all the mind that was in Christ . . . walking uniformly as Christ walked." For Wesley these properties were the inseparable fruit of perfect love. The letters by Fénelon in *The Christian Library* speak of love in a similar way: "This love requires nothing of us, but to do for the sake of God"; and even good works (*if* they are practiced) must be done "from a principle of love to God," not for honor or regard for oneself.[66] Inge traces the origin of this love through Fénelon's mystical "path to God." The illuminative stage, for example, requires one to concentrate all of one's faculties (one's will, one's intellect, and one's feeling) on God. Good works may continue but as fruits rather than virtues.[67]

Furthermore, Fénelon insists that when this love of God is perfect in us, it draws off our "inordinate affections" (an expression frequently used by Wesley) and gives us peace.[68] Consequently, this love sweetens our afflictions and evens our temper.[69] This awareness of God's presence (shades of Brother Lawrence), even amongst the trials of everyday living, was important to Wesley and his societies. Methodists needed a practical experience of God which would apply to ordinary people, and Wesley was constantly searching for appropriate illustrations of such an experience. Fénelon met that need. He states further, "[God] maintains his love in your soul, while you are surrounded with whatever tends to extinguish it . . . O how rich and powerful is a heart amidst adversities, when it carries this treasure within it."[70]

Similarly, Wesley speaks of perfection as a "constant communion with God and a heart filled with love."[71] Furthermore, Wesley believed that the force behind Fénelon's practice of the presence of God was the

---

[64]*Library*, 38:12.

[65]*Works*, 11:441f.

[66]*Library*, 38:6.

[67]Inge, *Mysticism*, 13. In the *Dissertation on Pure Love* (London, 1735) Fénelon states that Pure Love considers "the universal lump of mankind as one great family" and that it prefers the good of the whole to one's own particular interest (p. 2).

[68]*Library*, 38:7.

[69]Ibid.

[70]Ibid., 38:11. Cf. Wyon's section (*Desire for God*, p. 42) on "Holy Worldliness" where she reiterates Fénelon's ideal of Christian perfection, realized amidst conditions most alien to it. Cf. also Brother Lawrence (from whom Fénelon frequently quoted in his *Defenses*), *Practicing the Presence of God*.

[71]*Journal*, 4:367–70. Several testimonies of such are provided here.

love of God, having no other will but God's, and loving what Christ loved: poverty, humiliation, and sufferings.[72] The primary ingredient, therefore, was total resignation, or what Fénelon referred to as "disinterested love." In *Pious Reflections* he writes, "We cannot become good, but in the measure we become humble, disinterested, and free from self-love, so as to ascribe all to God, without arrogating anything to ourselves."[73] Inge claims that as a guide to purification the mystics are unanimous on disinterested love.[74] Although Fénelon was greatly misunderstood with regard to this term (his *Maxims of the Saints* was an attempt to determine and clarify the limits of true and false mysticism concerning the doctrine of disinterested love and passive contemplation) and although Wesley recognized the dangers of its extremes (to the place where salvation itself becomes unimportant),[75] he did not hesitate to use the term himself. On January 4, 1749, Wesley's description of a Christian underscores the humble abasement so important to the mystical scheme. Then he writes, "Above all, remember that God is love" and that the Christian's love "is in itself generous and disinterested; springing from no view of advantage to himself, from no regard or praise—no, nor even the pleasure of loving."[76]

One additional word regarding Fénelon's influence needs to be noted. As mentioned in the discussion on perseverance, although Wesley interpreted the experience of entire sanctification as instantaneous (that being the work of God to be received by faith as in the moment of justification), clearly a *process* both precedes and follows that "moment of grace." Like Macarius, Fénelon's understanding of "dynamic perfection" contributes significantly at this point, but as much by way of contrast as by comparison.

Although Wesley is by no means clear as to the process of perfection, one can tell, by comparing the extract from Fénelon with the original, that at least some differences of opinion occurred. Although Wesley agrees with Fénelon that perfection is never really absolute— that is, it is constantly improvable and can be lost at any moment or at

---

[72]*Library,* 38:65f.

[73]Ibid., 68.

[74]Inge, *Mysticism,* 13. This is his fourth mystical proposition. Cf. *Theologia Germanica* on disinterested love.

[75]Cf. Lavington, *Enthusiasm Compared,* 1, 35. (London, 2d ed., 1749–51, 3 vols.). Lavington cites the words of the dying man in Georgia (*Journal,* 1:226ff.) as an example of disinterested love: "I 'care not where I go, God put me where he will but set forth his honour and glory.' "

[76]*Letters,* 2:376f.

any level—he still apparently holds on to the idea that the actual experience of sanctification, like justification, is (or at least can be) instantaneous. Like most mystics both Fénelon and Wesley see personality as both and neither the "shifting *moi*" and/or the "ideal self." Wesley would agree with Fénelon's concept of the *moi progressus ad infinitum* to the *ideal*.[77]

It has already been established that this dynamic ideal is paramount to perseverance. Yet, Wesley takes special care to eliminate from *The Christian Library* any idea of growing *into* perfection. Perhaps Olive Wyon's quotation from Wesley provides the key: "You don't *grow into* it: you are *born into* it, and you *grow in* it."[78] Although Wesley is a little ambivalent, it is fairly easy to see that he is transferring to sanctification his concept of grace as applied to justification. With this in mind, it is interesting to study his omissions from the original (*Devotional Tracts*, especially "Of the Good Use of Crosses"). He omits Fénelon's denial of instant perfection on several occasions.[79] Wesley insists that one can grow *in* prevenient, justifying, or sanctifying grace but only *after* being *born into* it. The following comparative passage illustrates Wesley's reaction to Fénelon on this point:

> *By such a series of events,* which all appear natural, *he makes us die* to sin leisurely and by degrees. *We would gladly be consumed all at once, to escape the lingering sufferings of a* long and *tedious mortification*; [:] and we desire immediate perfection only from an excess of self-love. 'Tis, I say, *self-love makes us murmur at the length of our sufferings; and that is the very thing which God would destroy, for while it lasts, his work cannot be perfected.*[80]

Further along he writes, *"God prepares a train of events, which . . .* at last *weans us from self-love."*[81] Two facts emerge from the comparative study of this passage. First, although Wesley views perfection as dynamic, he still holds to the "miracle of grace" acting in a moment. Second, some struggle for years in the varying degrees of grace, but it is possible to be sanctified in a moment, and one should come to expect it and anticipate it. Wesley and Fénelon agree on the principle of perfection and the necessity of growth in perfection, yet Wesley discards Fénelon's

---

[77] Cf. *Letters*, 4:188f.; Todd, *Catholic Church*, 107; Inge, *Mysticism*, 12.

[78] Wyon, *Desire for God*, 67.

[79] Fénelon, *Devotional Tracts*, 161f.

[80] Fénelon, Ibid., 162f.; *Library*, 38:68f.

[81] Ibid. Again, the original text is in quotations while the extract is italicized and in brackets.

description of the slow, painful process (which Fénelon calls the "obscurity of faith")[82] necessary to attain perfection. Our hypothesis is once more supported when one realizes that it is again (as with justification) the problem of mystical (and therefore the struggle is again transferred to the inner life) works-righteousness. For Wesley, one was not only justified by grace through faith, but sanctified as well.

ON PRAYER

Another area where the mystics influenced Wesley (especially after the period of readjustment) concerns his doctrine of prayer. Wesley's concept of prayer as influenced by the mystics cannot be limited to the ejaculations discussed earlier and practiced so religiously by Wesley and the English mystics. This section deals more with the aspects of prayer in Wesley's experience which have areas in common with the more advanced stages of mystical prayer.

Early in his ministry (before 1738), Wesley encouraged prayer as a means of grace to be exercised at all levels of the Christian experience. Similarly, he criticized the mystics for disparaging prayer and the other means of grace. After 1764, however, he seems to view prayer more along the mystical lines as a *disposition of the heart,* questioning, for example, the wisdom of teaching the children of Kingswood to pray since prayer, like rejoicing, is from the heart.[83] Although between 1738 and 1764 Wesley strongly objected to the mystical use of prayer as a means of producing faith, after 1764 (even more than before 1738), he emphasizes prayer more and more in this mystical sense as a continuous state of mind. Wesley singles out Lopez and Brother Lawrence in particular for their practice of prayer as an uninterrupted communion— the practical result of praying without ceasing.[84] Although between 1738 and 1764 Wesley criticized the mystical approach to prayer as being too general and lax, he now begins to see prayer not just as an occasional communication with God, but as a disposition of mind and heart that involves all of our thoughts and actions.[85]

On October 16, 1771, Wesley writes, "A continual desire is a

[82] Ibid. The same idea is omitted from the works of Brother Lawrence. Cf. Fénelon, *Devotional Tracts* (1724), p. 46 with *Library,* 38:27. Wesley omits Lawrence's statement that perfection necessarily implies long and tedious diligence.

[83] *Letters,* 6:39; cf. *Sermons,* 1:430f.; *Letters,* 6:44.

[84] *Letters,* 5:283, 326. Remember Lopez's prayer "Thy will be done," which he uttered continually for three years.

[85] *Letters,* 1:208; cf. 7:375, 378f.

continual prayer." He goes on to say that there is also "a far higher sense, such an open intercourse with God, such a close, uninterrupted communion with Him, as Gregory Lopez experienced. . . ."[86] Wesley, even now, strongly discouraged the practice of wordless contemplation and mental prayer, but the mystics obviously influenced his emphasis on private prayer and silent (but systematic) meditation.[87] Dunn Wilson's implication that Wesley adopted the mystical "prayer of repose" is an interesting theory, but, unfortunately, this cannot be documented by the evidence which he provides.[88] As is evidenced by the extracts, Wesley systematically avoids references to contemplation and mental prayer, and likewise there is little or no evidence in Wesley's *Works* to suggest that he practiced this highest level of mystical prayer. Yet this still does not deny the influence on Wesley of the mystics as men and women of prayer and deep devotion.

Again on August 31, 1772, Wesley commends both de Renty and Lopez for their constant communion with God, the former while serving the poor, and the latter while writing. Furthermore, the mystics frequently appear as the standard of measurement to which the Methodists' communion with God is compared: Ralph Mather had as much grace as Lopez; Fletcher, as much as de Renty and Lopez; and Jane Bisson exceeded Madame Guyon.[89]

Fénelon's little tract on the words "Lord, teach us to pray" (Luke 11:1) illustrates the connection between prayer and disinterest. He writes, "I know what I should ask . . . O Lord, give to me, thy child, what is proper, whatever it may be: I dare not ask either crosses or comforts: I only present myself before Thee: I open my heart to Thee . . . Smite or heal; depress me, or raise me up: I adore all Thy purposes, without knowing them: I am silent, I offer myself in sacrifice."[90] Wesley's attitude relative to prayer and disinterest is comparable. He

---

[86] Ibid., 5:283. Wilson, "Influence of Mysticism," 308, interprets this as *ecstatic*; but, in light of the letter for August 31, 1772 (5:338), for example, where Lopez's sense and understanding are not suspended, this is highly unlikely.

[87] Cf. *Letters*, 3:229; 4:90, 100f., 103; 5:326; 6:44 (against mental prayer); *Sermons*, 1:429; *Works*, 8:322.

[88] Wilson, ("Influence of Mysticism," 293–314) cites *Works*, 11:379, 436; *Notes on the NT*, 1 Thess. 5:17; and several hymns as evidence. But this is far from conclusive. Wilson's assertion that Wesley practiced stages of mystical prayer has simply noted a development in Wesley's concept of prayer which deepened over the years. Cf. Wesley on prayer pre-1738, 1738–1764, and post-1764.

[89] *Letters*, 6:67; *Works*, 11:273ff.; and *Letters*, 8:18. Wesley reacts against Guyon's "prayer of quiet."

[90] *Library*, 38:67.

writes, "Any temporal view, any motive whatever on this side of eternity and any design but that of promoting the glory of God . . . makes every action . . . an abomination unto the Lord."[91]

To conclude this section, it is interesting to note that Wesley's *Collection of Prayers for Each Day of the Week* follows closely the earlier stages of the mystical scheme, especially as it is presented in the Preface to this collection.[92]

ON SIMPLICITY

Our hypothesis can be reiterated not only in Wesley's increased appreciation of the mystic gold, but also in the fact that he continues to have little sympathy for the main tenets previously established as mystic dross. Wesley's criticism of this dross at this time can be fairly well characterized by the discussion of his recurring theme of *simplicity* over and against the philosophical *refinement* of religion.[93]

Fénelon's treatise *On Simplicity* was read by Wesley while he was still at Oxford. Although Wesley criticizes the mystics in general for complicating the gospel with a mixture of philosophy and religion, he nonetheless admired Fénelon's emphasis on the simple purity of love. For both Wesley and Fénelon, pure love was lovely, simple, and patient. Wesley's own sentiments are expressed in Fénelon's words: "Seek Him in your heart with the simplicity of a child."[94] Wesley frequently uses the identical phrase! Furthermore, Wesley was not only attracted to this simplicity for its effect on Methodists, but he also used it as an argument against so much mystical dross.

Wesley, like Fénelon, also believed that life was brief, "an arrow passing through the air."[95] Fénelon writes (again with words similar to Wesley's), "Yet a few moments, yet (I say) a little while, and all will be finished. Alas! that which now appears long and tedious to us, because it is mournful, will seem short when it is over."[96] One can imagine the appeal of this message to a nation of "unfortunates." Wesley assured his

---

[91] *Sermons*, 1:429.

[92] *Works*, 11:203–72; the Preface to the sixth edition (1775) appears in 14:270–72. There is a great deal of emphasis on self-examination (p. 206); humility (p. 216); mortification (pp. 221, 230); and resignation (p. 225).

[93] Cf. *Letters*, 5:142, 187f.

[94] *Library*, 38:11; cf. p. 69. Wilson, "Influence of Mysticism," 169f., sees Wesley's attachment to Fénelon's simplicity as one of the most remarkable aspects of his influence.

[95] *Sermons*, 1:Preface.

[96] *Library*, 38:71.

listeners that their suffering was but for a short duration in comparison with eternity. They were to put their crosses to good use that eternity might be even brighter.[97] On October 23, 1772, Wesley writes that those at Bristol "have been in danger of being a little hurt by reading those that are called mystic authors. These (Madame Guyon in particular) have abundance of excellent sayings. They have many fine and elegant observations; but in the meantime they are immeasurably wise above that is written. They continually *refine* upon plain Christianity."[98] Wesley's soul is apparently still "sick of sublime divinity."[99]

Two days later Wesley again exhorts his reader not to refine upon plain religion that "is only humble, gentle, patient love."[100] He writes:

> You cannot imagine what trouble I have had for many years to prevent our friends from *refining*. . . . Therefore I have industriously guarded them from meddling with the mystic writers . . . these are the most artful refiners of it that ever appeared in the Christian world, and the most bewitching. There is something like enchantment in them. When you get into them, you know not how to get out.[101]

Wesley is undoubtedly speaking from personal experience. Again on December 5, 1772, he associates this refinement with the "insensible degrees" by which the mystics were led "to value extraordinary gifts more than the ordinary grace of God." He insists that "by this very thing Satan beguiled them from the simplicity that is in Christ."[102]

Wesley's continual emphasis on simplicity during this period also manifests itself in his renewed objection to mystic solitude. One letter is of particular interest. On November 30, 1774, he writes, "In every age and country Satan has whispered to those who began to taste the powers of the world to come (as well as to Gregory Lopez) 'Au désert!' Au désert!" Wesley again uses the mystics against themselves as he encourages his reader to hold to the simplicity found in Fénelon: "that

---

[97] Ibid., 67ff; cf. Wyon (*Desire for God,* 40) states that suffering for Fénelon was not a problem but a fact to be recognized, faced, and accepted.

[98] Guyon's *Life* had just been translated by a Quaker, James Gough, and published in Bristol. Incidentally, Gough seems prejudiced against Catholicism. Cf. the translator's note (p. 36, original) "of the gross abuse of language among the Papists" omitted by Wesley.

[99] Cf. *Journal,* 2:328.

[100] *Letters,* 5:341.

[101] Ibid., 342.

[102] Ibid., 349; in this same letter Wesley states that his caution against the mystics at this time arose from the excesses in London (George Bell, etc.; cf. John Wesley's *Journal,* 3:265; 4:94; and Charles Wesley's *Journal,* 1:429) that exaggerated the extraordinary revelations and manifestations.

grace 'whereby the soul casts off all unnecessary reflections upon itself.'"
He then quotes the following lines first written to Sally Kirkham during
his Oxford days:[103]

> In art, in nature, can we find
>   Colours to picture thee?
> Speak, Cambray's pen, for Sally's mind;
>   She is simplicity.

Related to his rejection of solitude is the fact that Wesley was also
interested in what might be called the psychological as well as the
spiritual effects of mysticism. His concern for a balanced yet wholehearted devotion to God prompted many exhortations which modern
psychiatry would label "good therapy." He emphasized, for example, the
need for personal relationships involving an open and honest sharing of
one's inmost problems.[104] He writes to Ann Loxdale that Lopez's
"horrid temptations" were due to his desert experience,[105] and urges her
to speak to him "without reserve."[106]

An interesting example of mysticism gone wrong can be seen in the
case of Ralph Mather. On January 13, 1774, Wesley states that Mather
has as much grace as Lopez, and goes so far as to say, "When I talk with
Ralph Mather, I am amazed and almost discouraged. What have I been
doing for seventy years!"[107] Then, just over two weeks later he notes in
his Journal that Mather is "a devoted young man, but almost driven out
of his senses by mystic divinity."[108] The danger of mysticism is
reiterated the following year in Wesley's judgment of the *Life of Mr.
Marsay*. Marsay is described as a man of "uncommon understanding"
and greatly devoted to God but unfortunately "a consummate enthusiast" who mistook his own imagination for divine inspirations. Wesley
adds, "I do not know that ever I read a more dangerous writer; one who
so wonderfully blends together truth and falsehood, solid piety and wild
enthusiasm."[109]

---

[103]*Letters*, 6:128; Wesley sent Sally a copy of Fénelon's *On Simplicity*.
[104]Cf. *Letters*, 3:220f.; 6:94f.; 7:53f.; 7:196ff.; 8:158.
[105]Ibid., 7:198.
[106]Ibid., cf. 6:280.
[107]Ibid., 6:68.
[108]*Journal*, 6:10.
[109]Ibid., 6:202f.; cf. 6:71; Vaughan's *Hours With the Mystics*, 2:391; and Overton's *Life
of Law*, 93.

ON SOCIAL JUSTICE: THE INEVITABLE FRUIT

At this point a "mysticism of service" finds its focus. Perhaps illustrations from the extract of the life of de Renty (although Lopez and others would serve as well) is the best example of just what this means. As mentioned in chapter 4, Gaston Jean Baptiste de Renty was a wealthy nobleman of France and counselor to Louis XIII. From Wesley's extract of de Renty's life we read that "during the war at Paris, he went 'himself to buy bread for the poor and carried through the streets as much as his strength would permit. . . .' "[110] Remember that de Renty was in frequent communication with Vincent de Paul. De Renty not only cooperated with de Paul in works of charity but on occasion directed the saint's special attention to them. De Renty, "a worthy co-labourer" animated with the same spirit, was always sensitive to those in need and was actually the one who brought to de Paul's attention the relief of the refugee nobility of Lorraine and the relief of the Catholic *and* Protestant refugees from England (those loyal to Charles I).

Wesley also mentions the fact that de Renty examined his faults twice daily and communicated three and four times a week (proof enough that *all* mystics do not despise the means of grace, at least in the initial stages). He then adds that de Renty had "an incredible esteem of the holy Eucharist," but he carefully omits de Renty's popish practice of confession. De Renty's works of charity still receive top billing: "One day in a week he visited the poor sick people of the great hospital *de Dieu*: another those of his own parish; a third the prisoners; and in the rest he used to meet at assemblies of piety."[111]

De Renty was a pattern of what St. Paul calls the "love of neighbor flowing from the love of God."[112] Several similarities can be noted between de Renty and Wesley with reference to this love manifesting itself in works of charity. Both attended to the needs of the poor.[113] De Renty frequently had the poor in to dine as did Wesley at the Foundery.[114] Both lived economically in order to give to the poor. Both visited the sick and took a considerable interest in the medical arts. Both

---

[110]*Extract,* 10.

[111]Ibid., 3.

[112]*Letters,* 5:268.

[113]Ibid. 10. Cf. *The Life of the Baron de Renty or, Perfection in the World Exemplified* (London: Burns and Oates, 1873), 197ff.

[114]Wesley refers to this practice at the Foundery as "a comfortable earnest of our eating bread together in our Father's Kingdom."

spent a great deal of time ministering to the imprisoned; de Renty assisted English prisoners captured during Buckingham's expedition to Rochelle, and Wesley ministered to French prisoners captured during the Seven Years' War. He undoubtedly interested Wesley in the *practical effects* of the mystical life with God which combined an "internal evidence firm and unshaken" with an external life of constant service. The following passage on "his application to our Lord Jesus Christ, in regard of his neighbor" contains many of the characteristics later to appear in Wesley's doctrine of perfection.

> We have observed in the first part of this history, that [*T*] *the grand exercise of M. Renty was, to apply and unite himself to our Saviour, and from that union, and his example, to derive all his vertues and good works:* [*.*] This was the general course he held in them all, [*T*] *to mould himself after him [was his general course, both in his inward tempers and outward behaviour. He]* for the composition of his external and internal, *never* taking [*took*] *his eyes off this divine copy, but endeavour*ing [*ed*] *to draw* each [*every*] *line exactly,* and [*to*] *pencil his true* lineaments [*likeness*], making [*and make*] *him his native and perfect original.*"[115]

This well describes a *mysticism of service.*

In his sermon *Marks of the New Birth,* Wesley writes, "An immediate and constant fruit of this faith whereby we are born of God, a fruit which can in no wise be separated from it, no, not for an hour, is the power over sins;—power over outward sin of every kind; over every evil word and work. . . ."[116] Although Wesley was more of an evangelist than a social reformer, his message of personal salvation to the disenchanted masses of the eighteenth century resulted in a social conscience as well. For Wesley, conversion transcended both wealth and poverty by placing all persons in the same class: the saved. The effect of this was (at least within the Methodist societies) that none had too much and none had too little. I've always been intrigued with this letter written to John Wesley and included in his Journal:

> Sir, I was yesterday led to hear what God would say to me by your mouth. You exhorted us to "strive to enter at the straight gate." I am willing so to do. But I find one chief part of my striving must be, to feed the hungry, to clothe the naked, to instruct the ignorant, to visit the sick and such as are in prison, bound in misery and iron.

---

[115]*Original,* 117f.; *Extract,* 36.
[116]*Works,* 5:214.

But if you purge out all who scorn such practices, or at least are found
in them, how many will remain in your society? I fear scarce enough
to carry your body to the grave! Alas, how many, even among those
who are called believers, have plenty of all the necessities of life, and
yet complain of poverty! How many have houses and lands, or bags of
money, and yet cannot find in their hearts to spare now and then to
God's poor a little piece of gold! How many have linen in plenty, with
three or four suits of clothes, and can see the poor go naked! They will
change them away for painted clay, or let the moths devour them,
before they will give them to cover the nakedness of their poor
brethren, many of whose souls are clothed with glorious robes,
though their bodies are covered with rags. Pray, Sir, tell these, you
cannot believe they are Christians, unless they imitate Christ in doing
good to all men, and hate covetousness, which is idolatry.[117]

And Wesley answers, "I do tell them so: And I tell them it will be more
tolerable in the day of judgment for Sodom and Gormorrah than for
them."[118]

Although early Methodism was not exclusively a movement of the
poor, most Methodists lived among the lower order of the laboring
class. As pointed out by Tom Albin:

Theologically, Methodism under the leadership of the Wesley
brothers maintained a stress on the importance of the inner life, and at
the same time insisted that an authentic spiritual life must find
practical expression in outward actions to benefit the poor and needy.
Methodism stood over against the more contemplative way of other
mystic and quietist options available during this period. And in
contrast to the deistic and Trinitarian controversies that ravaged
Dissent, for the most part Methodism was able to keep speculative
theology subservient to the larger issues of love, obedience and
humble service. In short, the Methodist Societies functioned like a lay
religious order which enabled men and women to work out their own
salvation, and at the same time maintain a socially redemptive
involvement with the poor and vulnerable around them.[119]

John Wesley wrote repeatedly that " 'faith working by love' is the
length and breadth and depth and height of Christian perfection. This
commandment we have from Christ, that the one who loves God loves
one's brother or sister also and that we manifest our love by doing good

---

[117]*Works*, 3:305.

[118]Ibid.

[119]Albin, "Early Methodism and the Poor," American Academy of Religion Lecture,
November 1988.

unto all people." For Wesley, conversion was two-sided—indeed, a *full* gospel. Religious zeal and social enthusiasm went hand in hand as inseparable, indivisible, "until Christ can be proved the fool and Scriptures a lie."

Wesley, taking his cue from de Renty, Fénelon, Lopez, and others, saw love as the motivation for social justice. Quite simply, for Wesley to know that God loved us is to love ourselves; to love ourselves is to love our neighbor. Love of neighbor is an imperative among all the mystics whom Wesley abridged. The bottom line on being a Christian was charity.

So although Wesley rules out the example of the mystics for those whose temperament did not require it or whose disposition could not absorb the gold without the dross, he continues to recommend and publish the Roman Catholic mystics throughout the rest of his life.[120] Admittedly, Wesley generally recommended *only* what he had edited personally, but the fact remains that the influence of the mystical gold and his distaste for the mystical dross are both undeniable.[121]

The closing years of Wesley's life are filled with the thoughts of a man who pauses on occasion to allow his mind to run back over the years, but who nonetheless marches on tirelessly and still within the sphere of the mystic influence.[122] Wesley, advanced in years, continued with remarkable regularity to peel away the mystical dross from the gold in order to improve one of his most effective tools, which he readily applied whenever the occasion arose.[123] Admittedly, much of this gold was not necessarily unique to mysticism alone, but the fact remains that the mystics in particular were most frequently used to illustrate the need for discipline and personal holiness. Although one of his strongest statements yet against mysticism was published in 1780 in his attack on Jacob Behmen,[124] Wesley continues at the same time to cite the example of mystics like de Renty and Lopez until the very end.[125]

---

[120]Cf., for example, *Letters,* 6:222f., 270 (de Renty's "experimental verity" or 7:379 where Wesley requests a copy of Guyon's *Life* to be sent to a friend who had just lost her books by fire. Cf. also *Journal,* 5:382f.

[121]Cf. *Letters,* 6:125; Wesley recommends only "what we have published."

[122]Ibid., 232f., 292f. Wesley recalls his mystical days at Oxford.

[123]Cf. Ibid., 373, 381 (de Renty on the efficacy of suffering); 7:143 (de Renty's "experimental verity"), etc.

[124]Wesley's "Thoughts on Behmen" (1780) *Works,* 14:509–18.

[125]*Letters,* 8:253. Less than two months before his death Wesley writes to Adam Clarke concerning the death of his child, "How did Mr. de Renty behave when he supposed his wife to be dying? This is a pattern for a Christian."

It is also interesting to note that with the reappearance of the Diary (which is missing for the period August 9, 1741, to December 1, 1782) one can readily see that Wesley's rules for holy living continued to form (in the words of Nehemiah Curnock) "the substratum of Wesley's daily devotional life, and kept him, as originally they made him, the most useful saint in the British Empire."[126] In addition to his early rising and constant prayer, à Kempis reappears within six pages after the Diary is resumed.[127] There can be little doubt that the mystic influence relative to the pattern and content of his quest for holiness enabled Wesley to tap the reservoir of divine power which sustained him throughout his life as an evangelist extraordinaire.

Although there are many more abiding influences that could be rightfully attributed to the mystics, time and space insist that we move on to the contemporary scene since so much of what John Wesley gleaned from his experience with the mystics is important (perhaps even more important) for today. The contemporary scene demands a relevant word.

---

[126]*Journal*, 6:370.
[127]Ibid, 386.

7

ISSUES RELEVANT TO THE CONTEMPORARY SCENE

Some would argue that it is a quantum leap from the eighteenth century to the present. Not so, at least with regard to the issues pertaining to mysticism. In fact, the issues here are perhaps even more relevant to the contemporary scene than they were to Wesley's day. To unravel Wesley's ambivalence caused by strengths in the mystical ethic and weaknesses in mystic theology teaches us much about certain mystical strengths and weaknesses today. After sorting through a number of theological implications to use as guidelines, we will examine some of the gold and dross on the present scene. For example, the gold of a "right-brain" awareness will be contrasted with the dross of a "pop" or "new age" mysticism that is leading many astray. Then, remembering Wesley's own struggle, we will conclude our study with an exhortation to press our noses against the "glass darkly" in order to catch a glimpse of a God present and a God at work.

THEOLOGICAL IMPLICATIONS:
A RADICAL MONOTHEISM

Genesis 1:1 reads, "In the beginning God created the heavens and the earth." Deuteronomy 4:39 follows up on that: "Acknowledge and take to heart this day that the Lord is God in heaven above and on the earth below. There is no other."[1] These two passages might seem self-

---

[1] Cf. Deuteronomy 4:35: "You were shown these things so that you might know that the Lord is God; besides him there is no other."

evident, but where mysticism is concerned the concepts affirmed here are crucial. Let me explain.

A Tendency Toward Dualism Among Some Mystics

Those within the Judeo/Christian tradition have strongly resisted the notion of multiple gods since at least the time of Abraham. The early Hebrew concept of creation acknowledges only one God who not only dwells in "heaven above" but who creates the "earth below." Humankind, for example, was created body, mind, and spirit in God's own image. Obviously, to be created in God's image relates to God's moral or immanent attributes (those remaining within, such as love and obedience), not to God's natural or relative attributes relating to God's deity or to God's ommipotence, omniscience, and ommipresence. We are clearly not "omni" anything. Yet the same God whose presence dwells within us is the creator God, and all of creation is subsequently good. Some, however, would attempt to alter that view.

As early as the fourth century B.C., Greek philosophers began to slip in among the Israelites when there was no longer a prophet to direct the nation. Contrary to the Hebrew understanding, Greeks introduced a form of platonism (later refined by the Gnostics and the third-century A.D. philosopher Plotinus) that had a view of creation or matter as basically evil. Since the "One" God is good and could not associate with evil, let alone create it, a lower deity or evil *demiurge* was surmised as responsible for creation.[2] This *demiurge* supposedly created the flesh and the world we live in and created them *evil*.[3] Body, mind, and spirit as God's good creation within Hebrew culture were replaced by body and soul. A graph of the two approaches would look something like that on page 169.

Again, the Hebrew concept depicts the One good God as creator and sustainer but not as an essential part of who we are as created beings. Creator and created are forever distinct. Although created in God's image we are good but we are not God.

The Greek *schema* envisions humankind in terms of evil flesh (body) and the good God (Soul) who dwells within, not as a separate entity but as an essential part of who we are. Salvation, therefore, is not to redeem

---

[2]*Demiurge* is from the Greek *démiourgos* and is used positively in the New Testament (Heb. 11:10) to refer to God's creative activity, but came to be used in a derogatory sense by the Greeks.

[3]Contrast the words from 1 Timothy 4:4: "Everything God created is good, and nothing is to be rejected if it is received with thanksgiving."

a good but fallen image but to deny the flesh and the world as evil, to come out of the flesh and the world by mortification and self-denial, to let the flesh and the world (as it were) go hang, that by contemplating the Divine Spark within we can be absorbed into some kind of a Divine Blob. Now we begin to understand some of the roots of the mystical philosophy that strongly influenced Wesley but that he just as strongly rejected.

EARLY HEBREW CONCEPT

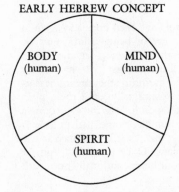

Humankind created by the *One* God (body, mind, & spirit) in God's own image and whose Spirit dwells within us but *not* as an essential part of who we are.

THE GREEK CONCEPT

Humankind whose body is created by a lesser deity (*demiurge*) and evil. The Soul is the contrasting divine Spirit as an essential part of who we are.

In the early church, aspects of this heresy surfaced in the form of a belief system called Gnosticism. The Gnostics, in a similar way, even applied this type of dualism to Christianity, perhaps most crucially related to the person of Jesus Christ. Since Christian doctrine insists that Jesus Christ was fully God *and* fully man, the Gnostics, naturally, denied his humanity. Because (remember the Greek *schema*) flesh is evil, the divine Christ could not possibly participate. He only appeared to be human. In fact, he only appeared to die. Added to this "knowledge" (the Greek *gnosis*) were the so-called "secrets," which were revealed only to the Gnostics by intermediary spirits or angels who led them beyond the Scriptures and apostolic teaching to a "new and better way." Predictably, Paul (cf. Colossians 3, 1 Timothy, and Titus), Peter (cf. 1 and 2 Peter), John (cf. 1 and 2 John), and Jude all warn strongly against the Gnostic heresy. Paul writes, for example, "See to it that no one takes you captive through hollow and deceptive philosophy, which depends on human tradition and the basic principles of this world rather than on Christ" (Col. 2:8). Again, "Do not let anyone who delights in false humility and the worship of angels disqualify you for the prize" (Col. 2:18).

Church apologists have had to combat various forms of Gnosticism throughout the centuries. Once Wesley, for example, fully understood the principles of justification by faith, the Gnostic tendencies in mysticism aroused his ridicule as well as his rejection. In 1772 he writes to Penelope Newman:

> In one point only our friends at Bristol have been once and again in some danger. They have been in danger of being a little hurt by reading those that are called Mystic authors. These (Madame Guyon in particular) have abundance of excellent sayings. They have many fine and elegant observations; but in the meantime they are immeasurably wise above that is written. They continually *refine* upon plain Christianity. But to *refine* religion is to spoil it. It is the most simple thing that can be conceived: it is only humble, gentle, patient love. It is nothing less and nothing more than this; as it is described in the 13th chapter of the [First] Corinthians. O keep to this! Aim at nothing higher, at nothing else! Let your heart continually burn with humble love.[4]

For John Wesley, God was one God as Creator, Redeemer, and Sustainer. Absolutely essential to Wesley's theology is the idea that creation is of God and that in spite of its lost image all of creation can be restored to its original righteousness (epitomized by humble love) by the power of the Holy Spirit.

Again, Wesley's rejection of the mystic dross continues to react against much of this same teaching. He writes, "My soul is sick of sublime divinity. Let *me* think and speak as a little child! Let *my* religion be plain, artless, simple."[5] For Wesley, God is *one* God and the plan of salvation for all humankind could be understood only in terms of good news/bad news/good news. We were created by God in God's own image only to lose that image through sin (good news/bad news). The ultimate good news is that God is in Jesus Christ reconciling or restoring us and the world to our created image. Salvation for us is not simply imitating Christ by contemplating some Divine Spark within. God was in Jesus Christ (fully God and fully human) that we might have life abundant through faith in him. In other words, God made it, we

---

[4] Wesley's *Works*, 13:165-66.
[5] Ibid., 1:256.

corrupted it, but God wants it back just as it was intended to be. That's the gospel: one God, Creator and Redeemer of us all if we but repent and believe.

On the contemporary scene a pernicious dualism has crept in among Christians under guise of so-called Eastern spirituality. We will discuss this at some length in a moment, but for now, with the importance of a radical monotheism clearly in mind, let's look at the more positive side of contemporary mysticism.

EMBRACING A "RIGHT BRAIN" AWARENESS

For all of their potential dangers (some that will be described in the section to follow), the mystics can assist us in getting in touch with a reality beyond the material world, beyond physics, beyond the so-called senses. Mystics resent the attempts of any culture to stuff its people into the left sides of their brains (the rational or the cognitive). Our own Western world seems to suggest that if it cannot be seen or heard (or perhaps reasoned), it does not exist. The mystics remind us that there is far more reality beyond the senses than can be experienced within them. Yet we in the West order our lives as if nothing really matters beyond the veil, that *that* reality, at best, is simply unavailable to the modern mind. Right-brain awareness (the intuitive, the creative, the mystical) is rarely portrayed as important in a society that measures success in terms of pleasure and things, position and power.

The Scriptures object to this left-brain mentality. "For what is seen is temporary, but what is unseen is eternal (2 Cor. 4:18). That could just as easily read, "The only things eternal are unseen." That perhaps is one of the most basic of Christian principles among the mystics. De Renty understood it: The only way to take it with you is to give it away. Lopez understood it: The only way to be great is to be a servant. Brother Lawrence understood it: The only way to be first is to be last.

John Wesley objected to this left-brain mentality. He was continu- ally looking for evidence that would suggest the reality of an existence beyond a five-dimensional world (height, width, depth, time, and motion). Wesley went so far as to defend those who believed in apparitions, insisting

> that if but one account of the intercourse of men with separate spirits be admitted, their whole castle in the air (Deism, Atheism, and Materialism) falls to the ground. I know no reason, therefore, why we should suffer even this weapon to be wrested out of our hands. Indeed, there are numerous arguments besides, which abundantly

confute their vain imaginations. But we need not be hooted out of one: Neither reason nor religion require this.

One of the capital objections to all these accounts, which I have known urged over and over, is this: "Did you ever see an apparition yourself?" No: Nor did I ever see a murder; yet I believe there is such a thing; yea, and that in one place or another murder is committed every day. Therefore, I cannot, as a reasonable man, deny the fact; although I never saw, and perhaps never may. The testimony of unexceptional witnesses fully convinces me both of the one and the other.[6]

Mystics are still objecting to this left-brain mentality, and with good reason.

The World Says: There is a time	The Mystic Says:
To eat,	but there is hunger that bread cannot satisfy
To drink,	but there is a thirst that water cannot quench.
To lie down,	but there is tired that sleep cannot rest.
To conquer,	but there is war that the forces of this age cannot win.
To cure,	but there is hurt that the sciences cannot heal.
To loose,	but there is bondage that ideology cannot free.
To redeem,	but there is price that the blood of bulls cannot ransom.
To clothe,	but there is nakedness that rags cannot cover.
To comfort,	but there is loneliness that crowds cannot dispel.
To seek,	but there is lost that the pilgrim cannot find.
To listen,	but there is truth that the ear cannot hear.
To perceive	but there is reality that the eye cannot see.
To cry,	but there is sorrow that tears cannot relieve.
To believe,	but there is faith that reason cannot reach.
To rejoice,	but there is joy that this world cannot supply.

---

[6] Ibid., 3:325. Wesley published several accounts of eyewitnesses to such phenomena in his Journal; cf. Ibid., 3:148, 202, 258, 293, 324–35.

To live,	but there is life that the womb cannot birth.
To care,	but there is love that only God can give.

For example, my young daughter is subjected to a half-dozen, thirty-second sermons (called commercials) every time she watches a thirty-minute Saturday morning cartoon program. Each of these "sermons" attempts to convince her that she simply cannot be fulfilled without certain things. She can be. So we talk a lot about right-brain reality, just to keep pace. We both believe in God and angels, in heaven and hell, even in signs and wonders. Like the mystics, we talk a lot about a reality beyond what I sometimes refer to as the five-dimensional box.

Within the Wesleyan tradition, mystics on the contemporary scene focus on the *presence* more than the profound, more on *piety* than power. Just as Wesley was impressed with Brother Lawrence of the Resurrection who practiced the presence of God among the menial chores of a monastery kitchen, I was impressed with the peaceful countenance of Frank Laubach, the "Apostle to the Illiterates." Although I met him only once as a boy in the living room of our home, his serenity made a lasting impression; and I confess that that impression makes much more sense to me now than it did then.

In his book *Letters by a Modern Mystic* he describes his mystical beginnings:

> We used to sing a song in the church at Benton [his boyhood home in Pennsylvania] which I liked, but which I never really practiced until now. It runs:
>
> > Moment by moment, I'm kept in His love;
> > Moment by moment, I've life from above;
> > Looking to Jesus 'til glory doth shine;
> > Moment by moment, O Lord I am Thine.
>
> It is exactly that "moment by moment," every waking moment, surrender, responsiveness, obedience, sensitiveness, pliability, "lost in His love," that I now have the mind-bent to explore with all my might. It means two burning passions: First, to be like Jesus. Second, to respond to God as a violin responds to the bow of the master.[7]

Laubach then relates an experience taking place some years later as a missionary in the Philippines when attempting to love the native Moros.

---

[7] Frank Laubach, *Letters by a Modern Mystic* (New York: Student Volunteer Movement, 1937), 11.

While watching a sunset, he had a mystical encounter that led him to spend every waking moment attempting to keep his full attention upon God. Suddenly, especially where the Moros were concerned, he became "color-blind." The love was there. The following quotation records the rest of his witness:

> This concentration upon God is *strenuous,* but everything else has ceased to be so. I think more clearly, I forget less frequently. Things that I did with a strain before, I now do easily and with no effort whatever. I worry about nothing, I lose no sleep. I walk on air a good part of the time. Even the mirror reveals a new light in my eyes and face. I no longer feel in a hurry about anything. Everything goes right. Each minute I meet calmly as though it were not important. Nothing can go wrong except one thing. That is that God *may slip from my mind* if I do not keep on my guard. If He is there, the universe is with me. My task is simple and clear.[8]

Wesleyans frequently define worship in terms of this awareness of God's presence. If mysticism really can be identified, quite simply, as the direct inward experience of a divine reality, then perhaps (consistent with Brother Lawrence and Frank Laubach) all of spirituality can be understood in these terms. It is most difficult for us to sin when we are most aware of God. It is tough to disobey with God looking at us. Our problem is that we are too frequently more aware of God's creation than we are of God. That is just how sick we are. To follow up on this, just as worship acknowledges God's presence within the community gathered to celebrate the God *who is* and the God *who is there,* so true spirituality acknowledges the presence of God "moment by moment," a true mysticism within the Wesleyan tradition. This is a right-brain awareness.

With the importance of this "presence" clearly in mind, it is good to realize that there is no real mystery in Wesleyan mysticism. John Wesley was quick to affirm that God is not the divine *Concealer.* God is the divine *Revealer* who is always seeking to make the revelation known to those who have eyes to see and ears to hear. Mysticism within the Wesleyan tradition gains most from those who by "practicing the presence" acknowledge the power of the Spirit who leads into higher and higher levels of "love and obey," the essence of Christian perfection. That is not to suggest a religion for the chosen few. Mysticism within the Wesleyan tradition is a mysticism for the common people, those who move in the work place, who sit in the pews, yet who nonetheless take God seriously but who have neither time nor the temperament for

---

[8]Ibid., 24.

the secluded cloister or a place in the desert. Contrast this with the downside of a "pop" mysticism which is primarily for the initiated elite.

CAUTION AGAINST "POP" MYSTICISM:
FROM SUN MYUNG MOON TO SHIRLEY MACLAINE

In recent years a "pop" or "new age" mysticism has surfaced in the West that has some aspects of religious experience that it shares with Christianity but that is by no means totally compatible. So-called mystics within the new age movement emphasize what some have referred to as "an ultimate non-sensuous [not receptive to the physical senses] unity in all things, a oneness or a One to which neither the senses nor the reason can penetrate."[9] Whereas the awareness of a non-sensuous reality is basic to Christianity, it is the "oneness" that causes concern for us here. In the first section of this chapter, we discussed the importance of a radical monotheism. The oneness of new age mysticism, however, refers not to God as One so much as it does to God as *in* all of life. Oneness here refers more to a shared deity in or among all beings so that what you and I have in common is not that God is our Creator but that God is an essential part of who we are, and this shared deity becomes one as we successfully shed the matter that is sense-related. To the extent that we shed sense-related matter, we break the bonds or cycle of a vast universal wheel of birth, death, and rebirth. More will be said about that in a moment. For now, this new age mysticism embraces the East more than the West, supporting titles such as *Zen and the Art of Motorcycle Maintenance* and the more recent *Zen Driving*.[10] Although Christianity is not a Western phenomenon as such, new age mysticism is more consonant with a Buddhist or Hindu culture than with the

---

[9]Walter Stace, *The Teachings of the Mystics* (New York: Mentor, 1960), 14f.

[10]Robert M. Pirsig, *Zen and the Art of Motorcycle Maintenance* (New York: Morrow, 1974). Here motorcycle maintenance is merely a mental phenomenon as catalyst to inner peace. Pirsig writes, "Peace of mind isn't at all superficial to technical work. It's the whole thing. . . . The specs, the measuring instruments, the quality control, the final check-out, these are all *means* toward the end of satisfying the peace of mind of those responsible for the work. What really counts in the end is their peace of mind, nothing else" (p. 294). My comment? Interesting philosophy but incredibly shallow when confronted with the realities of life and death, not to mention heaven and hell. *Zen Driving* by Kevin and Todd Berger (Ballantine Books, 1988) exhorts its readers to cope with freeway anxiety by being a "Buddha behind the wheel" and (just to cover all the bases) placing a plastic Jesus on the dashboard. My comment? If Jesus were only plastic, this would be just the book for every Christian. Apparently, many are reading it. It sold over 40,000 copies in the first six months since publication.

teachings of Jesus and his followers. The new age self-help philosophies imply: God helps those who help themselves. Christianity insists that God helps those who cannot help themselves but who are willing to be helped by God. The contrast really goes no deeper than the *profound* difference between Law and Grace, but that's another book in itself.

For now the disciples of new age thinking speak of the "truth that is within us," which brings peace to ourselves. Several of my best students were deeply involved in new age philosophy before coming to seminary. Their description of the "hook" (that which draws us in) and the deception is sobering. For example, one of the classical new age texts is entitled *A Course in Miracles*.[11] Miracles here are defined as "the change of mind that shifts our perception from the ego's world of sin, guilt and fear to forgiveness . . . being the means of healing ourselves and others; not to be confused with the traditional understanding of miracles as changes in external phenomena."[12]

New age creates its own reality in its own way. Consensus new age insists that though we are not separate from God we are masters of our own destinies and must take full responsibility for our actions. Again, new age creates a strange mix between pantheism and humanism. Although new age philosophy insists that we are one with God, matter for new age mystics is evil ("the world, being the expression of the belief in time and space, was *not created by God*, Who transcends time and space entirely").[13] Pantheism (God is *all* things), therefore, yields to humanism. Once again, although new age thinking insists that we are one with God, as creators of our own destinies a new humanism predominates.

Meanwhile, this philosophy of oneness in new age or Eastern thought assumes (as observed earlier) that God and creation are fundamentally separate (if not opposite) but that God is an essential part of who we are as persons. Deep within all beings God dwells, hidden from the senses by the coverings of created matter (necessarily opposed to God as the emanation of a lesser deity). The bottom line seems to be this: remove the coverings and become God.[14] Walter Stace writes:

---

[11]*A Course in Miracles* (Foundation for Inner Peace, 1975); vol. 1 is the *Text* ; vol. 2 is a *Workbook*; vol. 3 is the *Manual for Teachers*. There is also a *Glossary-Index* by Kenneth Wapnick (Foundation for a Course on Miracles, 1982). Cf. *Choose Once Again*, selections from a "Course on Miracles," 1981; and *God's Way of Life*, given through (and copyrighted by) Adele Tinning, 1975.

[12]*Glossary-Index*, 115.

[13]*A Course in Miracles*, 1:367f., italics mine (the world as illusion); cf. 2:402f.

[14]According to new age, "separation from God never truly occurred," and accepting

This vast universe is a wheel. Upon it are all creatures that are subject to birth, death, and rebirth. Round and round it turns, and never stops. It is the wheel of Brahman. As long as the individual self thinks it is separate from Brahman, it revolves upon the wheel in bondage to the laws of birth, death, and rebirth. But when through the grace of Brahman it realizes its identity with him, it revolves upon the wheel no longer. It achieves immortality.[15]

This, at least in part, sets the stage for a whole host of neo- or pseudo- (if not bogus or counterfeit) mystical phenomena, some relatively harmless (if not misleading and naïve), but some extremely dangerous (if not demonic and blasphemous). Astrology, witchcraft, black magic, and Satanism, employing such devices as clairvoyance, charms, amulets, and pentagrams, come immediately to mind. Many of these start innocently enough (making them all the more dangerous). Ouija boards, tarot cards, even children's games and TV shows to many appear harmless but can stir the imagination and whet the appetite for experiences which in effect void the mind and lay us open to "principalities and powers." First Peter 5:8 warns us, "Be self-controlled and alert. Your enemy the Devil prowls around like a roaring lion looking for someone to devour."

It is interesting (curiously tragic is perhaps the better way to say it) that Geraldo Rivera can take on such issues as Satanism as (according to some) a mind-teaser to boost TV ratings (it still received bad reviews), or as a genuine concern (according to others) for an evil influence, especially among the young, while the church, for the most part, sits idly by, yielding needlessly to the "rulers of this present darkness."

For my part, I register my solemn protest. As one deeply committed to the mystical strengths, I am deeply opposed to the mystical weaknesses which open the door to the occult. Fifteen years ago Georgia Harkness in her book *Mysticism* warned us about such things on the contemporary scene.[16] More recently, Michael Green and many others have joined in sounding the alarm. Green's *I Believe in Satan's Downfall* describes the present fascination with and the biblical ban on such experiences.[17] For example, the Bible "explicitly forbids all

---

this basic principle restores to awareness "our true identity as God's Son, our Self." *Glossary*, 85.

[15] Stace, *Teachings*, 40.

[16] Georgia Harkness, *Mysticism* (Nashville: Abingdon, 1973), ch. 8 "Neo-Mysticism Today." This entire book is an excellent study of mysticism, its meaning and message.

[17] Michael Green, *I Believe in Satan's Downfall* (Grand Rapids: Eerdmans, 1981), ch. 5, "The Fascination of the Occult," and ch. 6, "Counterfeit Religion."

three main divisions of occultism: magic, fortune-telling, and spirit-ism."[18]

> When you enter the land the Lord your God is giving you, do not learn to imitate the detestable ways of the nations there. Let no one be found among you who sacrifices his son or daughter in the fire, who practices divination or sorcery, interprets omens, engages in witch-craft, or casts spells, or who is a medium or spiritist, or who consults the dead. Anyone who does these things is detestable to the Lord, and because of these detestable practices the Lord your God will drive out those nations before you (Deut. 18:9–12).

Likewise, Jesus and the New Testament authors not only acknowl-edge that for every good gift Satan has a counterfeit, but they actively oppose the demonic.[19] Their overall advice is not to place yourself under the control of that which is not from God. Furthermore, do not seek knowledge of things beyond the boundaries set by God. Do not seek power or domination over the supernatural. Know that the demonic is dangerous and ultimately destructive.[20]

Perhaps less dramatic but nonetheless just as misleading are the more mystically oriented philosophies (to mention just two) of Sun Myung Moon and Shirley MacLaine.

Sun Myung Moon's Unification Church illustrates one of the more vulnerable sides of the mystic weaknesses. Again, radical monotheism is under attack. Although creation is not the product of a Greek *demiurge,* according to their "holy book," *Divine Principle,* we are the offspring of Satan: "What were the circumstances surrounding the affair which made the descendant of the fallen angel, Satan? These circumstances are related to the fact that adultery was committed between the first human ancestors and the angel. From this act, all men came to be born of Satanic lineage, apart from God's."[21]

This attempts to mix Christian and Taoist thought. Since the first Adam failed, the second Adam also failed as demonstrated by the crucifixion (the cross in Unification theology is the symbol of Satan). The "Moonies" proclaim Sun Myung Moon as the third Adam who will

---

[18]Ibid., 121.

[19]Cf. Acts 16:16–18; 19:19; 1 Corinthians 8:4; 10:20; Revelation 9:21; 18:23; 21:8; 22:15.

[20]M. Green, *Satan's Downfall,* 123f.

[21]*Divine Principle,* 73. It is important to remember that God has no opposite. Satan may be the opposite of some archangel but is not the opposite of God. Again, God alone is God who creates and sustains.

complete the work of Christ who redeemed spiritually but not physically. From this point the movement quickly degenerates even further into hero worship and spiritism. Moon himself claims to have spoken with Jacob, Moses, and Jesus about the questions of life, the universe, and creation and that all of these subjected themselves to him. The Unification Church is just one of many cult movements, some from Christian roots and most with so-called mystical affinities. Divine Light Mission, Hare Krishna, scientology, and even Transcendental Meditation (portrayed as a harmless, non-religious means to relaxation, but is, in fact, a branch of Hinduism) are all very much alive.

Also within new age categories "est," "actualizations," and Life Spring characterize the so-called "self-help movement." Mix with this a somewhat bizarre fascination with reincarnation (a new age trademark) and the name Shirley MacLaine quickly surfaces. Her *Out on a Limb,* and *Dancing in the Light* captured the imaginations of thousands as her books remained on the best-seller lists for months. Reality for MacLaine is simply what she chooses it to be, a product of her own creation (or perhaps imagination is the better word).

The theology which best exposes this misguided (though perhaps well-meaning) philosophy has already been established. A radical monotheism denies the dualism essential for any such belief. Reincarnation builds on the Greek separation of a God whose Spirit dwells within and the God who creates matter. Once again, here, salvation demands the denial of flesh so that spirit can be free to unite (or perhaps reunite) with the Spirit of God and others or be condemned to return in another form until the cycle is broken and immortality achieved.

Christian mysticism, although vulnerable at this point, nonetheless insists on one God whose Spirit is at war with the flesh but who nonetheless can recreate in such a way as to perfect our fallen nature into an image consistent with our original righteousness.

To conclude this section with a note even more relevant to mysticism, we reiterate that an experience that does not focus on and come through Jesus Christ is dangerous. Even meditation can open us up to forces over which we have no control. At worst, we could subject ourselves to demonic influences and at best we could be caught up in an activity which is selfish and (since poverty and oppression in the physical world are illusory) does nothing for anyone else. Only mysticism within the Judeo/Christian tradition is inescapably linked with love and compassion. Again, Michael Green writes:

> A mystic approach to the impersonal "One" has absolutely no necessary link with ethics. I have no doubt whatever that spiritualism,

no less than witchcraft, can induce healings. But that does not mean we should follow these avenues. I have no doubt that meditation through yoga and Hinduism can bring tranquility. But that does not mean these paths are unexceptionable. Mysticism is very attractive. It appeals to an age which is forever restlessly activist. It is glitteringly attractive to seek power over men through spiritual exercises. It is appealing to gain an esoteric knowledge through initiation and to some mystery, particularly if it goes beyond death. But all such quests are forbidden in Scripture.[22]

Although that rather long quotation perhaps overstates the "dross," the point is well made and we have registered our complaint against the abuses of something that can be of God. We should now be prepared to conclude our study on a positive note.

WALKING OUT THE LAND

If we have learned anything from the study of John Wesley and the mystics, we have learned to sift the gold from the dross. Although we have cautioned against self-styled or non-Christian mysticism, there is much to learn from the great Christian mystics, yet (like Wesley with à Kempis and Law), we follow them only insofar as they followed Jesus.

Mysticism in the Wesleyan tradition affirms a reality beyond sense-related experience. It acknowledges God present and God at work.

God Present

Mystical dross in Wesley's day and our own tends to deny God's involvement with created matter so that first the Incarnation (God with us in human flesh) and then our ministry to the physical needs of others are in serious jeopardy. Mysticism within the Wesleyan tradition, however, not only believes that God was with us in the human Jesus but that God is with us today empowering us for ministry (body, mind, and spirit) by the Holy Spirit. Note the importance here.

No self-respecting mystic would deny the deity of Christ. Wesleyan mysticism, however, recognizes that if Jesus was also *fully* human then the ministry that he performed he performed by the Spirit, the same Spirit available to us today. Since the same Spirit available to Jesus is available to us now, the things that he did we can do: healing the sick, casting out demons, feeding the hungry, clothing the naked, and visiting the sick and imprisoned. Remember that a "mysticism of service,"

---

[22]M. Green, *Satan's Downfall*, 191.

empowered by the Spirit, so appealed to Wesley that he remained open to the mystic gold for the rest of his life.

Jesus introduces the work of the Holy Spirit in his farewell discourse (Jn. 13:31–16:33) with these words: "I tell you the truth, anyone who has faith in me will do what I have been doing. He will do even greater things than these, because I am going to the Father" (Jn. 14:12). Little wonder that Christianity takes its cue from the experience at Pentecost. In fact, there were no Christians as such prior to Pentecost. To be sure, there were men and women in right relationship with God, but none was a Christian since to be a Christian is to be baptized by the Holy Spirit into the body of Christ, the church. The God who is with us, not as an essential part of who we are but as unique and separate, nonetheless dwells within the believer as both enabler and friend.

John Wesley realized after years of struggle that although Christianity is not a Western phenomenon, neither is it, in essence, mystical. Yet he admired the mystical ethic that embraced a compassion for those who suffer, and a holiness of life consistent with the mind of Christ whose Spirit with and within, for and among, empowers and sanctifies. Now, that is a mysticism in the Wesleyan tradition!

God at Work

Mysticism within the Wesleyan tradition not only acknowledges the presence of God but God at work. God is not only *here,* God is at work with far more invested in our ministry than we have. The Holy Spirit speaks of a God present who goes out ahead of the people as a cloud by day and a pillar of fire by night. It clearly portrays a God who speaks from the burning bush and out of the holy mountain. It speaks of a God who goes into the land ahead of the nation and promises victory for those who trust in God. The "I Am" God is not only ever-present but ever at work preparing a chosen people for victory over the enemies of God. Just as God sought to prepare Israel for conquest and occupation of the land promised in the Old Testament, God in the New Testament goes out ahead of the people as the Spirit, "convincing the world of sin, of righteousness, and of judgment." The New Testament clearly portrays a God who speaks from the light on the Damascus road and out of the mountain of Transfiguration. It speaks of a God who goes into the land ahead of the church and promises victory for those who believe. The "I Am" God is not only ever-present but ever at work, preparing those called for victory over principalities and powers. Just as God sought to prepare the church for the abolishing of strongholds in the New Testament, God today goes out ahead of us and prepares those within our spheres of influence for our ministry consistent with the gifts and graces divinely appointed. To acknowledge that God at work and to participate under the leading and empowering of the Spirit are mysticism in the Wesleyan tradition. In order to increase our vision for what God can do and what we can do with God's anointing, let's retrace some of our steps relevant to the three areas just presented: God at work in the Old Testament, in the New Testament, and in the present.

God at Work in the Old Testament. The Israelites sinned in their refusal to take the land that God had promised. They were afraid. Satan would always have us overestimate the power of the enemy. Mysticism is always seeking a promise from God (there are 7,700 in the Bible) and then orders life consistent with the fulfillment of that promise. The mystic says, "If you can describe your vision, then I can predict your future, for those without a vision, consistent with the promises of God, perish."

Throughout the Old Testament God is at work as the "I Am" God. Just one Israelite with the "I Am" God was a majority—one stood against a thousand. Moses, Joshua, Deborah, David, Gideon, Samson, Daniel (to name but a few) were all aware of a power beyond them to sustain the causes of God and reject the bonds of oppression.

God at Work in the New Testament. Mysticism in the Wesleyan tradition affirms the power of the Holy Spirit available through faith in Jesus Christ. God is present, God is at work in every aspect of ministry. When Philip got to the eunuch, God was already there. When Peter got to Cornelius, God was already there. When Ananias got to Saul, God was already there, preparing the heart to receive the ministry of God's anointed.

God at Work in the Present. One of the things that concerns me most about seminary students today is that they cannot afford to embrace a ministry without God, without the anointing power that comes from God. Ultimately, power comes from God alone. Paul writes:

> For though we live in the world, we do not wage war as the world does. The weapons we fight with are not the weapons of the world. On the contrary, they have divine power to demolish strongholds. We demolish arguments and every pretension that sets itself up against the knowledge of God, and we take captive every thought to make it obedient to Christ (2 Cor. 10:3–5).

Our "wisdom" must also come from on high. The mystics can teach us to be open to God's revelation so that knowledge does not deceive us. "Knowledge puffs up, but love builds up" (1 Cor. 8:1). This brings us back to Wesley's focus on the heart of the mystic gold. The mystics loved both God and people. For Wesley, their love epitomized the heart of his doctrine of perfection. Their service epitomized Wesley's understanding of a gospel ethic that extended not only to individuals but to systems as well. The mystic gold was a formidable tool for Wesley in his attempt to abolish the bondage of sin that was manifest in individuals and society as well. Today our Wesleyan mystical heritage reminds us that the Spirit of God is still present and still at work, motivating and empowering us to "walk out the land," to anticipate a God already at work.

Perhaps John Fletcher's advice mentioned earlier best summarizes our concluding thoughts. As Christians we can learn from the errors of the mystic who "turns all into spirit," and we can learn from the errors of the philosopher who turns all into "bodies and natural phenomena." But we must then "preserve the way of truth equally distant."[23] Finally, I must pay tribute to my father, Robert Tuttle, Sr., a minister of Jesus Christ for over fifty years, who best exemplifies for me mysticism in the Wesleyan tradition. These words from his book of poems *All Heaven Broke Loose* could outlive his physical body a hundred years:

> God speaks—
>   And with a pulsing soul
> I know
>   The quenchless love behind the shadow
> Where I cannot see—
>   And feel
> The everlasting presence in
>   The sanctuary of my kneeling heart—
> And dimly see
>   The beckoning glow of that far-off distant land
> Where departed loved ones live in never shadowed light,
>   Understand new mysteries,
> And do the will of God![24]

Now that is mysticism in the Wesleyan tradition!

---

[23] Fletcher, *Works,* 388ff.

[24] Tuttle, *All Heaven Broke Loose* (Lima, Ohio: C.S.S. Pub. Co., 1986), 38.

CHARTING WESLEY'S RELATIONSHIP TO THE MYSTICAL GOLD AND THE MYSTICAL DROSS
Chart 1[1]
Before the Hypothesis is Applied

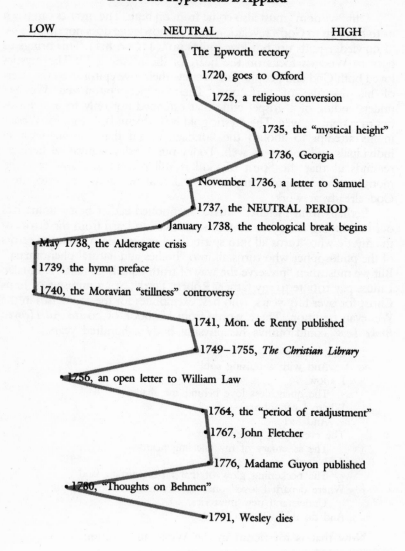

LOW   NEUTRAL   HIGH

The Epworth rectory

1720, goes to Oxford

1725, a religious conversion

1735, the "mystical height"

1736, Georgia

November 1736, a letter to Samuel

1737, the NEUTRAL PERIOD

January 1738, the theological break begins

May 1738, the Aldersgate crisis

1739, the hymn preface

1740, the Moravian "stillness" controversy

1741, Mon. de Renty published

1749–1755, *The Christian Library*

1756, an open letter to William Law

1764, the "period of readjustment"

1767, John Fletcher

1776, Madame Guyon published

1780, "Thoughts on Behmen"

1791, Wesley dies

[1]This of course is a general scheme and exceptions could be found for almost every year. These highlights, however, should serve to demonstrate the problem of judging Wesley's attitude toward the mystics.

Chart 2[1]
After the Hypothesis is Applied

LOW	NEUTRAL	HIGH

The Epworth rectory

1720, goes to Oxford

1725, a religious conversion

1735, the "mystical height"

1736, Georgia

November 1736, a letter to Samuel

1737, the NEUTRAL PERIOD

January 1738, the theological break begins

May 1738, the Aldersgate crisis

1739, the hymn preface

1740, the Moravian "stillness" controversy

1741, Mon. de Renty published

1749–1755, *The Christian Library*

1756, an open letter to William Law

1764, the "period of readjustment"

1767, John Fletcher

1776, Madame Guyon published

1780, "Thoughts on Behmen"

1791, Wesley dies

━━━ ━ ━ ━ : the mystic "gold"—Spiritual discipline, Holiness, Communion with God

▓▓▓▓▓▓▓ : the mystic "dross"—Speculative, Dark Passive, Unsocial

[1]This again is an oversimplification but it should serve to demonstrate the structure of our hypothesis at a glance.

BIBLIOGRAphy

Atkins, G. G. *Making of the Christian Mind*. Garden City, N.Y.: Doubleday, 1929.

Avila, Don Juan de. *The Spiritual Letters of Don Juan D'Avila*. Rouen, 1631.

Baker, Eric W. *Herald of the Evangelical Revival*. London: Epworth, 1948.

Bett, Henry. *The Spirit of Methodism*. London: Epworth, 1937.

Bouhours, Dominick. *Life of Ignatius Loyola*. Translated into English. London: Henry Hills, 1686.

Bourignon, Antonia. *An Admirable Treatise of Solid Virtue*. Translated from French. Published at Amsterdam by H. Wetstein, 1698.

Bouyer, P. Louis. *Du Protestantisme a L'Englise*. Paris: Editions du Cerf, 1959.

Brash, W. Bardsley. *Methodism*. London: Methuen, 1928.

Cannon, William R. *The Theology of John Wesley, With Special Reference to the Doctrine of Justification*. New York-Nashville: Abingdon-Cokesbury, 1946.

Coke, Thomas. *The Life of John Wesley*. London: printed by G. Paramore, 1792.

Cyprian. *The Writings of Cyprian* in the *Ante-Nicene Christian Library*. Edinburgh: T. and T. Clark, 1868.

Daniel-Rops, H. *The Catholic Reformation*. London: Dent, 1962.

Dimond, S. *The Psychology of the Methodist Revival*. London: Oxford University, 1926.

Edwards, Maldwyn. *John Wesley and the Eighteenth Century*. London: Epworth, 1933.

_____. *Family Circle*. London: Epworth, 1949.

Evennett, H. O. *The Spirit of the Counter-Reformation*. London: Cambridge University, 1968.

Fénelon, François de Salignac de la Mothe. *Dissertation on Pure Love*. London, 1735.

Fitchett, W. H. *Wesley and His Century*. London: Smith, Elder, 1906.

Fletcher, John. *The Works of the Rev. John Fletcher*. 9 vols. London: John Mason, 1860.

Flew, R. Newton. *The Idea of Perfection in Christian Theology*. London: Oxford University, 1934.

Foundation for Inner Peace. *A Course in Miracles*. 3 vols., 1975.

Green, Brazier. *John Wesley and William Law*. London: Epworth, 1945.

Green, Michael. *I Believe in Satan's Downfall.* Grand Rapids: Eerdmans, 1981.

Green, Richard. *The Works of John and Charles Wesley.* London: C. H. Kelly, 1896.

Green, V. H. H. *The Young Mr. Wesley.* London: Edward Arnold, 1961.

Guyon, Jeanne Marie. *Life of Lady Guion.* Bristol: printed by S. Farley, 1772.

Harkness, Georgia. *Mysticism.* Nashville: Abingdon, 1973.

Harmond, Rebecca. *Susanna, Mother of the Wesleys.* Nashville: Abingdon, 1968.

Heitzenrater, Richard P. *The Elusive Mr. Wesley.* 2 vols. Nashville : Abingdon, 1984.

Herman, Nicolas (Brother Lawrence of the Resurrection). *Abrége de la Vie . . . Maximes Spirituelles.* Paris, 1691.

Hughes, H. Trevor. *The Piety of Jeremy Taylor.* London: Moravian Publishers, 1923.

Hutton, J. E. *History of the Moravian Church.* London: Moravian Publishers, 1923.

Inge, W. R. *Christian Mysticism.* Seventh edition. London: Methuen, 1899, 1933.

————. *Studies of English Mystics.* London: John Murray, 1906.

James, William. *Varieties of Religious Experience.* New York: Longmans, Green, 1919.

Janelle, Pierre. *The Catholic Reformation.* Milwaukee: Bruce, 1949.

Jeffery, Thomas Reed. *John Wesley's Religious Quest.* New York: Vantage, 1960.

Jones, R. M. *Studies in Mystical Religion.* London: Macmillan, 1936.

————. *Flowering of Mysticism.* New York: Macmillan, 1939.

Kempis, Thomas à. *De Imitatio Christi.* Trans. by George Stanhope, 1660-1728. New Edition, 1809.

Kirk, John. *Mother of the Wesleys.* London: Jarrold and Sons, 1866.

Knowles, David. *The English Mystical Tradition.* London: Burnes and Oates, 1961.

————. *What Is Mysticism?* London: Burnes and Oates, 1966.

Knox, Ronald. *Enthusiasm.* Oxford: Clarendon, 1950.

Laubach, Frank. *Letters by a Modern Mystic.* New York: Student Volunteer Movement, 1937.

Law, William. *Works.*

Lawson, John. *Notes on Wesley's Forty-Four Sermons.* London: Epworth, 1946.

Lindström, Harald. *Wesley and Sanctification.* Stockholm: nya bokförlags aktiebolaget, 1946.

Losa, F. de. *The Holy Life of Gregory Lopez, a Spanish Hermit in West-Indies.* out of Spanish, 2nd edition. Printed 1675.

Lyles, Albert M. *Methodism Mocked: The Satiric Reaction to Methodism in the Eighteenth Century.* London: Epworth, 1960.

Macarius. *Primitive Morality: or, the Spiritual Homilies of St. Macarius the Egyptian.* London: printed for W. Taylor, 1721.

Macewen, Alexander. *Antonia Bourignon, Quietist.* London: Hodder and Stoughton, 1910.

Molinos, Michael de. *The Spiritual Guide*. Trans. from Italian and printed in 1699.

Monk, Robert C. *John Wesley: His Puritan Heritage*. London: Epworth, 1966.

Moore, Henry. *Life of John Wesley*. 2 vols. London: Kershaw, 1824–1825.

Newton, John A. *Susanna Wesley and the Puritan Tradition in Methodism*. London: Epworth, 1968.

Nuttall, G. F. *The Holy Spirit in Puritan Faith and Experience*. Oxford: Blackwell, 1946.

Orcibal, Jean. "The Theological Originality of John Wesley and Continental Spirituality," *A History of the Methodist Church in Great Britain*. Translated by R. J. A. Sharp, 4 vols. Rupert Davies, Gordon Rupp, eds. Vol. 1. London: Epworth, 1965.

Outler, Albert C. *John Wesley*. New York: Oxford University, 1964.

Overton, J. H. *John Wesley*. New York: Houghton, Mifflin, 1891.

Pascal, Blaise. *Thoughts on Religion*. Edinburgh, 1751.

Peters, John L. *Christian Perfection and American Methodism*. New York: Abingdon, 1956.

Piette, Maximin. *John Wesley in the Evolution of Protestantism*. London: Sheed and Ward, 1937.

Pinto, Vivian de Sola. *Peter Sterry: Puritan, Platonist, Mystic*. Cambridge (England): University Press, 1934.

Plumb, J. H. *The First Four Georges*. New York: Macmillan, 1957.

Pope, W. B. *A Compendium of Christian Theology*. 3 Vols. New York: Phillips and Hunt, n.d.

Purcell, Mary. *The World of Monsieur Vincent*. London: Harvill, 1963.

Rattenbury, J. E. *The Conversion of the Wesleys*. London: Epworth, 1938.

————. *The Evangelical Doctrines of Charles Wesley's Hymns*. London: Epworth, 1941.

Reynolds, John. *Anecdotes of Wesley*. Leeds, 1828.

Richter, Friedrich. *Martin Luther and Ignatius Loyola*. Westminster: Newman Press, 1960.

Saint-Jure, John Baptist de. *The Holy Life of Monsieur de Renty*. Trans. E. S. Gent. London: printed for John Crook, 1957.

Schmidt, Martin. *John Wesley: A Theological Biography* Trans. Norman P. Goldhawk. Vol. 1. 3 Vols. London: Epworth, 1962.

Scougal, Henry. *The Life of God in the Soul of Man*. London, 1707.

Simon, John S. *John Wesley and the Religious Societies*. London: Epworth, 1921.

————. *John Wesley and the Advance of Methodism*. London: Epworth, 1925.

————. *John Wesley and the Methodist Societies*. London: Epworth, 1923.

————. *John Wesley, the Master Builder*. London: Epworth, 1927.

————. *John Wesley, the Last Phase*. London: Epworth, 1934.

Southey, Robert. *The Life of Wesley*. 2 Vols. London: Longman, Brown, Green, Longmans, and Roberts, 1858.

Stace, Walter. *The Teaching of the Mystics*. New York: Mentor, 1960.

Stevens, A. *History of Methodism*. London: W. Tegg, 1864.

Stevenson, George. *Memoirs of the Wesley Family*. London: Partridge, 1876.

Syrus, Ephraem. *Rhythms of Saint Ephraem the Syrian*. Trans. by J. B. Morris, 1847.

_____. *Devotional Tracts Concerning the Presence of God and Other Religious Subjects*. London: trans. from French, 1724.

Telford, J. *The Life of Wesley*. London: Epworth, 1924.

Todd, John M. *John Wesley and the Catholic Church*. London: Hodder and Stoughton, 1958.

Tuttle, Robert G., Jr. *John Wesley: His Life and Theology*. Grand Rapids: Zondervan, 1978.

_____. *On Giant Shoulders*. Nashville: Discipleship Resources, 1984.

Tuttle, Robert G., Sr. *All Heaven Broke Loose*. C.S.S., 1986.

Tyerman, Luke. *The Life and Times of the Rev. John Wesley*. 3 vols. London: Hodder and Stoughton, 1890.

Underhill, Evelyn. *Mysticism*. Twelfth edition. London: Methuen, 1911, 1930.

_____. *The Mystic Way*. London: Dent, 1913.

Urlin, R. *Churchman's Life of Wesley*. London: S.P.C.K., 1880.

Vulliamy, C. E. *John Wesley*. London: Geoffrey Bles, 1931.

Wakefield, Gordon S. *Puritan Devotion: Its Place in the Development of Christian Piety*. London: Epworth, 1957.

_____. *The Spiritual Life in the Methodist Tradition 1791–1945*. London: Epworth, 1966.

Wapnick, Kenneth. *Glossary–Index*. Foundation for a Course on Miracles, 1982.

Warfield, B. B. *Biblical and Theological Studies*. Philadelphia: Presbyterian and Reformed, 1952.

Wesley, John. *The Christian Pattern: Or a Treatise of the Imitation of Christ*. London, 1735.

_____. *Extract of the Life of M. de Renty*. London, 1741.

_____. *The Christian Library*. 50 vols. Bristol: printed by William Pine, 1749–1756.

_____. *Works*. 32 vols. Bristol: printed by William Pine, 1771.

_____. *Extract of the Life of M. Guyon*. Bristol, 1776.

_____. *Ecclesiastical History*. 4 vols. London: printed by J. Paramore, 1781.

_____. *Notes Upon the New Testament*.

_____. *Poetical Works*

_____. *Works*. Thomas Jackson, ed. 14 vols. Grand Rapids: Zondervan, n.d.

_____. *Works*. Frank Baker, et al., eds. New York and Nashville: Oxford and Abingdon, 1975–1988. 8 vols. in print with more to follow.

_____. *The Journal of the Rev. John Wesley, A.M.* Nehemiah Curnock, ed. 8 vols. London: Epworth, 1909.

_____. *Standard Sermons*. E. H. Sugden, ed. 2 vols. London: Epworth, 1921.

_____. *The Letters of the Rev. John Wesley, A.M.* John Telford, ed. 8 vols. London: Epworth, 1931.

Williams, Colin W. *John Wesley's Theology Today*. London: Epworth, 1960.

Workman, H. B. *The Place of Methodism in the Catholic Church*. London: Epworth, 1909 (revised 1921).

Wyon, Olive. *Desire for God*. London: Fontana, 1966.

A. S. Yates. *Doctrine of Assurance*. London: Epworth, 1952.

A New History of Methodism. W. J. Townsend, H. B. Workman, George Eayrs, eds. London: Hodder and Stoughton, 1909.

Encyclopedia of Religion and Ethics. James Hastings, ed. Edinburgh: T. and T. Clark, 1910–1934.

The Oxford Dictionary of the Christian Church. London: Oxford University, 1957.

Periodicals

Faulkner, J. A. "Wesley the Mystic." *London Quarterly Review* 153 (April 1930): 145–60.

Jennings, Theodore. "John Wesley *Against* Aldersgate." *Quarterly Review* 8, no. 3 (Fall 1988): 3-22.

Lofthouse, W. F. "Wesley and the Mystics." *Methodist Recorder*. (September 6, 1945).

Turner, E. E. " Wesley and Mysticism." *Methodist Review* 113, (January 1930): 16–31.

For additional periodicals relevant to Wesley and the mystics see *Proceedings of the Wesley Historical Society*, IV:137ff.; XIII:29ff.; XVIII:43ff.; XXVI:114ff.; XXVIII:71ff.; XXXV:181ff., 65ff.; XXXVI:105ff.

Lecture

Albin, Thomas. "Early Methodism and the Poor," American Academy of Religion Lecture, November 1988.

Unpublished Material

Tuttle, Robert G., Jr. "The Influence of the Roman Catholic Mystics on John Wesley" (unpublished Ph.D. thesis, University of Bristol, 1970).

Wilson, D. Dunn. "The Influence of Mysticism on John Wesley"(unpublished Ph.D thesis, Leeds University, 1968).

index

Abridgments, 52, 123
  of Bourignon, 39, 133–35
  of de Renty, 18, 91–94, 162
  of Fénelon, 39, 133
  of Guyon, 18, 39, 126, 128,
    133n
  of John of Avila, 30, 33, 133
  of Law, 58
  of Lawrence, Brother, 33, 133
  of Lopez, 33, 133, 162
  of Macarius, 22, 26, 133, 146
  of Molinos, 37, 133, 135–38
  of Pascal, 36, 38n, 133
  of Thomas à Kempis, 58, 63
  Wesley's style of, 26–27, 32, 63,
    65, 91–94, 131, 133–38,
    149, 156. *See also The
    Christian Library*
Active mysticism, 26–27, 30, 31,
  34, 38, 128. *See also* Romanic
  mysticism
Acts of the Christian Martyrs, The
  (Wesley), 96
à Kempis, Thomas. *See* Thomas à
  Kempis
Albin, Thomas, 164
Aldersgate, 120–26
  factors leading to, 62, 84–85,
    87, 90, 100, 106, 111,
    113-14
  as a mystical experience, 70
  and perfection, 148, 152
  as turning point, 14, 15, 18, 79,
    89, 99, 107n, 130–31, 140

Alexandria, 22
Alfabetto et Lettera, 37
Alumbrados, 30, 37
Annesley, Samuel, 48
Anthropocentrism, 32, 37
Antinomianism, 24, 27, 48, 66, 88,
  135, 139–40
Archbishop of Cambrai. *See*
  Fénelon, Francois
Arianism, 74
Aristotelianism, 24
Arminianism, 122–23
Arnauld, Angélique, 34–35
Arnauld, Antoine, 35–36, 42
Ascent of Mount Carmel (John of
  the Cross), 70
Asceticism
  and contemplation, 26–27, 37,
    96
  of Puritanism, 47n
  of Thomas à Kempis, 26–27,
    59, 62–63, 65
  of Wesley, 67, 75–79, 148
Assurance
  and Aldersgate, 62, 120–21, 124
  and mystic faith, 24n, 86n, 99,
    153n
  versus Quietism, 37
  Wesley's search for, 71, 79–81,
    90, 106–10, 113–14
Atonement, 113–42
  mystic denial of, 15, 85n, 89,
    104, 106, 108, 111

193